YO-BQD-671

WITHDRAWN

CARL A. RUDISILL
LIBRARY

Gift of

Dr. James Lawton Haney

JOHANN CONRAD BEISSEL

AND THE

EPHRATA COMMUNITY

MYSTICAL AND HISTORICAL TEXTS

Edited by

Peter C. Erb

CARL A. RUDISILL LIBRARY
LENOIR-RHYNE COLLEGE

Studies in American Religion
Volume Fourteen

The Edwin Mellen Press
Lewiston/Queenston

Library of Congress Cataloging in Publication Data
Main entry under title:

Johann Conrad Beissel and the Ephrata community.

(Studies in American religion ; v. 14)
English and German.
Bibliography: p.
1. Spirituality--Addresses, essays, lectures.
2. Mysticism--Addresses, essays, lectures. 3. Ephrata
Community--Addresses, essays, lectures. 4. Beissel,
Conrad, 1690-1768--Addresses, essays, lectures.
5. Ephrata (Pa.)--Imprints--Catalogs. 6. Bibliography--
Early printed books--18th century--Catalogs. I. Erb,
Peter, C., 1943-   . II. Series.
BV4501.2.J49 1985   271'.8   85-3015
ISBN 0-88946-658-0

BV
4501.2
.J49
1985
Dec 2003

This is volume 14 in the continuing series
Studies in American Religion
Volume 14 ISBN 0-88946-658-0
SAR Series ISBN 0-88946-992-X

The Johann Conrad Beissel *Maxims* (pp. 95ff) and the Peter
Miller "Selected Letters" (p. 249ff) are reproduced by the kind
permission of the Pennsylvania German Society.

Copyright © 1985, The Edwin Mellen Press
All rights reserved. For information contact:

The Edwin Mellen Press   The Edwin Mellen Press
Box 450   Box 67
Lewiston, New York   Queenston, Ontario
USA 14092   Canada L0S IL0

Printed in the United States of America

The ray and light of a lamp
    without the true life's power
Is a painted image
    made up by art and wit.
                --Johann Conrad Beissel

TABLE OF CONTENTS

INTRODUCTION

INTRODUCTION

Among the numerous Christian sectarian communities of colonial America, perhaps the most noteworthy is that of the solitary Seventh-Day Baptists at Ephrata, Pennsylvania.[1] It flourished for less than fifty years in the eighteenth century and died eighty years after its inception (although a less significant daughter house did continue for another eighty), but during its relatively short life it produced a large body of significant artistic,[2] architectural,[3] musi-cal,[4] and literary[5] work and evolved a striking spiritual life drawn from Old World norms but especially developed to grace New World expectations.[6]

A History of the Ephrata Cloisters

In February of 1732 Johann Conrad Beissel, pastor of a dissident Church of the Brethren community at Conestoga, Pennsylvania, resigned his charge and travelled in midwinter some eight miles to the north-west to take up residence as a hermit on the banks of the Cocalico Creek, Koch-Halekung as the Indians called it, Den of Serpents. One man, Emanuel Eckerling, in whose cabin Beissel lived, had preceeded him. Beissel's action marks the beginning of the Protestant monastic community later to be called Ephrata, a community whose history in the main cannot be separated from the biography of its founder.

Of Beissel's early life we know little. A Brother Lamech of the Cloisters (d. 1764?) kept a chronicle of the community during his residence there. On Lamech's death, the chronicle was continued by Peter Miller, the learned Reformed pastor who had joined the Ephrata congregation in 1735 and was chosen Prior after Beissel's death in 1768. Miller's history of Ephrata, based on the chronicle which he prefaced with a life of the founder to his arrival in America, was printed on the Cloister press in 1876 under the title <u>Chronicon Ephratense, Enthaltend den Lebens-Lauf des ehrwürdingen Vaters in Christo Friedsam Gottrecht</u>.[7] It closes with Beissel's death. Although the difficulties in the use of the work are obvious because of its hagiographic intent, there seems little reason to doubt the pattern of Beissel's early life which it outlines or to question seriously its depiction of the later events in the development of the Cloisters.

Numerous materials are available to corroborate and correct the description of events in the Chronicon and to outline the life of the community following the death of Beissel to the close of the Cloisters in 1812. Non-members visited the religious at Ephrata with regularity throughout the period and often recorded their experiences.[8] The many literary and theological productions by members of the society were printed on the Cloister's press up to the nineteenth century or copied by the Sisters into the beautifully illustrated and illuminated manuscripts for which they have been justly praised.[9]

Beissel was born in 1690 at Eberback in the Palatinate, the posthumous son of a drunken baker. When he was eight his mother died and the precocious child was apprenticed by his brothers to a baker under whose direction the boy learned, not only to bake but to play the violin and to dance, both of which activities he indulged in.

All of Germany and paticularly the Palatinate abounded
with religious options in Beissel's day. In 1675, Philip
Jacob Spener, Senior of the ministerial consistory at
Frankfurt am Main, was approached by the publisher of a new
edition of Johann Arndt's postills on the church year to
write an introductory preface. Arndt (1555-1621) had early
reacted against the growing post-Reformation Lutheran schol-
asticism and had advocated greater concern with Christian
life and growth in piety than with mere formal acceptance of
a credal position. That position was admirably developed in
his lengthy and highly popular True Christianity.[10] Spener's
preface to the Postills, reprinted the following year as Pia
Desideria,[11] took up Arndt's basic concern and rapidly became
the manifesto for a new religious movement, dubbed by its
enemies as Pietism.[12]

After outlining the social, moral and spiritual corruption of the day as evidenced in the three estates, Spener
in the Pia Desideria goes on to outline some basic solutions
he feels should be implemented. Wider use of the Scriptures
was to be encouraged, the role of the laity in the church
enlarged and the practice of piety developed to a greater
extent than previously. Against scholastic orthodoxy which
reigned in the universities, Spener called for a new spirit
in religious controversy, a spirit centred in the heart
rather than the mind, and drafted a reformed outline for
pastoral education which would emphasize the spiritual
growth of the proposed pastor rather than his intellectual
progression alone. Sermons of moral earnestness in place of
the rhetorical dogmatising all too common at the time were
urged for the good of the entire congregation. Central to
the whole of Spener's teaching in the Pia Desideria and
later was praxis pietatis. Again and again he urges
Christians to direct their thoughts inward, to meditate on
the Word, to grow in the likeness of Christ, and to use in
their meditation such classics of the spiritual life as the

Theologia Deutsch and the Imitatio Christi. Spener's
seriousness in this matter is clear from the fact that he
later edited both works as well as the sermons of Tauler.[13]

Especially important for later church history was
Spener's introduction in 1670, perhaps under the influence
of the Reformed pastor Jean de Labadie,[14] of collegia pietatis, bi-weekly gatherings of committed Christians for Bible
study and mutual encouragement, and his defense of, in fact
demand for, such collegia in the Pia Desideria. The purpose
of such gatherings, free from quarrelsome sentiments, was
God's glory and the spiritual growth of the members alone,
although other advantages were foreseen. Both pastors and
laity would learn to know each other better through such
groups, and the laity could play out the role assigned them
in what Spener considered the ultimate spiritual economy.
The Bible would be studied and the theology of the church as
a sharing, growing community fulfilled. The emphasis on
growth was central. Members generally experienced, after a
deep sense of sin and guilt, the joy of new birth. The
reborn having died and risen anew in Christ, carried out a
careful devotional life to maintain that sense of spiritual
joy and to increase it throughout their lives. Spener's
concept spread rapidly. In later life he gained the ear of
the King of Prussia and with the influence of the latter was
able to direct the foundation and development of the
University of Halle, where his disciple August Hermann
Franke immediately gained a leading position. In the
Wurttemberg area Pietism flourished under the friendship of
both the local authorities and the University at Tubingen,
and throughout the other German states it grew at various
rates despite the often harsh treatment of the authorities,
who were able to persecute persons with Pietistic leanings
under the Treaty of Westphalia, which condemned any quarta
species religionis within German territory.

Neither Spener nor Franke ever intended their conventicules as such to be a quarta species, but the originally
orthodox movement soon developed a radical wing under the
growing influence of the writings of Jacob Boehme and other
Protestant and Quietist mystics. Radical Pietism was pro-
tean, but despite the significant differences between the
various groups represented in it, there was one common
characteristic: separatism. The orthodox conventicules
founded by Spener and Franke emphasized their close association with the established church, their desire to reform its
abuses from within. The radicals simply left Babel. Johann
Conrad Beissel left with them. What spiritual crises the
young Beissel experienced are not known. The Chronicon
simply states that his conversion from his old life occurred
in 1715 and shortly after it he took up a wandering life.
Travelling to Strassburg, Manheim and Heidelberg, he kept
within radical Pietist circles. At Manheim, after offending
his landlord's wife by drawing her husband's attention from
her to religious concerns, he decided upon a life of
celibacy. At Heidelberg, antagonism with local bakers led
to his arrest as a separatist, his refusal to take the
sacrament once a year and his expulsion. He moved on to the
county of Wittgenstein.

Little can be said with certainty regarding the
religious traditions with which Beissel came in contact or
digested in Europe. He may have known the society of the
Rosenkreutzer.[15] Nor is there any need to suppose any close
knowledge on his part of Roman Catholic monastic communities. The development of the cloistered life at Ephrata
was directed to a large extent by the availability of
housing and the speed with which more could be provided.
Beissel's vision for the community, in fact, was likely
influenced much more by the descriptions of the gathering of
hermits in the Vitae Patrum[16] and the demands of a
chaste life in pursuit of the divine Sophia than by any

particular knowledge of Catholic traditions. He had,
indeed, numerous other examples to choose from. One
suspects that already in Europe he had heard of the
Labadists, and he may have visited their settlement in
Maryland shortly after his first attempt at the
establishment of a hermitage. The concept of communal
Christian life went back to the Reformation[17] and was inher-
ent in the very fact of Pietist conventicules, many of which
after separating formed into tightly united bodies. The
addition of a theology of an Adamitic existence to such
separation resulted in the growth of monastic bodies of
celibate members leading a life of constant devotion. In
the main the similarities between such bodies and those of
the Catholic church, although striking, were in almost all
cases coincidental.

Among the radical Pietist conventicules with whom he
associated in Europe Beissel must have learned the main
outlines of the Sophia mysticism as passed down from the
Silesian visionary Jacob Boehme and popularised in late
seventeenth-century Germany. The hypostasis of Wisdom
(Sophia) had already been completed in the Old Testament[18], and that hypostasis was used both by the Fathers
and the gnostics in the early years of the church and by the
Jewish and Christian Cabbalists in the Middle Ages and
Renaissance. It remained for the humble shoemaker of
Gorlitz, Silesia, Jacob Boehme (1575-1624),[19] to tie together the various threads of tradition and pass on a
unified and poetic theology to the modern world.

Grappling with the problem of theodicy, Boehme posited
Ungrund (Urgrund), an absolutely simple, primordial Nichts,
transcendent and unknowable, which as fire desires to become
Grund and as light wills such a becoming. The Father wills
his desire, speaks his Word, begets his Son. The spoken
Word forms a mirror in which the eye of the speaker sees
itself. In the seeing, in the self-knowledge which it

signifies, the Holy Spirit proceeds from the Father and the Son. The act of self-contemplation is at one and the same time the act of self-revelation. All members of the Trinity are consubstantial and that consubstantiality Boehme defines as Sophia or the Divine Wisdom. The relationships of Wisdom with the Son are exceedingly close, so close in fact that in Boehme's disciples and in Beohme himself it is often difficult to differentiate between them. To realize perfectly its desire, the Ungrund had to be perfectly manifested and therefore the free being, man, was created. The image in which God created man was his own image, divine Sophia and the man created, Adam, was androgynous, partaking of both male and female. Non-elemental, Adam lived on paradisical food and loved the Divine Sophia continually until the day he slept spiritually and awoke a fallen man, having lost the divine Sophia, divided sexually. The fall consisted in the sleep; tasting the fruit was merely a further step along a path, now predirected. With the eating of the fruit man entered elemental existence, incapable of redemption. His body was bound by death, his soul by the destruction of self-desire and his spirit, originally the receptacle of divine light, fell under the power of that desire. Yet the light remained, reminding man of the loss of his bride Sophia, inciting him to search out his salvation. With the incarnation of the androgynous Jesus of Nazareth the unity lost in Adam was restored, and fallen man, in the humility and resignation of repentance and faith, partakes of redemption achieved by the restored unity.

Boehme distinguished, then, between (1) the Church of the reborn as did the later Pietists and (2) the established Steinkirche (Stone Church), the church of Heucheley (hypocrisy), Babel, and Babylon, and maintained that external dogmas and practices were unnecessary. Nevertheless, he himself emphasised the useful value of such externals, noting the relationships between the Eucharist and the original paradisical food which Adam ate in the garden. He had, however, laid the foundations for any future separation and the chiliastic note in his theology was continued by his followers.[20]

In Wittgenstein, to which Beissel had fled after his expulsion from Heidelberg, he came in contact with two groups, both of which would play a significant role in his theological development. At the village of Schwarzenau, Alexander Mack (d. 1735), strongly influenced by the Pietist movement of the day and the Anabaptist tradition,[21] separated with his followers from the established church, and in 1708, in accordance with his understanding of the Biblical pattern of Baptism, he immersed eight followers three times forward in living, i.e. flowing, water. In 1719, after some inter-communal strife part of the group moved to America where they were followed by the remainder in 1729.[22] It was in America that Beissel became closely tied to this sect. His first contacts with them in Europe do not seem to have been at all affable, for the Chronicon notes that he considered them much too sectarian.[23] Even more indicative of his feeling is the fact that he joined the Church of the Free Inspiration[24] a few miles away at Marienborn, a sect against which Alexander Mack of the Schwartzenau Brethren had written a tract.[25] The Inspirationalists had come under the influence of the French Prophets or Camisards[26], and centred their theology on prophesyings. A prophet among them would undergo various physical experiences during worship, producing phenomena similar in appearance to later Shaker manifestations[27]. His head would twitch, his body shake, he would enter a trance and speak. His words had to be written down for when the trance passed he could remember nothing of what he had said.[28] Beissel's later preaching follows the pattern closely. He may also have first thought of the establishment of a communistic religious community while among the Inspirationalists.[29]

In the religious climate provided by the Inspirationa-
list at Marienborn Beissel's peculiar personal and religious
attraction began to manifest itself. What fully comprised
all the circumstances of the incident which led to his
dismissal from the sect and his emigration to America is not
known. The Chronicon merely notes that during a prayer
meeting, the sister on either side of him was strongly
attracted and interpreted the attraction sexually.[30] One of
the two asked him to leave. Seemingly a sexual interpretation was placed on the occurrence by the whole community
and Beissel was ostracized. In company with several friends
he left for America and arrived in Boston in the autumn of
1720. Shortly after, he travelled to the -- for a sectarian
at least -- more affable colony of Pennsylvania.

Finding no need for his skill as a baker, Beissel
served a year's apprenticeship in Germantown under Peter
Becker, a weaver and leader of the Church of the Brethren in
the New World. At the close of his apprenticeship, disappointed with the religious indifference in the area, he
travelled some sixty miles to the west and, with three
companions, set up a hermitage on Mill Creek in what is now
Lebanon County. His contacts with the numerous religious
bodies of the colonies continued. It is possible that he
visited the Labadists in Maryland and the Chronicon does
note that Matthew Bauman, founder of the sect of the Newborn
searched him out. When Bauman stated his central principle,
claiming he could no longer sin, having achieved the state
of the first Adam, Beissel, never particularly given to
tactful behaviour, suggested Bauman investigate closely his
own excrement.[31] The first attempt at a monastic community
broke up in a short time and Beissel moved up the river to
where he built a cabin and was joined by a Michael
Wohlfahrt, a kindred spirit who remained with his master
throughout his life.

In 1724 Beissel underwent a spiritual crisis, a crisis inherited with the radical Pietist tradition. That tradition emphasized an experiential faith worked out within a theology of the church which distinguished between the reborn remnant and the pretence of such rebirth in Christendom at large. It emphasised the antagonism necessarily existing between the two and the need on the part of the remnant to delineate clearly the distinctions, yet it took the Christian community essentially for granted, defining it as the need came within its own experiential boundaries. Beissel's Pietism expected of him, as one of the reborn, a vigorous devotional life, carefully patterned and scrupulously carried out, a life of prayer and praise ever seeking closer union with God. Beissel met those expectations. He renounced all things for God; his scrupulosity included, within those things renounced, all the pretences of organized religious life not fitting one of the remnant. The crisis occurred, writes the author of the Chronicon, when Beissel realized that "with all his renunciation, he still had not renounced himself."[32] Indeed, he could not. Beissel, in proper Anabaptist tradition, felt the need to be rebaptized. God had ordained such baptism, but such an act was communal and Beissel had eliminated, in accordance with the rigour of his Pietism, all communities. He made a futile attempt to baptise himself. His conscience was not satisfied. There were not witnesses to certify the act, a fact which eventually let Beissel to seek baptism, as he saw it, at the hands of one unworthier than himself and a fact which brought him to face the pathos of his situation.

At the peak of the crisis, Peter Becker, Brethren leader in America, appeared on the scene. Having undertaken an evangelistic visitation of all Church of the Brethren congregations in Pennsylvania, he stopped to visit Beissel and Wohlfahrt in Novembr of 1724. On November 12 he held a meeting which Beissel attended, and at which six persons

requested baptism. The service adjourned to a nearby stream
and Beissel's conscience went to work again. He solved the
situation by calling to mind the example of Christ who had
been baptized by one unworthier than himself and stepped
into the water, to become the seventh person to accept
baptism that day.

Since no Brethren church existed in the area, Becker
and his colleagues organized one before they left. Shortly
after, much to the regret of the evangelists, Beissel was
chosen pastor of the new church body. The Brethren had good
reason to regret the choice. Beissel had Judaizing tenden-
cies, and the effect of these were beginning to make themselves shown throughout the area, although often to
Beissel's regret. Two of his friends would not eat pork or
drink from vessels improperly cleaned. Two others circumcised each other. By May of 1725 he had baptized seven more
members, some of whom, notably Michael Wohlfahrt and Rudolf
Nagle openly adhered to his doctrines of celibacy and worship on the seventh day. The offense increased when, much
to the antagonism of local Mennonites and the Brethren themselves, he proclaimed the doctrine that children who die
without baptism die in sin and are purged of that sin in a
purgatorial fire. For Anabaptists who held to the innocency
of children until the age of accountability to support their
understanding of adult baptism, the doctrine was totally
unacceptable and offensive. Beissel in the meantime moved
to a cabin on the farm of Nagle to be nearer his congregation and in a short time others had built small huts near
his, much like those described in the Vitae Patrum. In 1726
two sisters asked to be given permission to undertake a life
of celibacy and a cabin was built for them on Mill Creek.

Beissel's influence among his neighbours continued to
grow throughout the following years. In 1728 Israel
Eckerling, the erratic mystic who was to cause Beissel much
trouble a decade later was baptized. In the same year

Beissel had his first treatise, on the observance of the seventh-day Sabbath, published[33] in which, through a dialogue of father and son, he expressed his views on the need for the keeping of all laws, whether those of the Old or the New Testaments, and his praise of and counsel for worship on the seventh day. Not only did such worship fulfill the demands of the law but it directed attention to the final seventh age, shortly to dawn when the true image of God, Wisdom, would be fully restored in man and all things would be returned to their origin through it. Shortly ater the publication of the treatise he began peaching in the city of Philadelphia, at one point addressing a Quaker meeting.

With the publication of the tract on the Sabbath in 1728, Beissel's congregation as a whole took up the practice, gaining some support perhaps from the English Seventh-Day Baptists who had been travelling through the area.[34] Such a custom, however, caused no end of unrest among the other denominations, for unlike the English believers, Beissel's group refused to rest on the first day of the week as well as the seventh and were as a result continuously harrassed under the acts of the colony which regulated the Lord's day.[35]

Beissel's Mystical Proverbs[36] were printed on the Franklin press in 1730. Although striking one as mere commonplaces on a first reading, the ninety-nine sayings must be interpreted in their seting in Beissel's theology as a whole. With few exceptions, they can be interpreted within the Anabaptist - Church of the Brethren framework, and the writings have often been so interpreted with the exceptions explained away as mere driftings from an orthodox core[37] under the influence of other American sects such as the Sabbatarians, the Kelpius group[38] and the Universalists,[39] not to mention alchemists, Free-masons and Rosicrucians. Certainly all those sects had their influence on the growth of Beissel's theology and the Cloisters at Ephrata, but Beissel's thought is rooted first in the Boehmist tradition.

His mystical proverbs serve as an example. All might be understood within the typical Anabaptist, Pietist or Brethren rhetoric, but Beissel's understanding was not such. Beissel was not ultimately interested in metaphysical speculation but in the salvation of human personalities and in the growth of Christian faith, hope and love within those personalities. He therefore counsels Christians with, among others, such _sententiae_ as follow:

> 1. To know truly himself, is the highest perfection: and to worship and adore right the only, everlasting and invisible God in Jesus Christ, is Life eternal.
>
> 2. All wickedness is Sin: yet is none so great but to be separated from God.
>
> 3. Whoever loveth God is from God, and hath the unigenite Son remaining in himself, for the same did proceed from God.
>
> 4. The highest Wisdom, is, to have no Wisdom: yet he is the highest, which posseseth God, for He is alone wise...
>
> 17. Whosoever is wise with himself, is a Fool: for all Wisdom is from God, and all those, which love him, honour the same.
>
> 18. All actions of a Man bring him to the same End, for whose sake they are done, either for Life or Death: therefore let no works be found on thee, whose Possessor is Death.
>
> 19. Nor is he great and high, which is looked upon as flesh: but he is highly to be esteemed, which hath his Conversation in the Meekness of the Son of God.[40]

All such mystical sentences might have originated from the pen of a Christian of almost any denomination, certainly from any within the Anabaptist-Pietist tradition. Beissel does not, however, so understand them.

In 1765, three years before his death, Beissel had published in English A Dissertation on Man's Fall[41] which had been circulating in German some time previously, the only properly systematic work in theology he wrote. Although his

thought underwent changes throughout the years, and the
marks of Boehme and Bromley[42] are clearer in A Dissertation
than in his writings, the work does help to outline the
pattern of the universe as Beissel understood it throughout
his life. Beginning in an autobiographical vein, Beissel
tells of his experience as a youth attempting "to live a
life of superlative purity in a state of amorous sanctity
with heavenly light."[43] The results however were not satisfying and he was driven to meditate upon the meaning of
his failure.

> ...rebellion increased in proportion to my indus-
> try... and I discern'd when my spiritual zeal
> cool'd by neglect, I had peace, and the violent
> resistance of evil abated in proportion. These
> aforesaid discoveries drew me into a deep concern
> to search into the Abyss of that, which is good,
> in order to discern, how it was from all eternity,
> before any evil was discovered.[44]

The Boehmist theme of the work follows. It will be

> ...the heavenly God-femalety, for the fall of
> Lucifer was the occasion that her manifestation
> was postponed. This was She with whom I was then
> so deeply enamoured, tho' then unaquainted with
> her will and pleasure, and being ignorant of my
> own Adam, I thought it sufficient to communicate
> with the mother of Eternity, or everlasting vir-
> ginity.[45]

Every attempt made to reach the "God-femalety" failed
for the male life within him, the male fire reacted against
the aim, knowing that with its consummation its own power
would decrease and die out. All endeavours to conciliate
the two failed until God revealed to Beissel the true way in
which Adam must be conquered. All that was male, that was
part of the first Adam must be crucified. That crucifixion:

> was typified by Jesus, the second Adam, for his
> side, which was closed up with flesh was opened
> again at the cross, and now the everlasting mother
> findeth a free entrance, and taketh possession of
> her true heritage... My ascending self-will was
> crucified with Christ, so that now consequently
> his firey male property is made sinking down,
> which sinking is the female property, from which
> font mercy flows out for the salvation of the
> whole world.[46]

Beissel then goes on to explain the restoration from the rise of its need to its final end, systematically rather than autobiographically. In the beginning the Godhead was one, an abyss of perfect simplicity, of fire and light, of male and female. Although Beissel does not elucidate, we are given to understand that the angels, as in Beohme's system came forth with the manifestation or the objectification of God. No dialectical being broken into fire and light or male and female existed, however. The tension remained unbroken until

> the rebellious Hierarch [Lucifer] began to revolt against the goodness of God, and by his ardent ascending broke off from the Meekness of the Deity: he attacked the fort of eternity and excited within himself the hidden abyss, therefore God now was under a necessity to abandon his fort, for the union being now broken he must, ever contrary to his property and nature raise within himself his male property, & suspend [to] govern with his Divine femalety (id est) his goodness, because the rebellious Hierarch had stirred up within himself the hidden abyss of fire in which he exalted himself above the meekness of femalety of God. And if God then had not left his sacred tent, the apostate angel would have took possession of God for his Bride, and consequently the Divine Goodness would have been made subject unto him.[47]

God then necessarily separated all into male and female, so that no female part could be governed by Lucifer with his male, firey element. Indeed, God himself separated. He left the fort as male, leaving behind his "femalety", no widow. The division of things into the two "tinctures", Beissel designates the two elements, was complete.

To effect a restoration of the whole, God created man in the image of the Divine Wisdom. Man was not created of the two tinctures but was an androgynous being. All things were put under his dominion.

> If man in his probation had kept that state in which he was placed by creation, he might have redeemed all creatures subordinate to him, from the separtion of the tinctures to the Godly harmony and union; for he had within him the temper (or balance).[48]

Man was not initially an elemental creature. He was created
in the "quint-essence", the first of all created essences,
through which all creation might have been restored. Had
man subdued his quintessence he might, as Beissel puts it,
have

> dissipated, disanulled and abolished in the whole
> creation all venom, which was introduced by the
> fall of Lucifer: & in due season having put off
> the body, the image of God would have appeared
> again in perfect brightness.[49]

Man did not, however, so conquer the body. Lusting after
the division as manifested in the animals over which he had
dominion, man fell into a spiritual sleep. In that sleep or
lust, Divine Wisdom, Sophia, abandoned him and God created
out of his side a female patterned after Adam's lusting Eve.
The fall had not yet fully occurred. Rather Beissel sees
the fall as manifested in a number of progressive occurrences, as did his tradition. Eve was innocent and good.
had she been able to overcome the temptations of the
serpent "she might have been the throne-princess of Adam and
his paradisical rosary."[50] In fact she would have fulfilled
her role in the restoration had she "remained as a certain
shadow of the primitive intention of God"[51] which she was.
Had she not fallen, she and Adam would have lived a day,
i.e. a thousand years, in Paradise and together they would
have raised spiritual children. After the lapse of time,
the virgin fair as the moon could have returned and taken
the two under her wings and restored all things. Eve,
however, tasted the fruit and seduced Adam to do likewise.
With the eating, man fell into the elemental body which he
now has and frustrated the goal of the restoration further.
The hope of restitution now rested in a second Adam. In a
summary paragraph Beissel sums up the role of that second
Adam, Jesus of Nazareth.

But how should this matter be brought to a good end? that the afflicted God-femalety may be re-united to her true husband (even to such a one, that would re- frain to govern with wrath;) and on the other side, that the Divine male-property might be discharged from her office in the relation of righteousness, and dressed again in a female attire, in order to pacify all things again and disanull all separation. To bring this to pass the heavenly femalety must of necessity beget her own husband out of the eternal maternity, which should be invested with the Divine male and female properties, & besides this he should bear his government on his shoulders. Now is a virgin big with child being impregnated with the seed of the heavenly woman. Now the abolishment of all elevated selfishness is begun, so that the same returneth unto the bosom of the everlasting mother. This man Jesus was not male [although created in the figure of a male] but female..., for he liveth in subjection and obedience even to the death of the cross.[52]

With the incarnation of Christ, the wrath of the fiery rul- ing male principle was enraged and could not rest until he had destroyed "the female or heavenly property" wrapped in the male person of Jesus. The result was the crucifixion. The cross became then the battle-ground on which the final struggle for the restoration of things was fought. It in- volved essentially an absorption of the fiery male spirit by the spirit of Christ. Attacked with all the wrath and fire of the male property, Christ did not give way to it but prayed for his enemies. Had he not so prayed he would have been consumed with the fire. As it was the water of meek- ness in Christ, the female, held off the male. "Therefore is now Christ the reconciliation of fire and light, and has made one of the twain."[53] That reconciliation can be best symbolized by the opening of Christ's side on the cross. Through it the virgin Sophia entered once again into the androgynous body of mankind.

With Christ then, all must conquer the male prin- ciple. For Virgin Sophia will assume no male pro- perty burning in the fire into her chaste embraces, and if you want to be called a consecrated favor- ite of her, you must first indispensibly become a priest, bearing in your heart the seal of atonement

> for the whole world. And if a virgin desired the
> title to be a wife of the priest Jesus, she must
> first be a virgin in body and spirit else the
> priest will not associate her unto his side: for
> the everlasting virginity doth disanull all sep-
> aration whatsoever.[54]

The battle between the fire and the light, the male and the
female will continue but only for a short time. The restitution of things has begun with Christ. Sophia draws all
men to her but the male in them fights. In Christ the battle ends. In him one finds "an exact balance of temper,
where the male fire continually is clothing himself into
water and light, and has crucified whatsoever is not mitigated therein."[55] Therefore, concludes Beissel,

> If I want to be united with virgin Sophia to heav-
> enly fructification, I needs must in that body,
> wherein I am dressed, suffer with Jesus before the
> city-gate, where the reproach of Christ is my hon-
> ourable garb, and his death my life.[56]

Within this technological system, then, all of
Beissel's works are to be interpreted. Clearly, the early
works are more under the influence of Pietist thought and
the Boehmist-Bromley rhetoric of A Dissertation is distant,
but the Boehmist schema is not. That schema grew in the
Cloisters under the influences of such men as John
Hildebrand[57] and the alchemist John Martin.[58] Thus, the Mystical Proverbs as well as A Dissertation emphasise the role
of Christ in human salvation, but the role is not understood
in terms of the sacrificial or ransom theories of atonement
in either the early or the later work. Christ's work was to
open to man, as the nineteenth sentence states, the possibility of a life walked in the meekness of the Divine
Sophia, after conquering through a vigorous ascetic life the
principle of wrath in the universe.

Difficulties with the parent congregaton at Germantown
continued throughout the late twenties and early thirties.
In 1728 after the change to seventh-day worship, Beissel had
himself rebaptized and then rebaptized six others. First of
the seven this time, he explained the action by noting that

as John's disciples had left him and were rebaptized by Christ so was the baptism of the Germantown Brethren replaced with a greater baptism. The arrival of Alexander Mack and the remaining Brethren from Friesland did nothing to alleviate the disagreement, although Mack was well respected by the separatists under Beissel.

The two communities of celibates grew with rapidity and communal life was introduced at the instigation of Beissel. Israel Eckerling's brothers joined and led by them the celibates began to dress in Quaker costumes which they wore until the habits of their respective orders were introduced. One of the particular difficulties was the fact that women of the area were leaving their husbands to join the Sisters under Beissel's direction. The height of the scandal came when the wife of Christopher Saur left her husband. Saur[59] was a strong leader among the Brethren and his Philadelphia press, specializing in German works rivalled that of Franklin. The scandals continued to increase. A paternity suit was brought against Beissel but turned out to be based on misunderstanding and gossip. Then a Brother Amos, who had been most dedicated to the suit of the virgin Sophia, went mad and raped a local woman. Surprisingly enough he was allowed to return to the congregation but he escaped, and ran naked to Philadelphia where he mounted the courthouse roof and began to shout loudly to the gathering crowd. Again he was allowed to return and he seems to have remained at Ephrata to his death some years later. Shortly after this incident another irate husband beat Beissel and might possibly have killed him had not his parishioners come to his rescue. One would have expected a rather quiet retreat for a few years but at the height of the uproar in 1730 Beissel had the Franklin press print his book on marriage which attacked the state of matrimony and strongly upheld the superiority of the celibate life.[60]

Besides these concerns the problems of administration were weighing heavily on Beissel. He was drawn by the celibates to devote full time to their spiritual welfare and was mistrusted when he refused their request. The house-holders (married members of the community) also demanded his attention and he had, in addition, concerns in a Brethren congregation some miles away in which his ideals had begun to take root. It was perhaps all these responsibilities and problems taken together which brought him finally to a decision in the early months of 1732 when he appointed Elders for his somewhat surprised congregation and withdrew to the wilderness retreat on the Cocalico, eventually to found the Economy of Ephrata.

There seems little doubt that Beissel wished once again to live the life of a solitary. That he still considered himself part of the community he had founded is clear since he allowed opportunity to those of the householders he had established as elders in the congregation to come to him for consultation. Nor did he reject those solitaries who were soon clamouring to live near him. In the winter of 1732 a house was built for the solitary brethren who followed him and in May of the following year the residence for sisters was completed on the other side of the stream. Shortly after, a bake-house and supply shelter were constructed.

Perhaps the greatest coup of Beissel's career came in 1735 when he was able to attract two members in particular of a neighbouring Reformed congregation to his sect. One of the members was the pastor of the Reformed congregation, John Peter Miller,[61] a Heidelberg graduate and perhaps the most learned German in the Americas. Miller was later chosen Prior of the Brethren and took over leadership of the whole Ephrata congregation after Beissel's death in 1768. The other convert was the Indian scout Conrad Weiser.[62] Weiser remained some time within the Cloister confines but his talents and knowledge of Indian ways and Pennsylvania terrain were needed by the government of the colony and he was slowly attracted from Ephrata to serve as a judge.

1735 was an important year in many ways. The first church building was erected and dedicated with the name Kedar. The solitary sisters moved into the upper story and worship services were held in the Saal below. The sisters undertook a communal life and in the autumn, when the remaining solitary of the area moved to Ephrata the communal life was inaugurated for all. A visitation was undertaken by 12 brothers to the New Jersey English Sabbatarians and some time after their return another church was built leaving Kedar free for the sisters. Four years later the church was razed to the ground by Beissel for no particular reason. The Chronicon indicating something of the respect with which the master was held, suggests that no reason was needed and that even had one been given it would surpass human understanding.[63]

Two major innovations were made in the spiritual life in Ephrata in 1735. At twelve midnight, each night, the solitaries gathered for a four hour service in anticipation of the return of the Lord. Because it was necessary to go immediately to the day's work from the service, the time was later cut to two hours but the rigour of the practice was upheld. The second innovation was equally rigorous. Beissel introduced the practice of lectiones, whereby each member had to examine his conscience and prepare a written statement which was read to the whole congregation on the Sabbath.[64] Habits were designed for all orders. The brethren were particularly happy when they discovered that their new design matched that of the Capuchians almost perfectly and the sisters, not to be outdone one suspects, delighted in being told that unawares they had decided to wear scapulae. The married householders also chose a habit.

Need for a hymnal brought the Ephrata members to the press of Christopher Saur with a bulky manuscript which included both new creations by Beissel and other members of the community, many of which had been previously printed,[65] and hymns already popular among all Pietists.[66] Saur, upset by his wife's desertion and a recent split in the Germantown congregation which resulted in another influx of new members to Ephrata, nevertheless undertook the work. His anger must have grown as he worked on the volume and it broke out when he came to Hymn 400. In that hymn, written by Beissel, Saur noticed a wording which closely related Beissel and Christ. He wished to expunge the verse and questioned the corrector from the Cloister about it. The answer he received met all his expectations. Did Saur, the corrector asked, believe in the possibility of only one Chirst? Saur's only course of action was to write against Beissel, not surprisingly discovering that "Conradus Beusselus" is numerically equivalent to the number 666.[67]

Before the publication of the hymnal, the solitary brothers found their residence crowded, and after some discussions of site it was decided by Beissel to build on a hill which was renamed Zion. The new residence was completed in late 1738 and throughout the next year the brethren moved in. Leadership was finally given to Israel Eckerling, not without much disagreement, Eckerling being Beissel's equal in demanding absolute subjection of all to his own will.

Contention between the householders and the solitary brethren grew during the early years of the settlement. It came to head with the question of Beissel's name. Each new member of the solitary changed his or her name on entering. Problems arose over Beissel's new name. The householders called him simply "brother" but the solitary wished to make use of the title "Father". The householders, fortified in their demands by the Boehmist John Hildebrand, who moved in and out of the Ephrata membership throughout his life, felt that the title Father should be applied only to God, and perhaps felt that its use would be extended to the solitary

brethren who had already gained precedence over them because
of the regard in which they were already held as celibates.
Beissel stayed out of the matter for the most part, attempting to pacify both sides. He accepted the first name
"Friedsam", which caused little problem, but the question of
the title plagued the community even after the founder's
death.

Somewhat earlier the name "Ephrata" was officially
chosen[68] and baptism for the dead introduced. By the end of
1739 a large prayer Saal was built, and a bell sent from
well-wishers in Germany hung which, rung every midnight
sounded for four miles and roused the householders, still in
their first love, to worship. A mission was set up in New
Jersey. At the request of the solitaries, a vow of perpetual chastity and the tonsure were introduced and the
Virgin Mary chosen as patroness of the order.

Israel Eckerling was a demanding Prior and a powerful
personality. From the time of his choice as Prior until he
left the settlement in 1745 his position grew rapidly, and
in fact during the few years of his leadership his direction
went virtually unchallenged. Beissel's power slowly waned.
He continued to write. In 1741 his old friend Michael
Wolhfahrt died. The major activity in Ephrata at the period
clearly centred around Zion. Eckerling had to employ two of
the brethren to copy his works, and he preached regularly,
but although his writings were kept by his admirers after
his death, they had disappeared almost completely by 1786.[69]
By 1741 Eckerling was already making plans to set up a
lumber mill to establish the economy of the Cloisters on a
surer footing. In the same year, yet a third house of
worship, Peniel, was constructed[70].

Sporadic but highly serious illness incapacitated
Beissel at points throughout the next several years and may
explain partially the rise to power of Israel Eckerling and
his brothers. The Eckerlings pressed the growth of

industries within the community. In a few short years the solitary were involved in the manufacture of paper, printing, the operation of a tannery, a saw mill, an oil mill, and a quarry as well as a profitable agricultural establishment. In addition, they brought the ritual of free-masonry into use and developed highly elaborate rites and costumes. Beissel stood by, either unable to do anything or aware that the self-will of Israel Eckerling would soon run its course. The latter did indeed happen. After a visit to the Sabbatarians in New Jersey the Prior returned to find that his high-handed tactics and his humiliation of the founder had run their course. The brethren rebelled and the attempts of Israel to make hasty changes, in addition to some hasty bribes, failed to have any effect. On September 25, 1745, unable to bear the humiliation, he left, thirteen years after the establishment of the Cloisters. He was to return in 1750 but again left with some other members. During the French and Indian war he was captured by the Indians, taken to Montreal and spent the rest of his days, happily one may suppose, in a Roman Catholic order in France.[71]

Beissel immediately inaugurated changes. The profitable orchard was cut down and the brethren moved out of Zion. The bells which the Eckerlings had placed throughout the community and the spires they had built were torn down. Many of the industries were curtailed, much to the concern of others in the area who had worked out a good business with the industrialized Cloisters. In his solitude Beissel must have confided much in Peter Miller, the first of the brethren who had led the revolt against the former Prior. He and thirteen other brethren, sought rebaptism and were granted it. On September 15, 1747, the flour and oil mills were mysteriously destroyed by fire, God's final comment, as Beissel saw it, on the work of Israel Eckerling. The rule of the Eckerlings was at an end but one ought not to see

their rule as totally negative. Their paper mill remained
and the productions of the scriptoria flourished under them
and continued after.[72] Of greatest importance was their establishment of the press, which turned out Ephrata works and
other materials throughout the rest of the century.

The disappointment Beissel suffered in 1749 when the
householders turned to the fashions of the society around
them was alleviated to a large extent with the arrival, in
November of that year of the first converts from Gimsheim in
the Palatinate.

In the French and Indian War, Ephrata was several times
in danger but the solitaries remained steadfast and served
the needs around them, taking those driven from their homes
into their community for relief. At one time the danger was
only thirteen miles away. The war must have been of continuous concern to the Cloisters but their spiritual life
continued at a relatively high peak throughout the period.
With the exception of one important occurence of visionary
activity,[73] the most important occurence before Beissel's
death was the growth of a daughter church in York county,
some one hundred miles to the south-west. A number of the
"awakened" who arrived from Gimsheim were not satisfied with
Beissel's autocratic rule and moved to York country to
settle on the Bermudian river shortly after their arrival.
Reconciliation eventually followed and Beissel sent Heinrich
Lohamnn to them who with the aid of George Adam Martin and
Official visits from Beissel and others of the solitaries
kept the two settlements in close contact. Martin, with
George Horn, both former members of the Germantown Baptists
who were baptized at Ephrata in 1763 moved shortly after
their arrival on the Bermudian to found a settlement on the
Antietam river in the southern part of the county. The
settlement on the Antietam, later to be designated Snowhill
after its most illustrious family, eventually incorporated
the languishing Bermudian congregation and flourished when

its parent foundation Ephrata was dying.[74]

The period of growth within the cloisters at Ephrata closed in the 1760's. On June 6, 1768 Beissel died, at the age of 77 years and 4 months according to his tombstone and leadership was assumed by Peter Miller the Prior of the solitary brethren and certainly the most qualified person in the Cloisters. His scholarly abilities were recognized throughout the province.[75] He cultivated friendships with the Penns, Franklin and Washington[76] and was an active member of the American Philosophical Society.[77] Little of his work has survived and of that even less of any importance has been published.[78] That he served as a fine spiritual advisor is clear from his letters to the settlement on the Antietam;[79] his interest in scientific concerns of his day is marked.[80] His scholarship is probably responsible for the belief that he was commissioned to translate the Declaration of Independence into the necessary international languages by the Continental Congress.

During the Revolutionary War, Miller led the solitaries in nursing the wounded soldiers in the great Prayer-House. Yellow fever broke out among the hospitalized but the sisters and brethren, racked with the disease continued their care of the wounded. The result was the loss of many lives and the final blow to the strength of Cloister life. Fewer and fewer volumes were printed on the press, the last publication being in 1793. Three years later Miller died. In 1812 the Cloisters closed and the buildings were taken over by the householders.[81] The glory of Ephrata marked by its literary, musical, artistic and theological productions and its spiritual life had come to an end.

The Life of the Ephrata Cloisters

In October of 1730, Johann Adam Gruber, son of the founder of the Community of True Inspiration, wrote to his co-religionists in Germany describing briefly the separated

church at Conestoga under Beissel. Although the community
had not yet begun to build on the Ephrata site, Gruber's
letter indicates how early the life of the community had
been closely organized.

> At Conestoga, some twenty miles from here, there
> has arisen a new awakening among some of the
> Brethren. Their leader is the well-known baker
> Conrad Binsel [sic]. They find a great response
> among the people. They insist upon renunciation
> of the world and ones-self. Their life, in cloth-
> ing and nourishment, is limited to the bare nec-
> essities. They discard superfluous property and
> livestock. They greet none they meet in the street
> but walk straight ahead. To outward appearance
> they live in great harmony. Both sexes hold ser-
> vices and communion almost daily. They observe the
> seventh day and claim in general that it is their
> goal to achieve a perfect life and continual union
> with God, and this with great power and
> zeal.[82]

The goal described by Gruber did not change throughout the
history of the community, although the emphasis of the
various segments of Ephrata society did differ. The
householders were always, we are led to believe, somewhat
envious of the roles of leadership granted to the solitary
brothers; the brothers developed, under the influences of
Free-masonry and Rosicrucianism elaborate rituals, habits
and devotions. Of the brothers' practices little is known,
but an elaborate rule was in use among the sisters.

For the householders the central religious event of the
week was worship on the Sabbath, when they travelled with
their families from their respective farms to the Saal at
Ephrata. They had for some of the early years worn a distinctive costume and risen with the celibates in the night
to pray when the great bell sounded from the Cloister, but
their first love, as the Chronicon describes it,[83] died and
they settled into a life which, we are led to believe, was
fairly much like that of their Church of the Brethren
neighbours. The householders, in fact never seem to have

imbibed much of the mystical speculation of Beissel and the celibates. Beissel indeed, seems not to have pressed it on men in particular. They were after all the weaker brethren, married as they were and, as a result, more in need of simple moral and doctrinal nurture than of close direction in the ascent to and suit of the virgin Sophia. As the years went on, they continued in close alliance with their Church of the Brethren associates, so that after the death of Beissel, whom one suspects, was, rather than doctrinal differences, the major reason for their separating from the Brethren in the first place, they continued a spirituality which differed from that of their parent body only in the practice of worship on the seventh-day.[84]

The Sabbath worship centered on Beissel's sermon. Many of the marks of the Inspirationalists remained with him and were likely responsible for Sangmaiser's later charge that he entered the chancel drunk. The <u>Chronicon</u> gives a fine description of the sermons.

> He conducted all meetings, however, with an aston-
> ishing strength of spirit, and used so little ref-
> lection over it, that even in the beginning he was
> not suffered to use a Bible; so that the testimony
> in its delivery might not be weakened by written
> knowledge. He began his discourse with closed eyes
> before a large crowd of hearers; and when he opened
> his eyes again the most of them were gone, not be-
> ing able to endure the spirit's keenness. On such
> occasions, wonderful mysteries of eternity were
> often revealed through him of which he himself had
> before been ignorant; but these were soon sealed up
> again, and then he would say: "The Spirit retires
> again into his secret chamber." Whenever he felt
> that persons were present who sought to catch and
> confine his discourse in the meshes of reason, he
> would suddenly be moved to hold a discourse direct-
> ly contradictory of his former one, and that too
> with equally strong reasoning, so that his hearers
> were thrown into a holy confusion. At the same
> time he was very sensitive to any hidden obstacle
> that might be present at the meeting, and in such
> a case never ended until everything was right
> again.... He was a born orator, and could carry
> out a proposition to great lengths, especially if
> he had rationalistic persons before him... In his
> delivery however, he was too fast because he had
> to hurry after the spirit, when he often concerned
> himself but little about the rules of language.[85]

It might be added that he also concerned himself but little about the rules of time.

The other major religious event in which the house-holders had a part was the celebration of the "Liebesmahl," held with regularity throughout the year. At the centre of this even stood the commemoration of the Lord's Supper accompanied with singing, prayer, the practice of foot-washing and the eating of a common meal, to which all and sundry came. The event was practiced by the Church of the Brethren as well, but the ritual patterns of the solitaries drew many to Ephrata and Snowhill, the daughter colony, at the time of the Love-feast. No one was turned away and at Snowhill when the practice reached financially ruinous proportions in the mid-nineteenth century, the community had to make moves to curtail the large crowds of non-members with diplomacy, secrecy, restrictions and somewhat less lavish meals.[86]

The unique spirituality of the life at Ephrata, however, was that of the solitary brethren and sisters. During the reign of Eckerling large amounts of alchemical, masonic and Rosicrucian teaching were incorporated into the rule under which the Brotherhood of Mont Zion, as the male celibates styled themselves, lived, but much of it disap-peared after Peter Miller was chosen as Prior. Because of the secrecy with which the Brotherhood protected its doctrines little knowledge of its practices remains but some scraps of its rituals exist.

The antiquarian, Julius Sachse, describes the ideal of the brotherhood, basing his account on information he re-ceived in an Ephrata manuscript.[87] The manuscript has since then disappeared but Sachse's details fit in general those of a contemporary account by Johann Frantz Regnier, a traveller among the numerous sects in the province.[88] According to Sachse, a neophyte was taken into the wilderness by another brother where he remained for forty days. The departure was made under the full moon in May and during the period he lived on a scanty diet and was offered drops of a white elixer during the early stage. On the thirty-third day the first grain of the prima materia[89] was taken which immediately caused convulsions. Two more grains of the materia were administered throughout the next several days. After the second a fever set in bringing the adept to the point of delirium, but after the third grain the convulsions and fever ended and a deep sleep ensued. The physical manifestations caused by the drug are testified to by Regnier who says he was driven to madness by the ritual and beaten by the brethren to bring him back to sanity. On the conclusion of the forty days the novice was received back and was thought to have achieved the ability to live for 5557 years. Each brother was to undergo the ritual every forty years. There is no doubt that such a practice was carried out but the doctrinal significance of the various stages is not known. It is not likely that the brethren, working in a highly symbolic thought-world, understood the process literally and with the departure of the Eckerling brothers in the fall of 1745 and the rule of Peter Miller as Prior and Beissel once again as leader, its practices were eliminated. The life of the male celibates from then on may be understood to have followed a pattern somewhat similar to that of the sisters, based on a more traditional concept of th contemplative life. It is the spirituality of the period after 1745 which marks the highest level of Ephrata religious life. Alchemy remained and was practised and the writings of Boehme and Bromley were studied but they were all kept within the scope of the development of a Christocentric life.

The Rule of the Sisters of Sharon[90] remains and offers a fine picture of the devotional practices and contemplative life of the Cloisters after the alien influences of the Eckerlings were rejected. Ephrata time was marked by hours,

twelve in the day and twelve at night. None of the clocks
of the community had minute hands, the passing of time being
indicated by the striking of bells as the hours moved on. A
concise passage in the Rule of the Sisterhood clearly
outlines the daily life of the Cloisters.

> The hours of sleep amount to six hours, as after the
> evening meal it happens that from the time of the
> second to the fourth hours the time is occupied in
> school instruction and practice, be it writing, read-
> ing or singing, after which the three hours... are
> devoted to sleep. The seventh hour is devoted to
> midnight mass, where the Christian and divine psalms
> and hymns are sung and the holy prayer attended un-
> til the ninth hour after which three hours... are
> devoted to sleep. Thus the time is passed from
> night until morning and everything is done within
> divine bounds and order.
>
> The awakening takes place at the twelfth hour and
> is done in the greatest order, the time being de-
> voted to holy contemplation until the striking of
> first hour when each and everyone goes to their
> regular vocation or employment given them by the
> overseer until the fourth four which hour is also
> devoted to spiritual and bodily refreshment. Little
> can now intervene to prevent us from keeping at our
> bodily employment until the twelfth hour when we
> again devote an hour to holy and divine contempla-
> tion until the first hour when our meal is prepared
> with great care and takes place, at which more
> attention is again given to obedience and moder-
> ation than to the kinds of viands.[91]

The regulations for disposal through the working period were
stern. Gossip and laughter were forbidden and no outside
visitation was allowed. When the short three hour periods
of sleep finally came, the sisters and brothers had for
comfort only a hard wooden couch with a wooden pillow.

The only period of relaxation was the three hours after
the evening meal when the members devoted themselves to
reading, writing hymns, instruction and singing. All
visitors to the Cloisters mention the peculiar quality of
the singing. The effect of the music on Governor Penn when
he visited was typical.

> The counter, treble, tenor and bass were sung by
> women, with sweet, shrill and small voices, but
> with a truth and exactness in time and intona-
> tion that was admirable.... The performers sat
> with their heads reclined, their countenances sol-
> emn and dejected, their faces pale and emaciated
> from their manner of living, their clothing ex-
> ceedingly white and quite picturesque, and their
> music such as thrilled to the very soul. I almost
> began to think myself in the world of spirits and
> that the objects before me were etherial. In
> short, the impression this scene made upon my mind
> continued strongly for many days, and I believe,
> will never be wholly obliterated.[92]

As a youth, Beissel had revelled in secular music and had
played the violin, but had not learned any music theory.
Early in the life of the Cloisters he introduced the singing
schools and directed them in the evenings with singular
severity. The results were spectacular. Perhaps with the
help of Leonard Blum, a musician who belonged to the community for a short while, Beissel developed the harmony
peculiar to the Cloisters. Hymns were written by him and set
to either, four, five, six or seven-part harmonies. The
four-part melodies were sung in three female parts and a
male. For the five-part music a second lower male voice was
added, for the six-part, a second higher female voice. An
additional high female voice made up the seven-part music.
All Ephrata endeavours were dedicated to the goal of perfect
life lived in union with God in the image of the divine
Sophia; and song was no exception. Perfect song was the
enactment of the union itself, for in it the singer was
angelic, returned in his primal image to paradise to praise
his maker in a perfect harmony of intellect and will. The
lyrics are not properly to be separated from the music, in
fact, are subordinated to them. The music dictates the
thought. To achieve the height of the musical experience
and the mystic union in it, Beissel demanded of his singers
an even more rigorous life. Food was especially important
and the singers were not allowed to eat any animal flesh,
including eggs, milk and butter. Such foods led man into the
elemental and encumbered the voice in the male so much that

it was not able to rise up into the female.[93] Music was the center around which Cloister was spiritually rotated. Hymns then, and not mystical or theological treatises are the most significant creation of the community although the proper manner of singing them has been lost.

Music, too, was responsible for what was, after harmony, what the Cloisters are most remembered. Among the numerous occupations in which members of Ephrata were engaged, work in the scriptorium played a major role in the life of the sisters. There manuscripts were copied and illuminated in a distinctive fraktur which has earned the respect of generations. Of the many music manuscripts which were copied by the sisters, some fifty remain. Several complete hymnals were copied,[94] as well as theological works[95] and the beautiful wall charts used to decorate the Saal.[96] Perhaps the sisters also were engaged in retail trade since two manuscripts of Schwenkfelder hymns exist which in likelihood were copied in the Cloisters.

Of the numerous other vocations practised at Ephrata,[97] among the most important were those which centered around the press. Some time shortly before 1745 a press was purchased, a paper-mill established and shortly after a bookbindery put into operation. The brethren occupied themselves with the continuation of these industries, the only ones of all those which the Eckerlings inaugurated which were not discontinued. Not only did the press serve to publish works by members of the Cloisters but it offered a service to other denominations in the area and provided a basic income to supplement Ephrata's economy. In the forty-eight years of its existence, eighty-eight pieces were printed, some few only broadsides to be sure, but many substantial volumes. In 1743 work on Theileman Jans van Braght's Het bloedig Tonsel der Doops Gesinde en Werelose Christen, commonly known as Martyrs Mirror, was begun. Van Braght, a Dutch Mennonite of the seventeenth century had

gathered together a bulky collection on the martyrs of the
Anabaptist movement and had introduced the martyrology with
a long history of the many who had died for the cause of
believer's baptism from the first century and thereafter.
The German Mennonites in Pennsylvania found themselves
increasingly unable to read the work in the original Dutch
and came with the proposal of translation into German to
Ephrata. Because of the Cloisters' interest Peter Miller
undertook the translation and the large volume was printed
1748-1751.[98] On its completion the Mennonites declined to
purchase a greater number of the copies, which, ironically,
having been stored at Ephrata, were turned over to
Washington by Miller during the Revolutionary War. When the
American general ran short of wadding, the stories of
pacifist martyrs were used on the field of Brandywine to
achieve military victory.

     The Mennonites made much use of the press. Their
devotional work Güldene Aeppfel in Silbern Schalen was the
first work printed on the press and several editions of the
Lutheran prayerbook Die Ernsthafte Christenpflicht, perhaps
the most important of their prayerbooks despite its origins,
were published under Mennonite sponsorship[99] as was Gerhart
Roosen's Christliche Gemütsspräch.[100] Numerous other works
of Quaker,[101] Universalist,[102] Anglican,[103] Pietist[104] and
general interest[105] were published throughout the years
along with the many imprints of Ephrata composition.

A Note on the Anthologised Texts

     An appendix at the end of this anthology provides the
reader with a chronological listing of the major works which
appeared on the Ephrata press or were written by Cloister
members. From these works I have chosen selections which
represent as fully as possible the breadth of Ephrata
spirituality, theology, and literary genres. The work of
Johann Conrad Beissel is emphasised. One literary genre

not well represented in this anthology, but of great significance for the Cloisters is hymnology. Hymns and poems are
'omitted' because a second volume on Ephrata is planned
which will include a selection of Ephrata hymns in German
with English prose translations, and a complete index to the
Ephrata hymnals, hymns, and hymn writers. In the first
selection of this volume, Mystical Proverbs and Poems,
however, a number of poetic passages are translated, albeit
in prose translations. Unfortunately in a volume such as
this, little attention can be given to the importance of
Ephrata music and art.

Unless otherwise noted all translations are by the
editor, who is responsible for the final version of the
complete volume. Special thanks go to Klaus Lindner and
Elizabeth Sauer for their translations, to Alice Croft for
help with proof-reading, to Charlotte Cox for her typing of
early drafts and to Gail Presley for her preparation of the
pages to be printed.

NOTES to Introduction

1.   The community was located approximately 70 miles to the
west of Philadelphia, some 12 miles north of Lancaster. A
small municipality of the same name has since been
established there.

2.   For studies and examples of Ephrata Fraktur and manuscript illumination see John Joseph Stoudt, Pennsylvania
Folk Art, An Interpretation, (Allentown, Pa.: Schlechter's,
1948), 74-90, 129-179 and Donald A. Shelly, The Fraktur-
Writings or Illuminated Manuscripts of the Pennsylvania
Germans, (Allentown, Pa.: Schlechter's 1961), 101-107,
plates 103-131. Both volumes were published under the
monograph series of the Pennsylvania German Folklore Society
as volumes 11 and 23 respectively. See above all Frederick
S. Weiser and Howell J. Heaney, The Pennsylvania German
Fraktur of the Free Library of Philadelphia (Breinigsville,
Pa.: The Pennsylvania German Society, 1976).

3.   See Edwin G. Brumbaugh, Colonial Architecture of the
Pennsylvania Germans, (Proceedings of the Pennsylvania
German Society, vol. 41, 1931), 47-51, plates 54-72 and
Julius F. Sachse, The German Sectarians of Pennsylvania,
1708-1800: A Critical and Legendary History of the Ephrata
Cloister and Dunkers, 2 vols., (Philadelphia, Pa.:   the
author, 1899-1900), passim.

4.   See Julius F. Sachse, The Music of the Ephrata
Cloister (Lancaster, Pa.: the author, 1903). Note also the
lengthy and historically accurate account of Ephrata music
by Thomas Mann in Doctor Faustus, chapt. VIII.

5.   During the first 30 years, members of the Cloisters
produced some 800 hymns and numerous theological works. For
a full bibliography of works by members of the Cloisters see
Eugene E. Doll and Anneliese M. Funke, The Ephrata
Cloisters: An Annotated Bibliography, Philadelphia, Pa.:
Carl Schurz Memorial Foundation, 1944, (Bibliographies on
German American History, ed. Wilbur K. Thomas and Felix
Reichmann, No. 3).

6.   Zionitischen Stiffts I. Theil. (Ephrata, 1745), 98:
"Awake you who are drunken. Awake you who sleep... The day
draws nigh and the end is hastening... Asia is fallen and
its light has gone out. In Europe the sun has gone down at
bright noonday. America sees a lily blooming."

7.   Chronicon Ephratense, Enthaltend den Lebens-Lauf des
Ehrwürdigen Vaters in Christo Friedsam Gottrecht, Weyland
Stiffters und Vorstehers des geistl. Ordens der Einsamen in
Ephrata in der Graftschaft Lancaster in Pennsylvania.
Zusammen getragen von Bruder Lamech u. Agrippa... Ephrata:
Gedruckt Anno MDCCLXXXVI. (hereafter cited Chr. Ephr. with
page no.).

8.   All contemporary accounts of the Cloisters have been
edited and translated in Ephrata as seen by Contemporaries
eds. Felix Reichmann and Eugene E. Doll (Allentown, Pa.:
Schechter's, 1953). One extensive account not included in
the collection is that of the disgruntled Ephrata Brother,
Ezechiel Sangmeister who left the community in 1745.   His
lengthy and antagonistic history of Ephrata was published in
Ephrata by Joseph Bauman 1825-1827 under the title Leben und
Wandel des in Gottruhenden und seligen Bruders Ezechiel
Sangmeister, weiland ein Einwohner von Ephrata von ihm
selbst beschrieben. Bauman claimed his edition was based on
a secret diary of Sangmeister and promised to print it in
six volumes, only four of which appeared. The peculiar circumstances relating to the discovery of this diary and its
subsequent disappearance in addition to its too striking
relationships with the Chronicon led Felix Reichmann to a
full investigation of the work published in the Pennsylvania
Magazine of History and Biography 68 (1944), 292-313.
Reichmann was able to show that the Leben und Wandel was the
actual work of Bauman who had the Chronicon before him,
along with some genuine Sangmeister letters. One such letter
exists in a collection of manuscripts now in Harrisburg Pa.
at the Pennsylvania State Archives (Broadsides and MSS from
the Cloister at Ephrata, Pa., 1723-1817.) The letter accuses
Beissel of drunkenness and has been incorporated into the
Leben und Wandel. Because of the dubious credibility of the
source, it has not been used in the following brief history.
Unfortunately no full history of Ephrata published to date
has been aware of the true character of the Bauman material.
The works of both Walter Klein (Johann Conrad Beissel,
Mystic and Martinet, Philadelphia, Pa.: Schlechter's, 1963
and James Ernst (Ephrata: a History, Allentown, Pa., 1963)
suffer accordingly although the former more so. The best
study of the community still remains the two-volume work of
Julius Sachse, The German Sectarians of Pennsylvania,
1708-1800: A Critical and Legendary History of the Ephrata
Cloister and the Dunkers. Sachse's limited edition is not
readily available but his materials were used by Corliss

Fritz Randolph in his lengthy study, "The German Seventh Day Baptists", Seventh Day Baptists in Europe and America, (Plainfield, N.J.: The Seventh Day Baptist General Conference, 1910), II, 935-1257.

9. See above, notes 2, 5. Also of great help for a historical description of Ephrata is the recent archeological investigation of the Cloister buildings, the findings of which are shortly to be published by the Pennsylvania German Society.

10. Des hocherleuchteten Sel. Herrn JOHANN ARNDS...sechs Geistreiche Bucher vom Wahren Christentum... Benebst 1, der Wiederholung und Verantwortung solcher Lehre vom wahren Christentum, 2. dazu gehörigen Send-Schreiben und gute Freunde, wie auch 3. dessen Bedenken über Tauleri teusche Theologie. Endlich des seligen autoris Paradiesz-Gartlein... herausgegeben von M.A.W. Schmalkalden... 1736. It was in many cases Arndt who passed on to later Pietists Luther's love for the sermons of Tauler and the Theologia Deutsch and directed their use of the works in meditation. See Johann Arndt, True Christianity, intro and trans by Peter C. Erb (New York, Paulist Press, 1979).

11. For text see Philip Jacob Spener, Pia Desideria, hrsg. Kurt Aland (3 Aufl.; Verlag Walder de Gruyter & Co., 1964). The problems relating to the various editions are fully discussed by Aland in his Spener-Studien (Berlin: Walter de Gruyter, 1943). See Peter C. Erb (ed.) Pietists (New York, Paulist Press, 1983).

12. The most substantial and reliable treatment of Pietism, despite the author's antagonism to the movement remains Albrecht Ritschl's Geschichte des Pietismus (3 vols., Bonn: Adolph Marcus, 1880-1886). The background to the movement in the church of the Netherlands is outlined in Heinrich Heppe, Geschichte des Pietismus und der Mystik in der Reformirten Kirche, Namentlich der Niederlande (Leiden: E.J. Brill, 1879). Of special value for students of the radical wing of the Pietist revival is the 3 vol. work of Max Goebel, Geschichte des christlichen Lebens in der rheinischwestphälischen Kirche (Coblenz: Karl Badeker, 1849-1860).

13. Spener's edition of Tauler's sermons was first printed in 1681. It included The Sermons, Das arme Leben Christi, the Medulla Animal of Staupitz, The Theologia Deutsch and

Thomas a Kempis Nachfolgung Christi with other volumes by
Staupitz and Arndt. The 1692 reprint added commentary and a
life of Tauler and was popular in America. A well-annotated
copy has been found at Snowhill, the daughter house of
Ephrata, which came from the Cloisters.

14. The Frenchman Jean de Labadie (1610-1674) withdrew from
the Jesuits in 1650 and joined the French Reformed Church in
which he held pastorates. Called to serve the Reformed
congregation in Middelburg (Holland), he was removed from
his office there in 1668 because of his attacks on the
established church. Some time previously he had begun to
hold small ecclesiolae in ecclesia for the spiritual benefit
of the more serious Christians within the congregation.
Separating from the Reformed Church, he and his followers
suffered continued persecution and finally achieved a brief
period of peace when they settled on the estates of Princess
Elizabeth of Herford in Westphalia, only to be banished
again. At Altona, Labadie died and the community, by now
living a corporate life, returned to Holland settling in a
castle at Wiewerd where they continued until they dispersed
in 1732. Several attempts at colonization were made. A
colony in Surinam failed but another in Maryland prospered
for a time. Discipline was exact, strict obedience demanded,
and a rigorous devotional life maintained. See Ritschl, I,
194-268, Goebel, II, 181-273, and Heppe, 241-374. Shortly
after 1659, Spener had met Labadie in Geneva. Labadie was
then at the height of his influence as a Reformed pastor and
had deeply impressed the young Spener. Certainly his influence is clear. It is not likely however that Spener
consciously imitated Labadie's La reformation de l'eglise
par le pastorate in his Pia Desideria as was maintained by
Kurt Dietrich Schmidt, "Labadie und Spener", Zeitschrift für
Kirchengeschichte, 46 (1928), 566-583.

15. Sachse, Sectarians, I, 140 maintained that Beissel was
initiated into the Brotherhood of the Rosy Cross while he
lived at Halle. His associations there may possibly suggest
this but the evidence is small.

16. The numerous comparisons between the solitary at
Ephrata and Beissel's earlier life in the wilderness with
the hermits of the Egyptian desert in the Chronicon may be
the result of the learned Peter Miller reading into earlier
history his knowledge of the Vitae. It is highly likely,
however, that Beissel knew the work or at least knew stories

of the hermits. A student of Arnold (see below), he must
have read parts of that historian's work which praised the
life of the earlier Christians, and imbued his love of
Macarius. See Ernst Benz, Die protestantische Thebais, Zur
Nachwirkung Makarios des Agypters im Protestantismus des 17
und 18 Jahrhunderts in Europa und America, (Wiesbaden:
Akademie der Wissenschaften und der Literatur in Mainz in
Kommission bei Franz Steiner Verlag GMBH., 1963), 101-117.

17. Cf. the revolutionary Anabaptists at Munster and the
pacific followers of Jacob Hutter, both of whom organized
themselves into closely knit religious and economic units,
the Hutterites maintaining the organization to the present
day. For details on both groups see George H. Williams, The
Radical Reformation, (Philadelphia, Pa.: The Westminster
Press, 1962), 362-386 and 417-452 respectively. The background to the Munster episode is well outlined in Norman
Cohn, The Pursuit of the Millenium: Revolutionary
Messianism in Medieval and Reformation Europe and its
Bearing on Modern Totalitarian Movements (London: Mercury
Books, 1962). For a fuller discussion of the relationships
between Anabaptism and Pietism see below.

18. See Wis. 8:2. Cf. I Cor. 1:24 in which Christ is the
Wisdom of God.

19. For biography see Will-Erich Peuckert, Das Leben Jacob
Bohmes, in Will-Erich Peuckert, hrsg., Jacob Böhme,
Sämtliche Schriften (Stuttgart: Fr. Fromann Verlag, 1961),
vol. 10. Fine studies on Boehme's thought are available.
See especially Ernst Benz, Der vollkommene Mensch nach Jacob
Bohme (Stuttgart, 1937) Alexandre Koyre, La Philosophie de
Jacob Boehme (Paris, 1929) and John Joseph Stout, Sunrise to
Eternity: A Study in Jacob Boehme's Life and Thought,
Philadelphia, Pa., 1957. See Jacob Boehme The Way to
Christ, intro. and transl. by Peter C. Erb (New York,
Paulist Press, 1978).

20. Note especially Boehme's influence on his disciples
Abraham von Frankenberg (1593-1652) and Johann Theodore von
Tschech (1595-1649). Frankenberg wrote a biography of his
master and wrote against the external religious tradition,
emphasizing the need for the new birth within all men. His
ideas were taken up by Tschech the wandering poet and
epigramist. Both men, unlike Boehme, hung in the fringes of
Lutheranism rather than living within it. The English
quickly assimilated the ideas of Boehme and in their

transformed character in the late seventeenth century writings of Jane Leade, the visionary founder of the Philadelphia society, her teacher John Porage and the highly
popular works of William Law (1686-1781). They were read
among many German Pietists. All English Boehmists leaned to
the doctrine of universal redemption. This fact has not been
fully taken into consideration by Bouyer, La Spiritualite
Protestante et Anglicaine (Paris, 1965), 225, in his discussion of Beohme's influence. For general discussion see Rufus
M. Jones, Spiritual Reformers in the Sixteenth and Seventeenth Centuries, (New York, 1914), 208-265. Boehme's influence was particularly strong on the great German mystic
poets Friedrich von Spe (1591-1635), Jacob Balde (1604-
1668), Daniel Czepko (1605-1660), Angelus 1689), and
Quirinus Kuhlmann (1651-1689). Note in particular, however,
Gottfried Arnold, the fullest biographies of Arnold remain
Franz Dibelius, Gottfried Arnold: Sein Leben und Seine
Bedeutung für Kirche und Theologie (Berlin, 1873), the introduction to K.C.E. Ehmann's Gottfried Arnolds Samtliche
geistliche Lieder (Stuttgart, 1856) and Goebel II, 698-735.
See also Ritschl, II, 294-321. His position as an historian
and his historical works receive fine treatment in Erich
Seeberg, Gottfried Arnold, Meerane, 1923 and H. Doerries,
Geist und Geschichte bei Gottfried Arnold (Goettingen,
1963).
Radical Pietism in Arnold's day felt the impact of Beohme in
particular. Besides Arnold, significantly affected was his
friend and companion for the years following his resignation
from Giessen to his marriage in 1701, Johann George Gichtel.
For a full discussion of the numerous sectarian visionaries
who fell under Beohme's influence, see Goebel, II, 681-690,
736-856, III, 71-234.

21.   The third spiritual movement in addition to Lutheranism
and the Reformed churches of Switzerland and the Netherlands
has been variously referred to as the Anabaptist tradition,
the left wing of the Reformation and the radical reformation. Of all three, George Williams' term "radical" is best
suited, for the movement was not one in outlook. As Williams
in the introduction to selections edited and translated by
himself and Angel Mergal (Spiritual and Anabaptist Writers,
Philadelphia, Pa., 1957) notes, the movement is characterized by two distinct strains, a spiritual looking to the
future, dividing clearly between spirit and letter in both
scriptural exegesis and the interpretation of dogma, and an
Anabaptist which directed its attention to the past, to

the Bible, attempting to live a life in close accordance with its norms. Each of these movements can be divided into parties characterized under the heading, contemplative, evangelical and revolutionary. Of all these groups, the only ones which have continued to the present day are the evangelical Anabaptists, represented by the Mennonites, Hutterites and Amish and the evangelical Spiritualists, represented by a small body of Schwenkfelders in the eastern section of Pennsylvania.

22. The movement started by Alexander Mack has gone under various names throughout the years and is designated the Church of the Brethren during the greater part of the last two centuries. Because of this, the term has been used retroactively throughout the discussion which follows. On the origins of the movement and its removal to America see the two fine source volumes by Donald F. Durnbaugh, European Origins of the Brethren (Elgin, Ill., 1958) and The Brethren in Colonial America (Elgin, Ill., 1967). Still of value is the early history by Martin Grove Brumbaugh, A History of the Brethren (Mount Morris, Ill., 1899). All volumes contain lengthy sections on Ephrata.

23. Chr. Ephr., 11.

24. On the Inspirationalists see Donald F. Durnbaugh, "Johann Adam Gruber: Pennsylvania-German Prophet and Poet," Pennsylvania Magazine of History and Biography, 83 (1959), 382-408.

25. Eberhard Ludwig Grubers Grundforschende Fragen, welche Neuen Tauffern, in Wittgensteinischen, insonderheit zu beantworten, vorgelegt waren. Nebst beygefügten kurtzen und einfältigen Antworten auf dieselben, vormals schrift-lich herausgegeben von einem Aufrichtigen Mitglied der Gemeine zu Wittgenstein...1713. See also Goebel III, 26-165 for a study of the Inspirationalists.

26. On the French Prophets see Ronald A. Knox, Enthusiasm: A Chapter in the History of Religion. (New York, 1961), 256-271.

27. See Edward Denning Andrews, The People Called Shakers: A Search for the Perfect Society, (New York, 1953), 138.

28. For an excellent description of the experience see Durnbaugh, Gruber, 384-385.

29. Cf. the establishment of a communistic society in Iowa by the followers of Gruber at a later date. The Amana community, although no longer purely communistic still exists. See Frank S. Mead, Handbook of Denominations in the United States, (5th ed; Nashville and New York, 1970), 22-23.

30. Chr. Ephr., 11.

31. Ibid., 16-17.

32. Ibid., 20.

33. The tract may have been printed as early as 1735 in an earlier version. No copy of the original German printing of 1728 is known but the translation by Michael Wohlfahrt, Mysterion anomias. The Mystery of Lawlessness; or Lawless Antichrist Discover'd and Disclosed. Showing That All Those Do Belong to That Lawless Antichrist, Who Willfully Reject the Commandments of God, amongst Which, is His Holy, and by Himself Blessed Seventh-Day Sabbath or His Holy Rest of Which the same is a Type... Printed in 1729 has survived.

34. Among the English Seventh-Day Baptists travelling throughout the colony, was Abel Noble, a particularly active preacher from Eastern Pennsylvania. For an overview of the early mission work of the Seventh-Day Baptists in America see L.A. Platts, "Seventh-Day Baptists in America Previous to 1802," Seventh Day Baptists in Europe and America, I, 119-146.

35. Legal action was taken against two members of the congregation in 1731 after which it ceased for some time. Snowhill, the daughter colony was plagued with such action in the nineteenth century.

36. Only one copy of the volume entitled Mystische und Sehr geheime Sprueche, welche in der Himmlischen Schules des Heiligen Geistes erlernet... Den Liebhabern und Schuelern den Goettlichen und Himmlischen Weisheit zum Dienst. Vor die Saeu dieser Welt aber, haben wir keine Speise, werden ihnen auch wohl ein verschlossener Garden. und versiegelter Brunnen bleiben. exists in the Curtis collection of the University of Pennsylvania. Fortunately a translation was made of the Spruche for Franklin by Peter Miller which has been printed in the Pennsylvania German Society proceedings, 21 (1920), 1-14 by Sachse, entitled "A Unique Manuscript by the Rev. Peter Miller (Brother Jabez)".

37. Note, for example, the otherwise fine volume by
Durnbaugh, The Brethren in Colonial America, which takes the
fact for granted.

38. With the exception of Ephrata, the most well-known of
the Pietist sectarian communities estblished in America was
that of Johann Kelpius, who after leaving Germany with a
small group of associates in 1693 visited both Dutch separatists and Jane Leade and the Philadelphians in London. He
arrived in America in 1694 and took up residence on the
Wissahicon, in north Philadelphia. There he and his group
practiced alchemy and astrology, taught local children and
lived a patterned devotional life. Kelpius is best remembered by his hymns, never fully edited (Historical Society
of Pennsylvania, Philadelphia, Pa., Ms Ac 189), his manual
on Prayer (ed. E. Gordon Alderfer, New York, 1950) and his
diary (ed. Julius F. Sachse, The German Pietists of Prov-
incial Pennsylvania, (2 vol; Philadelphia, 1895), I, 1-297.

39. The doctrine of universal redemption grew in
Pennsylvania throughout the eighteenth century and affected
numerous denominations. See Richard Eddy, Universalism in
America, 2 vols; Boston, 1884.

40. Sachse, A Unique Manuscript, 11-14.

41. A dissertation on man's fall, translated from the High-
German original by Peter Miller was printed in German on the
Ephrata press with a number of Beissel's sermons in 1773
(Deliciae Ephratenses, Pars I.) and again in 1789 under the
title Gottliche Wunderschrift...

42. Thomas Bromley, 1629-1691, an English non-conformist,
was one of the triumvirate with Jane Leade and John Prodage
who founded the Philadelphian Society in London. His most
famous work The Way to the Sabbath of Rest was translated
into German and exerted a great influence on all radical
Pietists
43. Diss., i.

44. Diss., 2.

45. Diss., 2-3.

46. Diss., 4-5.

47.   Diss., 6-7.

48.   Diss., 8.

49.   Diss., 9.

50.   Diss., 11.

51.   Diss., 11.

52.   Diss. 18.

53.   Diss., 20.

54.   Diss., 19.

55.   Diss., 21.

56.   Diss., 27.

57. Hildebrand was a powerful personality and excellent preacher and was chosen by the Ephrata congregation to represent them at the synods held under Zinzendorf in 1741 (see below note 81). His daughter married Valentine Mack, son of Alexander Mack, all of whose sons were at one point among the solitary brethren. Two tracts against the Moravians by him (perhaps with the help of Miller) were printed on the Saur press in 1743 and exhortatory works were published by the same press under his name in 1747 and 1754. One manuscript letter by him to Saur exists (Juniata College Library, Huntington, Pa. MS 48).

58. Numerous astrological and alchemical treatises by Jacob Martin, a member of the Cloisters are available in the Pennsylvania State Archives Collection of Ephrata Manuscripts and Broadsides.

59. Christopher Saur Sr. was born in Wittgenstein and emigrated to America in 1724. For a short time he lived near Ephrata but returned to Germantown and in 1738 opened his press, the first German language press in America. He is remembered for his publication of the Bible, his annual Almanac and his Newspaper, the latter two of which, in German, enjoyed great popularity in the colony and elsewhere, so much in fact that Franklin, despite his hatred of Germans began a German language newspaper. His son continued their press after his father's death in 1758, see Oswald Seidensticker, The First Century of German Printing

in America (Philadelphia, 1893), John S. Flory, Literary Activity of the German Baptist Brethren in the Eighteenth Century (Elgin, Ill., 1908), Edward W. Hocker, The Saur Printing house of Colonial Times (Norristown, Pa., 1948), and Felix Reichmann, Christopher Saur, Sr., 1694-1758: Printer in German town, An Annotated Bibliography (Philadelphia, Pa., 1943).

60. Die Ehe das Zuchthaus fleischlicher Menzchen (Philadelphia: Benjamin Franklin, 1930). No copy known.

61. Miller was born in the Palatinate in 1810 and educated at Heidelberg. He came to America under the auspices of the University in 1730 and the following year took direction of the reformed church at Tulpehocken near Ephrata. Miller seems to have been throughout his life a retiring person, more at home among his books than among the problems of the frontier, a fact which may well explain his rather sudden move to the Cloisters in 1735. See Joseph Dubbs, Historic Manual of the Reformed Church in the United States, (Lancaster, Pa., 1943), 16.

62. On the wide ranging and significant career of Weiser as a scout, diplomat and judge see Paul A. Wallace, Conrad Weiser, 1696-1760, Friend of Colonist and Mohawk Philadelphia, 1945.

63. Chr. Ephr., 40.

64. Many of these lectiones were published in 1752 as the Erster Theil der Theosophischen Lectionen, Betreffended die Schule des einsamen Lebens. They exhibit some redundancy, indicating either that they have been edited carefully before publication or, more likely, that their original authors knew what terminology and sins were expected of them in the weekly confessional.

65. In 1730 the Franklin press printed a number of Beissel's hymns under the title Göttliche Liebes und Lobes Gethöne.... to which more pieces were added in 1736 and printed as Jacobs Kampff-und Ritter-Platz...

66. The book published in 1739 was titled Zionitischer Weyrauchs-Hügel Oder: Myrrenberg, worinnen allerley liebliches und wohl reichendes nach apothekerkunst zubereitetes Rauchwerk zu finden...

67. The piece is readily available in Reichmann Doll, 13-27 based on that made from the original in the early twentieth century by Samuel W. Pennypacker from a copy in his possession.

68. Cf. Mic. 5:2, usually used as a prophecy for Christ's birth, as Beissel well knew. Ephrata was for him to fulfill the birth of Christ throughout the world.

69. On the departure of Eckerling from the Cloisters in 1745 his works were burned. All that survived were those held by his friends. Of these only three broadsides printed prior to 1745 remain along with two lengthy manuscript sermons (Historical Society of Pennsylvania, Ms Ac 1927 and State Archives of Pennsylvania, Ms Ephrata Roll I).

70. The Lutheran Pietist and restorer of the ancient Unity of the Brethren or Moravians, Count Zinzendorf (1700-1760), followed his people to Pennsylvania in 1741 and immediately undertook to organize an ecumenical church from among the numerous and varying sects and churches in the colony. The Sabbatarians at Ephrata attended the first few meetings but remained for the most part aloof and withdrew from the idealistic attempt after the third conference.

71. The passages from Bauman's edition of Sangmeister, and other material which discusses the later life of the Eckerlings are conveniently collected and translated with introductory material in Durnbaugh, Brethren in Colonial America, 149-169.

72. Two Schwenkfelder manuscripts exist which seem to have been copied at Ephrata. (See Historical Society of Penn-sylvania Ms Ac 1921 and Moravian Archives, Bethlehem, Pa., uncatalogued Ms hymnbook, Schwenkfelder). For full treatment on the use of the manuscript tradition among Schwenkfelders in America see Allen Anders Seipt, Schwenkfelder Hymnology and the Sources for the First Schwenkfelder Hymn-Book Printed in America, (Philadelphia, Pa., 1909), 17-36.

73. Shortly after her marriage to Christoph Bohlerin in 1760, Elisaba Bohlerin began to receive communications from the spirits of Christoph's previous two wives. They dragged her physically to hidden money which she was to turn over to their children but when the communications began to disturb her life, she and her husband went to Beissel who exorcised the spirits. The full account by Elisaba Bohlerin was

published on the Cloister press in 1761. At about the same time a Brethren woman was having visions of heaven which caused considerable stir throughout the area. The Chronicon makes special mention of this affair of Christian Hummer. When she married, the visions abruptly stopped, proof for Beissel that marriage is a detriment to the movement of the spirit.

74. The last celibate at Snowhill died in 1895. With his death the married householders took over the Nunnery, as the residence of the celibates was called, and retain it yet in their possession. The last remaining Seventh-Day German Baptists live near the area. See Charles M. Treher, Snow-Hill Cloister, Publications of the Pennsylvania German Society, II (1968) for a full history of the daughter house.

75. Miller's learning was praised throughout his life. Some small idea of it can be gained from the few volumes known to have been in his library. Some time prior to 1765 Miller donated to the Juliana Library in Lancaster, Pa., a copy of the Corpus Juris Civilis, Justinian's Codex, the Lectiones Antiquarium of Rhodiginus, the Opera Mathematica of Johannes Wallis, and Benedict Aretius' commentary on the four Gospels in Latin. See Charles I. Landis, "The Juliana Library Company in Lancaster" Papers and Addressed of the Lancaster County Historical Society, 33 (1929), 230-231.

76. On Miller's association with major figures in American history see Sachse, Sectarians, Ii, 401-438.

77. Miller was elected a member of the American Society for Promoting Useful Knowledge Apr. 8, 1768. The Society was modeled on the English Royal Society. One year later it united under the American Philosophical Society.

78. Only a few letters of Miller have been printed to date. They deal with some theological concerns but are on the whole intended as defenses of his community. A lengthy manuscript of selections from his Rettung der Lehr der Wiederbringung has been preserved (Juniata College Library, MS11X), the only significant and at all complete piece of his writing remaining with the exception of some spiritual letters (See below note 91).

79. A large selection of Miller's letters of spiritual counsel are found in Seventh-Day Baptist Historical Society, Plainfield, N.J., Ms. Sachse 15.

80. The scientific interests of Miller are not properly reflected by the letters which remain although they do indicate his interest in agriculture, geology and physics.

81. The married householders owned the Cloister buildings up to the 1940's but they fell into a state of disrepair, until the State government of Pennsylvania finally took control and rebuilt the community.

82. Reichmann, Doll, 3-4.

83. Chr. Ephr., 90.

84. The remaining 15 Seventh-Day German Baptists (who can no longer read German) for example differ from The Church of the Brethren only on the matter of worship on the Seventh Day although they do not share the doctrine of non-resistance.

85. Chr. Eph., 36.

86. For details see Treher, 76-79.

87. A letter from Sachse to Obed Snowberger, the last of the celibates at Snowhill, remains among the stacks of material in the Nunnery. The letter indicates that Sachse had in his possession a manuscript on the way to purification which only Beissel, Miller and Eckerling had ever read, and that he (Sachse) will send it to Obed. A thorough search for the manuscript has been in vain, it being likely that Obed destroyed it sometime before his death. Sachse himself notes the great danger that might befall the world should the manuscript get into the wrong hands. Superstition regarding such treatises still continues among Pennsylvania Germans in the area who will, for example, go to great lengths to burn the Sixth and Seventh Books of Moses, a document used for charming, if they are not certain that it can be kept from the hands of evil men.

88. Reichmann, Doll, 9-12.

89. Prima materia was the equivalent of the quint-essence from which man had been originally created. The whole description of the ritual is from Sachse, I, 358-363.

90. Two copies of the rule remain in the Historical Society

of Pennsylvania, Ms Ac 1924 and Ms Ac 1925. A partial copy exists at the Seventh-Day Baptist Historical Library, Ms Sachse 17.

91. Quoted from Randolf, 1105-1107.

92. Ibid., 1087.

93. Beissel's theology of music is outlined in his preface to Das Gesang der einsamen und gelassenen Turtel-Taube, Nämlich der Christlichen Kirche, the first hymnal to contain only hymns written by members of the Cloisters. It was printed in 1747.

94. The hymnal Paradisische Nachts-Tropffen, die sich in der stille zu Zion als ein lieblicher morgen kam über die Kinder Gottes ausgebreitet... of 1734 is the most significant example although numerous hymns were likely copied on single sheets. Examples of such copies remain in the hundreds at Snowhill.

95. Although a complete catalogue of Ephrata manuscripts has not yet been completed, all the major ones likely to be found have been listed. Among them are copies of theological treatises and spiritual letters, corroborating the stagements in the Chronicon and elsewhere of the practice of circulating such treatises in manuscript.

96. See Guy T. Hollyday, "The Wall Charts of the Ephrata Cloisters," Pennsylvania Folklife, 18 (1969), 244-257.

97. When Beissel had first settled on Mill Creek he began to instruct local youths in the rudiments of education. His interest remained with him but he never again found the time to undertake such teaching. In 1739 Ludwig Hocker entered the Cloister and immediately a school was opened. Sabbath School was inaugurated shortly after. Members of the community were engaged in instruction under Hocker's direction who wrote a manual on education for their use which was printed on the press in 1786. Many other vocations were practised at the Cloisters; agricultural and construction skills were fully used.

98. The work, the largest printed in America during the colonial period, was published under the title Der blutige Schau-Platz oder Martyrer Spiegel der Taufs-Gesinten oder

Wehrlosen Christen, Die um das Zeugnuss Jesu ihres Selig-
Seligmachers willig gelitten haben, und seyen getötet waren
von Christi Zeit bis auf das Jahr 1600...

99. For discussion see Friedmann, 158-165, 189-198.

100. Roosen was a seventeenth century German Mennonite
theologian who travelled much among his brothers in Europe
and wrote a number of devotional and exhortatory works. His
devotional manual Christliches Gemütssprach has remained
in use among Mennonites.

101. Works by the Quaker Anthony Benezet were printed in
1763 and 1780. In 1754 a reprint of the Quaker John
Freame's Scripture Instruction was done.

102. In 1793 James Bolton's treatise on universal restoration was printed.

103. Thomas Barton's A Family Prayer Book for the use of
members of the Episcopal denomination was printed in 1767.

104. Cf. the Ephrata prints of works by John Bunyan, of
special interest to Pietists; Johann Arndt; the Lutheran
Pietist Christian Anton Roemeling, banished from his church
in the early eighteenth century who later joined the
Mennonites and the great reformed pietist of the eighteenth
century Gerhard Tersteegen.

105. Religious broadsides, travels, volumes on folk
medicine, prophecies, visions, a treatise on education, an
almanac, a book on metallurgy and numerous editions of the
Bible were printed while the press was in operation.

Preface

to

SPIRITUAL LETTERS

by

Johann Conrad Beissel

SPIRITUAL LETTERS

Consider your duty

Preface

It is written: All Scripture is given by God and is profitable for doctrine [II Tim. 3:16]. If a composition is to be edifying, it must have this characteristic: it must be given by God, that is, it must not carry with it anything human when it brings forth the hidden Word, or the Word's power will be taken from it with the result that it will neither control nor satisfy our inner hunger. From this it is clear that the most difficult task given to us is to bring the Word of life purely and fully to the light of day. For this to occur, nothing of ourselves is to be mixed with it. Therefore we read that men of God, when this power was taken from them, would rather have remained silent and borne insult than in unbelief stir up the tinkling filth of their reason and thereby remedy the situation [for themselves].

Moreover, when the taste for the divine Scripture was lost to men, commentators endeavoured to make the divine mysteries probable and acceptable to reason. Because of this the power of the Word was greatly weakened so that the dearest mysteries of God, which in earlier times the saints purchased with their blood, were now in the hands of every man made useless, were despised and without power, as a thing which has been fully explained and in which there is nothing particularly to be gained, whereas, in fact, all the truths of salvation which are described in their purity always have the power to appear in new ways and to win the heart and mind of the reader. As a result it must be that their spiritual taste is too greatly taken in by worldly love and earthly thoughts.

Writing the following words under the tests which were given to me, I fully experienced how all of divine Scripture is always new, and can assure each person who reads it for his edification that the seed of the new man which lives in it will forcibly win him over completely. The hidden pearls expressed here and there in simple ways are not a mishmash of divine and natural light, but disciplines which are learned in the school of the Holy Spirit, in a fifty year apprenticeship and which can result in nothing other than to bring us out of our own regions into the region of Emmanuel. In this region, the author has now travelled for a long time, suffering much in his natural body so that it may easily be said that he is like a field on which one is always at the same time labouring and harvesting.

Before I close this preface, I must add one further note: in these words the author has revealed to all a high level of divine simplicity; the reader will do well if, in reading, he tames his earthly reason, the black woman, and takes the truths of salvation contained in these words to his heart. Thus through these letters he will be attracted to the life in which one becomes a partaker of the divine nature. For the reader and to all the children of God, I wish constant growth in these truths so that he might reach to the honour and the glory of our God.

To God, the Father of our Lord and Saviour Jesus Christ be all honour, praise, thanks, power and glory now and forevermore until the eternity of eternities.

Amen.

MYSTICAL PROVERBS AND POEMS

by

Johann Conrad Beissel

MYSTICAL PROVERBS AND POEMS

Proverbs 3:13-14

Happy the man who discovers wisdom and the man who gains
    understanding.

For gaining her is more rewarding than silver and to receive
    her is better than gold.

Wisdom 3:3, 8

She is the mysterious counsel in the knowledge of God and
    the director of his works.

If one is eager for wide experience, she can tell of the
    past and the future; she understands hidden words and
    can solve riddles.

Ninety-Nine Mystical Proverbs

1. To know oneself truly is the highest perfection, and to worship and adore the only, everlasting, and invisible God in Jesus Christ properly is life eternal.

2. All wickedness is sin, but none is as great as separation from God.

3. He who loves God is from God and has the only-begotten Son remaining in him, for the Son proceeded and came from God.

4. The highest wisdom is to have no wisdom, yet the highest person is the one who possesses God, for He alone is wise.

5. All works which a man works bring him to that end for which they were done, either for God's or his own sake.

6. Build for God no Temple except Jerusalem, so that you do not bring your gifts to a foreigner, and he also reward you.

7. Carry no fire in a wooden vessel, lest it burn you, but build an altar from new stones, and put good frankincense on it, and let the fire of the love of God penetrate it. Then a pleasant odour will rise before his holy nose.

8. Be always meek and humble in a high position, and do not build beyond yourself before you have measured the depth, lest in your ascent you rise above the measure, and your building be destroyed.

9. And build not for yourself a seat in heaven before you have made the earth your footstool, lest you choose the earth for the heaven.

10. Fight with nothing which is too mighty for you; yet keep good watch over yourself, lest you be killed by your own servants.

11. Build your house with industry, and make its foundation deep. Set it on pillars, and when you come to the top, endeavour to make a good roof over it, under which you can hide in difficulties and not perish in time of need.

12. Guard your heart against night thieves, yet be very careful, lest the noon-day devil with his angels enter into your garden and bite off the eyes of your vines, which is worse than when the wild boars break in for they only rout the soil.

13. At night, when it is cloudy and dark, turn your eyes continually towards the east, for when the sun rises, all wild beasts hide themselves in their holes.

14. And when the sun rises, go about your own business and work with industry in your daily work, and turn your eyes often towards the sun's rising and setting to see how much of the day has passed, lest the sun set and night overcome you before you have finished your work, and you are forced to spend the night in the fields when the city gates are shut. But if you have finished your work during daylight, then go and help your brothers, and you will have a fine abode in the land of the living, and your fruit shall grow and blossom in its proper season, and you shall refresh yourself in the evening of the day when the sun shall scorch you no more.

15. Do not be lazy in your activities, so that you fill your measure either in good or evil. Always prefer the best.

16. Do not trust nor have confidence in yourself, lest your enemy catch you in your own net; for no one is good but God alone.

17. Whoever is wise in himself is a fool, for all wisdom is from God, and all those who love him honour it.

18. All actions of a man bring him to the end for which they are done, either for life or death. Therefore let no works whose possessor is death be found in you.

19. He is not great and high who is looked upon as such, but he is highly to be esteemed who is found in the meekness of the Son of God.

20. Neither the heights nor depths are yet measured; but he who thinks little of himself has seen both.

21. He has travelled far who has come close to himself, and he raises himself very high who lives in the deep.

22. Go straight to Jerusalem, and do not look back, for in Babel the languages are confused.

23. Be upright in your activities, and visit your house at night, so that you are able to walk in the day.

24. If you have sowed a seed, put it in due time under ground, or the birds of heaven will eat it up, and you will suffer famine in harvest-time.

25. Do not build a house outside of your fatherland, nor have a dwelling-place where you are not at home; but dwell continually in the Temple at Jerusalem. Then you have a secure habitation, for there the Lord promises peace to his inhabitants and is himself in their midst.

26. Whoever follows his own thoughts misses the true Way, and whoever attends to the singing of birds will never grow wise.

27. All works of the Lord are commendable with the wise, but fools walk in darkness, even if they travel with vain goodness.

28. Goodness and sincerity meet one another on the way; truth and righteousness kiss one another [cf. Psalm 85:10].

29. Whoever observes the wind will not sow, and whoever will not plough because of the cold, will not reap. And whoever has meddled with unnecessary things must perish.

30. No one can fall unless he first stand, and he whom the Lord lifts up must have fallen.

31. He is great and highly learned who always willingly occupies the lowest station.

32. If you have cultivated your land and sowed your seed, rest. But take good notice of the time, lest you sow your seed in the winter, when the sun has no strength.

33. Let peace dwell in your gates, and righteousness in your paths. Then no plague shall approach your tents, and no unlucky accident touch your house.

34. Whoever associates with the wicked is a fool, and whoever loves mockery kills his own soul.

35. The fruit of the wise is peace and concord, but folly is found where men hate peace.

36. The gates of Jerusalem shall be open for the children of my people until midnight, but hypocrites must remain outside even if they walk in daylight.

37. Whoever builds his house with the goods of others gathers fire for its destruction.

38. Whoever worships God in a strange garment will have his folly revealed before the whole congregation.

39. My son! beware of thievery, lest you waste another's goods, and thereby destroy yourself, but let your soul be satiated with the works of your own hand. Then you shall have a blessing from the highest God, for stolen and robbed goods will never repay you.

40. Let no one praise or despise you, other than your own works, which were begotten in your soul.

41. Do not meddle with a foreign office, nor involve yourself with strange business; but take care of your own, so that you finish your task. And take care of that which is your responsibility, so at last the growth of your righteousness will serve you in the time of need, and you have abundance in time of want and famine. But whoever meddles with unnecessary things must perish.

42.   Do not be double-hearted, nor have a forked tongue; for a forked tongue sets princes at variance, and a double heart destroys those who have great peace, and never has rest for itself.

43.   Be more prone to hear than to talk, for the ears of the wise man listen, but a fool's heart lies on his tongue.

44.   He who guards his tongue guards his life. Therefore take good care, lest she become your master. But if she is it already, put her into the stocks until the Lord changes her captivity. Then the tongue of the speechless will give praise.

45.   Let a thing be ever so innocent, the superfluity of words must be avoided. Therefore we are never to make more words than what belongs to the matter.

46.   A wise man is in all this very practiced and knows that whoever will speak well must first learn to be silent.

47.   A man of understanding takes notice of a matter first, before he asks; but a fool breaks through like water in a broken dam.

48.   To speak brings honour, and sometimes to speak brings shame; a wise man knows how to yield to both, and waits for his time.

49.   Silence also has its time and sometimes serves to honour, sometimes to shame; but a wise man will hit the mark in both, for he waits for the time.

50.   The works of the Lord are praiseworthy with the innocent, but they who travel on perverse ways shall be ashamed.

51.   Whoever despises wisdom and the rod is unhappy, for his works are lost, and his end is death.

52.   Whoever converts to his Creator but not properly, shall have pains for his reward, and tempests for his harvest.

53. Wisdom is a fine thing, yet she has not many courtiers, for she is chaste.

54. Men are more prone to commit adultery with another's wife than to content themselves with that wife which God has given them.

55. No adulterer nor whoremonger shall enter into the Kingdom of God, but only those who live in holy matrimony.

56. No single man shall see the Face of God, for he lives for himself and brings forth no fruit. But whoever lives in holy matrimony, lives not for himself, for he studies to please his wife, for in her he is fruitful.

57. Whoever lives without matrimony is like a tree which blossoms and has fine leaves, but bears no fruits.

58. Therefore shall we in early time concern ourselves for one which we may love, and be fruitful in her. Yet we must take good care not to marry an ugly farmer's or a poor citizen's daughter, where we must gain our bread with hard labour all our life, and at the last receive an evil reward for all our labour.

59. Therefore concern yourself for a fine, rich, and noble one, who is of noble blood. Then you need not work hard for your bread and clothes, but can live very contented, and can rejoice in her beauty and provide yourself with her riches, so that you shall not be in want all your life.

60. But if you are grown up, and arrived at the years of maturity so that you are fit to beget children, and have not yet found that beautiful and noble woman, go with Jacob to the house of your mother's Father, to your mother's brother, who has two daughters, the one called wisdom, the other folly. Those you will gain by your hard labour for wives. But although the beautiful as wisdom (or Rachel) shall please you, yet you must lie first with foolishness or Leah, for with her you shall bear fruit. Yet you must take good care not to make the first-born son your heir, for he

shall through self-elevation stain your bed. Neither is it
the second or the third, for instruments of cruelty were
found in their habitations (Gen. 49:5). But it is Judah
whom his brothers shall praise. At last Joseph, the son of
wisdom, will be born; he is chaste and virginal, and if you
have acquired him, go on your journey to your native
country, for God, who has blessed you to this point, shall
be with you on the way, and shall also make subject unto you
your first-born brother, so that you may be the heir
forever.

61. Honour your mother, and forget not her travail
over you, for she carried you under her heart, and took care
of you, that the lines fell to you in pleasant places, and
she made you a first-born son, that you might have a good
portion in the land of the living [cf. Exod. 20:12; Psalm
16:16; 142:5].

62. Forsake not the wife of your youth, and be careful, lest your heart adhere to a foreign woman.

63. Always prefer the sunshine to the moonshine, yet
take care that your eyes be pure, lest the clear light
dazzle you, so that afterwards you travel in darkness, and
are deceived by a false light.

64. Have good care not to join with a woman in the
country where your mother has begotten you, lest you bestow
your seed upon a foreign one, and make common your blessed
lot and portion.

65. If you see the sun setting, do not look after it,
as if it will rise from there again, or darkness will catch
you, for it always follows the light. But turn your face to
the east. Then her clear light will again surround you, and
you shall be refreshed with a pleasant morning-dew.

66. Put no light before the blind, and do not talk
much with the deaf, for the costs and the pain are for
nothing. Yet give them no offence, lest guilt on their
behalf be laid upon you.

67. The Lord hates all who have double hearts and two souls. Woe unto those who are ensnared with them! How will they fare at that day when souls shall be judged by God?

68. The reproofs of the wise are acceptable to those who take them to heart, but the flattery of the hypocrite creates nothing but worms and moths.

69. The words of the wise are a fire, and burn the mocker to his very bowels, but the kissing of the hypocrite pleases him.

70. By the fruit is to be seen how the tree was tended. A man's being and behaviour indicate his thought.

71. Praise nobody for his deeds before the end, for in death and the end of works it will appear what a man was.

72. Death is the wages of sin [Romans 6:23]; therefore all works which precede death are foretellers of it; but those which follow after death indicate that a new life is born.

73. Happy are those who suffer for righteousness' sake [cf. Matthew 5:10]. They die a happy death, for the death of the saints is very precious.

74. Therefore take good care to die a happy death, for all works preceding death are a cause of a happy or unhappy death.

75. We receive the reward of our deeds, says the murderer. Happy is he who does not justify himself, for he can die a happy death.

76. Whoever loves his life shall lose it; and whoever loses his life shall find it [cf. Matthew 10:39].

77. The mocker and hypocrite must suffer much, for they want to possess two lives at once.

78. Death and life do not reside together at the same time in one house, for when one comes, the other goes.

79. Therefore do not propose to serve two masters, for both might at last give you evil wages [cf. Matthew 6:24].

80. In so far as is possible, serve God with your

whole heart, lest your situation turn worse, and at last you receive double stripes.

81. Whoever worships God with half a heart shall have worms and moths for his wages.

82. In all that you do, consider the end and issue of your works; thus you shall learn to know the beginning of them.

83. In all things for which you know that God cannot reward you at the end, leave at the beginning. Then you shall not come to a bad end.

84. Every master pays his servant according to his merits. Therefore take heed that no works be found with you which have merited bad wages.

85. Happy is he who does not need to expect in his work a bad end.

86. Happy is he who has a good conscience, and has left every bad beginning. He shall find a good end.

87. Therefore leave all works which do not have God for their beginning, for a thing in which God is not the beginning, He can also not reward at the end.

88. And be careful not to have your own scope in your works, for thus you miss the true way, and bring your works to an end, but not yourself.

89. Never be idle, but work with industry in your calling, so that you have something to give to the needy.

90. In all things take care not to eat another's bread for nothing, lest a famine come in the country and you pay dearly for it.

91. Therefore do not put your trust in another's table, even though you can have it, for the highest Recompenser, who sees all things, might put it on your account, and you might then have nothing to pay for it.

92. Do not love sleep, lest you be impoverished, for a drowsy fellow must wear worn-out clothes.

93. Therefore take heed never to neglect your own

business, and to eat bread of your own farm, so that you clothe yourself from the herds of your sheep, and grow warm from the skins of your lambs, and eat honey from the rock, and milk and butter from your goats, and grow fat from the rams and he-goats, and need not fear cold nor snow nor hunger, for all your house has double coverings, and your chambers are filled with provisions for many years, which will suffice you even in the greatest famine.

94.   Be neither a glutton nor luxurious, lest you ruin your estate by debauching in prosperity, and then suffer want in need.

95.   Distribute your bread among the hungry, and if you see any naked, clothe him. Then you shall gather a treasure in distress and provision for many years.

96.   Do not be wise with yourself, before you have travelled through the way of folly, lest you possess folly for wisdom.

97.   Put no trust in yourself, until you are confounded in your best works, for none is good except God alone.

98.   Do not ascend too high, before you have measured the depth, lest in your ascent you come too high, and another cast you down.

99.   To be meek and humble in his own eyes is victory in the power of God.

FINIS.

Poems

1

O man, consider well: you stand before the jaws of death;
If you live for pleasure, God can make nothing out of you.

2

O man, consider but this: leave the vain world,
Or you will never be counted among the holy choirs.

3

Leave your thoughts which rejoice in vain pleasure,
Or you will regret [your actions] in eternity.

4

You must be cast down and completely trodden under foot,
Or you will not be counted among God's holy choirs.

5

If you have begun to travel on the way to Heaven's gate,
Do not stand still but continue on.

6

A Christian is a marvellous human being in this vain world.
Why? He is directed toward heaven.

7

He who clings to the earth and remains bound to it
Will never be found with the noble treasure.

8

Go into the ground of the soul, away from all the world's
    turmoil;
There in yourself you will find the quiet heaven of God.

9

The life of this day is only a play of thoughts;
The wise man knows this and does not love it too much.

10

Leave the manifold and seek the one,
And your heart will enter into peace; you will be free of
    all pain.

11

He who has the fewest desires is the richest man;
He who finds himself in this state can be burdened by noth-
    ing.

12

If you wish to sit on high, dig deep below yourself;
Thus, you will find firm ground to grow above yourself.

13

If you have not yet seen the count of nothingness,
Build no nest in the house of security.

14

He who wishes to enjoy God must leave himself;
Then the heart will be prepared for God's temple.

15

The quiet rest of peace which God's children have
A man finds in the tents of Salem where soul and spirit re-
    fresh themselves.

16

He who loves Christ's messengers and the number of his
    saints
Exhibits his calling to the great Supper.

17

He who serves God in faith and honours him with obedience
Demonstrates that his heart is converted.

18

He who sings and speaks but does not prove [his words] with
    works
Is a hypocritical Christian even if he shines like gold.

19

The suffering which God's children experience is great,
But it seems like child's play if they find comfort in God.

20

How many a difficult path must the noble soul walk
Before it can sing with me the song of praise.

21

God's children shed many tears;
Blessed is he whose heart completely flows out in them.

22

God's children are hated, despised, cast aside;
O God, how comforted they are in many difficult tests.

23

I live in the pleasure of God and rest in his will;
I drink from his breast of love, and leave the world and the
    devil's raging.

24

He who possesses himself in God forgets time and place;
Is free from sorrow and pain and can rest in any place.

25

The mouth of the hypocrite speaks and postures, but is only
        talk and lies;
The wise word and appearance is power without the hypo-
        crite's emphasis.

26

The ray and light of a lamp without the true life's power
Is a painted image made up by art and wit.

27

The mouth of the hypocrite speaks much of Christ's miracles,
But he will be frightened and in dread when God judges him.

28

O how many cries will be heard on the appearance of destiny,
When those on the outside will eagerly wish to be God's
        people.

29

O evil Babylon, you exhibit a shining appearance,
But you will not enter where God's children are.

30

The watchman's judgment indicates that the end
Of Babylon the Great is at hand; therefore, leave her.

31

The cup of false doctrine from which Babel drinks
Is now filled with that by which Zion praises itself.

32

You pious ones, together flee Babel's abominable sins,
And you will never more share in her troubles.

33

Bear upon yourselves no more Babel's death-judgment,
So that her destruction cannot frighten you.

34

Force your way with power through the narrow gate of heaven,
Or you must stand outside and cry forever.

35

If you wish to live in God you must first die;
[Your] best appearance and light must first completely die
        in you.

36

Destroy self-love; you are a bitter death
To the heart which has given itself completely to God.

37

The narrow gate of life will never be found
By him who is yet tied to something here.

38

He who wishes to possess God must leave himself,
For he who possesses himself cannot grasp God within
        himself.

39

What hinders my way to joyous Eternity?
It is called: self-elevation, pleasing oneself.

40

O quiet rest of peace which the citizens of heaven have,
Since they rejoice in nothing except God.

41

O world, you deceiver with your vain appearance;
I have fled from you, and will never enter you again.

42

The vain light of the world will nevermore deceive [me].
Why? My heart is completely converted to my God.

43

The vain joy of the world is concealed death.
He who rejoices in it will never reach God.

44

O man, where are you going in your vain pleasure?
Are you not aware of the joy in the other world?

45

The vain pleasure of the world, which deceives many,
Causes great pain when they turn to God.

46

The way of life is narrow, filled with thorns and brambles.
O Christian man, press through; let nothing frighten you
     away.

47

God's children suffer much here.
How fortunate am I. My desire for joy stands in another
     world.

48

The mocking judgment of the world can no longer trouble me.
Why? My name is written in heaven.

49

He who sits in deep stillness and rests in the lap of God
Forgets pain and suffering and is free of all sorrow.

50

Many a man shouts at and reprimands the whore for her
    abomination,
But is not pure in his own heart.

51

The love-fount of wisdom remains firmly fixed in me;
Often it is completely sealed in the pious.

52

If I forget vain pleasure and arrogance here,
I will continually be hated, mocked, and laughed at.

53

I love only one thing and am firmly bound to it;
I enjoy pure joy because I have found the treasure.
The love-stream of wisdom refreshes my thoughts,
Gives me drink at her breast, draws my spirit away,
So that I can forget the arrogance of creatures
With all the vain appearances I have already laughed away.

54

The gate to heaven is small; if you wish to enter
You must remain a child or you will remain outside.

55

The name of virgin is beautiful but will not be seen
Where lamps are trimmed only with the sound of words.

56

How beautiful does it flourish here in the still soul
Which out of a desire for heaven betrothes itself to nothing
    here.
The joyous field of Zion shows forth its light and appear-
    ance
Where God's Spirit of peace draws into the heart
And makes an end to many difficult battles.
The power of all enemies must finally be destroyed.
O, how sweet a peace a man finds in such order
Where he only inclines his ear to the still words of the
    spirit,
Where in the still Sabbath peace without the words of the
    mouth,
A thank-offering is presented; at every point
He has chosen the best part, and reached
The noble valuable treasure. Many hope in pain and
With sorrow, dread, trouble, and much anxiety
    pass their time in pain and bitter suffering.
Man enters where nothing can be enjoyed but peace;
All tears which have been poured out on the way are at an
    end;
The silent Sabbath celebration finds its place.
Man finds here the best treasure.

57

The fruitfulness of love enlivens my thoughts;
While wisdom plays, my spirit draws away from here
To joyous eternity where my highest joy and
Peace of heart are. This is the one thing known to me
And therefore I let everything in this world go,
The light of the creature, and seek what is pleasing to God.
To him I completely give myself to live for him
In spite of whatever opposes me.

58

Because I forget the vain light and appearance here
I am stripped of all "I" and "mine"
So that nothing can possess the love of the dear spirit;
It raises itself up and journeys to God.
As a result it is freed and all burdens are lifted from it.
And already in time has found the eternal stillness
In which a man can enjoy peace which cannot be done away
    with.
Who is it who discovers this? The man purchased from the
    earth.

59

What sounds of praise and love one finds in souls
Who betroth themselves to nothing but Jesus,
And have completely offered up their whole heart together
    with everything they have
In suffering and pain,
And have walked forth to joyous eternity,
And are prepared to give him thanks and praise with every
    word,
And continually in complete stillness, completely detached
    from everything,
Rest in the will of God. They are truly satisfied
To live here according to his sign and counsel;
Thus they remain in peace and are blessed.

60

The day of full joy on which I have long waited has
revealed itself in the garden of my heart. Before my door
the true mother-heart has often waited with desire to embrace me fervently. Under great burdens, ill at ease and
troubled, I sought here and there to find joy and new life.
How weary I often was; I could hardly bear the many burdens
in so many days of difficulty.

But now in the chamber of my heart I catch sight of the true mother-heart; I forget all the sorrows which earlier troubled me in many ways, which trod on me in the years of my suffering. O folly, that I sought with so much weariness and sorrow the treasure hidden in me, in external forms.

But now I have heard the noble voice which calls so near before my door: "Come to me. Follow my teaching which will enliven you with the gift of heaven so that soul and spirit can rejoice." Therefore I followed her voice, the inner teaching of heaven, and took heed as to what it was. I will turn to nothing else. It is enough that I now rejoice in the still rest of peace. Can anyone suggest what is better?

61

O wisdom, go forth here with your firm discipline among your children who have often long sought the way to holiness with sorrow, weariness, and great difficulty until they experienced how your great love so faithfully bore [them], so that they were no longer controlled by what ruled in their hearts, the old abomination of sin with its vain pleasure, the enemy opposed to and ignorant of you.

O pure heavenly love! O true virtue of God! Because you have atoned for their sin and guilt, everything which is pleasing to you must hereafter be given to you throughout their whole life, so that they might fulfill your discipline in the true duty of love and live completely according to the judgment of your service, and thus only according to your will. Moreover they are to give their bodies continually up to your firm discipline until your hand of love has fully prepared them and you bring them into their Father's house.

There on the joyous day they will forget the many dry tears they often wept in trouble and difficulty, and the many problems when they were pressed, hemmed in, and

troubled. Because they found true rest in you, their state
of sorrow has disappeared into eternity.

On a God-loving Soul in Great Temptation

62

O where is my bridegroom, my soul's best friend? Has
he ceased to love her who so deeply desires him? His gates
are closed, his sun does not shine. A thousand tears flowed
from me because time and strength fail me. His sorrow lets
him leave me alone so that I was in many dangers; I was
never secure before the enemies who surrounded me. My soul
was in great dread; I sought for the life which earlier
enlivened me. But there was nothing to find which would
nourish my soul. O I poor hunted hind! Tears flowed as a
sea from me, because I saw myself surrounded by the fierce
raging of the enemy. I thought, how can I live? The
struggle reached the point of drawing blood.

O, I poor sheep who will save me from the enemies who
shout? Let us tread them down so that we can cool our
fierce raging. O, the great pain and need I must endure
because my best friends who are to counsel me act as if they
were enemies. The soul is pressed down by its enemies, and
in addition hemmed in even by its friends who once bore me,
a poor child, on their shoulders. They act as if they are
strangers in a difficult test, yet I received power and
strength in pain, for unnoticed I noted that nothing went
out from the heart. The counsels indicate to me that they
will change soon. Inwardly I note that the counsel is for
my good, that I am to stand before the ferocity of the
enemies and not to stand in shame, so that the friends may
rejoice in God's power which he has shown to me. Then he
brings about victory and adoration and is greatly praised by
the number of those chosen by love, who stand bound in
sorrows until we will all go there beautifully with the

sound of God's harp, glorious in the dance and singing without silence the song of victory and praise.

Sermon of a Christian Which His Teacher Gave Him to Teach

1. You must daily, indeed hourly, test yourself to determine how you carry out your activities and if you walk in a pure and clean spirit which is spotted by no foreign nature or creaturely love.

2. God is to be your one and everything; is this so?

3. Does it cause you as much pain when God suffers as it does when you are spoken against?

4. Do you have any intentions for your own person if you strive in an outward manner for God's honour?

5. Do you find it best in your activities to act purely for God or are there here and there intentional interests in yourself?

6. Do you stand calm before men in all matters both when you are elevated and when you are cast down?

7. Do you suffer as much when someone else is opposed for truth's sake as when you are?

8. In all matters do you seek nothing other in your neighbour than to be a cause of his salvation?

9. Or do you live for him according to your pleasure?

10. Do you remain in the same love if here and there he does something which is intended out of the will of God but which does not agree with your spiritual direction?

11. Do you always seek to place secretly your spiritual guidance before that of another and are you thus easily pleased if you see that you are no longer elevated by another above himself?

12. Is all your activity so carried out that in all your deeds nothing of your own nor any self-love shines forth?

13. In all things do you bear yourself as a man who desires and rejects himself?

14. In all your activities are you a good example for another?

15. Or, does something shine forth here and there which hinders another?

16. Is there something in you taken with more freedom from another than one would otherwise have in oneself?

17. Are all your words and deeds so salted that they always have a full taste in themselves, or do they not, many times, serve as a cause for the destruction or corruption of another?

18. Do you allow yourself inwardly and outwardly to be so seen in your activities that in all things you truly follow Jesus who denied himself and was mocked by the world?

A Deeply Considered Reflection on Subjection and Brokenness

To be pure in all ways it is necessary for me to keep myself under close scrutiny. I must increasingly endeavour to grow and to pray day and night, to walk in true brokenness of heart and while doing so to call upon God and say: "Lord God, redeem me from myself. Give me strength and purity so that I might walk perfectly in a pure and clean spirit and thus not be deceived by myself." O how carefully, closely, and with how firm attention I must walk if my path is to be pure. I must endeavour always to live inwardly and secretly so that my life is not sullied by arrogance or by too great attention to other men's opinions.

I must as a result shun all unnecessary conversation with pious men (although it appears to be good) for I must take great care that my walk is godly and not common. The moment it becomes common, godliness is lost and I lose my power. Above all I must see to it that my life increasingly becomes more and more like the innocent life of Jesus Christ. I must accept spiritual and physical nothingness as the mother and nurse of all other virtues. I must flee from eating and drinking as if they were an abominable beast which steps on and crushes all Christian virtue in me, and in its place uplifts and practises twisted thoughts and intentions, robs and destroys the divine oil of love, and makes the heart proud, arrogant, and haughty. I must thus take serious care not to become sullied by this beast.

This is to be my training and practice: all suffering which comes to me, I will eagerly and willingly accept without taking pride before men in this acceptance. I will thus guard my walk in humility and remain hidden in God.

He who has died to the world places his soul in God; Redeemed from need and death, he experiences the joy of heaven.

Another Sermon: A Description of Self-Deception Necessary and Useful

for Those who Follow and Study [the Life of] Jesus Christ

A follower of God, who devotes himself to a spiritual life, must examine himself closely and earnestly seek to discover if he is living in accordance with the duties of his life. He is not to clothe and adorn himself with an external virtuousness but with an internal one. He is to adorn and cover himself with godly virtues.

There are many souls who wish to change their outward state, but they themselves remain unchanged in their hearts. This is because their appearance is commonly directed to their own concerns rather than to God. When a man has God purely as his goal and intention, his soul cannot rest or remain still in any state, but always looks to its goal and end. There is no external state which the soul in and beyond itself directs to a spiritual life, which will not be hindered in becoming the most innocent state if a man looks more to the state than to God Himself. Nothing directs us to God except a pure eye.

Therefore it happens that few souls find themselves moved in the spiritual life even if they appear externally to have denied the world and all creatures. The state which they have chosen hinders them more than it helps them, since it is not [chosen and sought after] out of pure love for God, but rather out of a secret self-interest, even though a man denies his own intentions and points of view; in his heart, however, he looks to and seeks himself. This is then clear: such persons commonly remain still in their external state and do not enter their internal and spiritual work (for which the external state is only to be a means and a cause). As a result, in the state in which they think they are denying their own intentions, they are in fact seeking themselves, starving their own life and making their deceptive nature into a soft and restful bed.

Such souls always remain as they are. They know little or nothing of the inner growth of the spiritual life. They rest only in their external state and when this is changed they are changed with it. If the state is good and appears beautiful they shine as men full of virtue; if the state is changed into a poorer one, their beautiful light falls away and they stand naked and empty. They can say nothing of internal and spiritual battles. When things are as they think in their hearts they ought to be, they are at peace and they call this their well-being in God. But if things oppose them or do not go well, they are ill at ease and fall into temptation, and this they call spiritual battles. Such souls can be improved only with difficulty throughout their life because the eye is not cut off from the impure reflection on itself. Their good or evil states they measure according to the experience of their corrupted nature. As a result they can proceed no further. Since they are lovers and possessors of themselves, it is difficult to change them in a basic way, so that they can learn to deny themselves where they have sought themselves.

If a soul comes forth and [wishes] to attain a godly life, it must deny itself in all things which are central for it. In all stages it must often closely examine and test itself to see if it lives to please God or itself, and if the interest of its state commends itself to God or nature. When a soul keeps a careful order or watch over itself in this matter, it cannot fail to be hastened on its way. If it seeks no other interest than to increase its godly treasure, it will soon discover if this increases or decreases. This will be demonstrated when it notes that it dies daily from its natural affections and corrupted inclinations, and that at the same time it takes to itself and develops godly virtues. This can be best known in its relations with its neighbours. If a man lives according to his affections or his corrupted natural possessiveness, he always ascribes to his neighbour what he himself is guilty of. With the eye with which a man ought to see his own faults and needs, he looks upon his neighbours. The judgment and sentence which a man ought to ascribe to himself, he ascribes to his neighbour and forgets himself.

If a man lives for the virtues of God and [seeks] to possess them, things go much differently, for he rather considers himself guilty and demands nothing of his neighbour. What could be demanded, he pays himself.

All faults and shortcomings which a man sees in himself are punished with the sharpest judgments. He considers himself of no good. He ignores the word of his neighbour, considers him innocent and himself guilty, for he knows that he cannot mistake himself but only another.

Such souls always have a fierce eye toward themselves. They test everything they do very closely and sharply to see that nothing false is behind it. They know very well that it is a most deceptive path to trust oneself. They trust their neighbours rather than themselves, for they know that their neighbour's need or deception can do them no harm, but their own deception or need can. Because of this they turn the fierce eye away from their neighbour to themselves, and concern themselves only with themselves and forget their neighbour.

In this a soul can see and test the nature of its vocation. If it stands in the position of a judge over its neighbour, it is to know that in this station it is a vessel of the wrath of God and that the fiery dragon with its seven heads of falsehood rule in it.

If it discovers that it stands in the position of a judge over itself, it is undeniably in the Lord. As often as it comes before itself, it sees to it that it grants no mercy or God will grasp it in its vocation.

In all these ways one can test the way on which one walks.

If a man does not wish to be deceived, he must follow the lamb where it goes, for in its mouth no deception is found.

End.

MAXIMS

by

Johann Conrad Beissel

Selected and Translated

by

Peter Miller

A Collection of Maxims Taken From the Father's Writings

1. Be still and retire within yourself. In all things which you undertake to do, do not be moved by anything except that which brings you out of the quiet chamber of your own essentiality. For from the stillness of Zion proceeds the brightness of God; therefore always be still and attend to what the Lord speaks within you.

2. In all your doings carry yourself as poor and as a possessor of nothing in this world, which by the providence of God can be every hour transposed into an utter dependence on God, angels, and men. O what a happy gain! when a heart is emptied from the comfort of all creatures, and O! what gladness and comfort will it cause on the day of the happy eternity both for God and his Grace.

3. If you are mournful, then be joyful with the joyful; and when you are joyful, then be mournful with the mournful, lest you in an unbecoming manner trouble others with your burdens. Assist those in distress, and be merciful to the helpless. Comfort those who are dejected, and help the afflicted: as you wish God to be toward you, be toward others.

4. Do not despise those who are in favour with God, and do not love those who are hated by him. Let not your vessel be moved by the winds of your own thoughts; but when it is calm stretch out your sails. When your time is over, sleep; and when you awake, look around for the fine day-spring.

5. In dark times be bold and magnanimous; in prosperity be afraid. If it goes evenly, be the same. In glad days be mournful; in prosperity sorrowful. If it goes according to your wishes, mourn for it. And in all this have no other concern but that you do not neglect the sufferings which God has ordained for your salvation, as long you live on earth.

6. Be of humble mind, and do not clothe yourself in a strange form, lest you be puffed up by something which you are not. Also mind not what you are yourself, lest you abuse another's goods. Be emptied both of what you and others are, for an emptied mind is a tabernacle of God, and a possessor of nothing is His property.

7. Clothe yourself in white, and have no blood-coloured garment, except what clothes you for the cross (the purple cloak of Christ). What has in itself no remaining substance, tell not to others. You shall not lie either against God or men; but study both to talk and to keep silence well; then you shall be acceptable before both God and men.

8. Do not rest securly in your own station. The more you think you are safe, the more dubious you shall be of it, especially when you are not yet returned from weeping, for it is written: *He that goes forth weeping, bearing the seed for sowing, shall come home with shouts of joy, bringing his sheaves with him* (Psalm 126:6). O how many dangerous irregularities are found in our well-meaning contentedness with our own self. Therefore, if you want to be sure, entertain a continual disagreement with yourself; yet have the most confidence in God and your neighbour and last of all in yourself.

9. Whoever concerned himself for you in your distress, for him concern yourself in his welfare. If you prosper, bewail yourself; if things go ill with you, be glad. Carry no burdens which are heavier than you are, or else you shall

have no wages for your labour, and shall forget yourself besides, and neglect that which is the most necessary. Only carry yourself well, and you will have worked well.

10. In all your words and deeds have no other will and intention but to make your neighbour happy, and to be useful and edifying to him, and between him and yourself be neither his or your own judge, lest you pass judgment too severe for him and too mild for you.

11. In all your life meddle with nothing else but to love the only God from your whole heart, above all visible and invisible and created things. And if this seems too tedious to you, then spend your time in such things in which you can be useful and edifying to your neighbour. Do your own things also, so that you may be clear in your conscience at the Day of Judgment.

12. Do not be over-eager to pass judgment on that which is good or evil before you know another's scope, and the issue of it, for perhaps the one has with an imperfect thing, a good, and the other with a perfect thing, a bad intention. Therefore be careful not to embark into another's affairs; by such an action your own may suffer detriment.

13. Never be idle. Watch, contemplate, and meditate, who governs your actions, whether it be the chastising Spirit of God, or your own perverse nature. Besides this, be easy, and meditate only on such things which transcend your comprehension. Then you shall be qualified to receive advice from God, and sin not.

14. Be peaceable in all things: if you are despised, content yourself with it; if you are safe or put in eminence, suffer it as a malefactor, and watch yourself closely. Whoever hates you, for him make atonements. Bear him who loves you, and for him who prays for you, keep a medium stance.

15. Do not be against any person except your own self, for you can bear this without hurting another. Whoever is

not against you, do not be against him either. And if any person is your adversary, love him like yourself, and thank him, for he labours for you freely. Him who is concerned for you, neither praise nor revile, for you have no reward from either.

16. Rejoice at your God; rejoice at His Love; rejoice that He is so marvelous in His holy councils; rejoice that He has so marvellously predestined you to everlasting salvation; rejoice at that great work of grace in the new covenant; rejoice that a naked Jesus nailed on the cross has acquired for you such a high warfare for your own salvation; and therefore be glad at all times.

17. No better proof have we of the way to God than this, viz., if one gets rid of himself; for as much as a man possesses himself, so much is he an evildoer, and has an unlawful property, and can therefore not escape being punished. And therefore so far as a man is emptied of himself, so far is he free from sin, and so far he is free from sin, so far he begins to love God.

18. Before all things be watchful *not* to lose the love of the holy being of God, when your neighbour, brother, or friend sins against you; and, what is the most, beware of that sin carefully, of which the good is the cause, for this sin is the plague which spoils at noon-time, because we think to render God a service by it. In all winds and storms sit calmly in your hut, and think on God.

19. If you want to be sure of your salvation, it will be necessary sometimes to raise within yourself a doubt and mistrust against that good, which you have acquired by your conversion, viz., whether it is derived from grace or your own natural property; and if you find that your good is too much mixed with nature, you still owe God a conversion; therefore take heed not to be too careless in your life.

20. Love to be in a low station; yet do not only be low, but also upright, lest you fall into hypocrisy. As it

is necessary for you to be low-minded, even so you shall learn in it to boast about your greatness, or else you rob God of His own.

21.   Do not neglect the time of your youth so that you may recommend your age to God.   You shall neither mourn nor rejoice at any thing which has in itself no cause for life eternal.   If you are distressed, remember the vanity of this life and the joy of the life to come.   And be concerned for nothing, except that you possess your soul with God in peace.

22.   Do not be either a glutton, or luxuriant.   Neither in temporal nor spiritual things elevate yourself, lest you appear in another form than you are, and afterwards at another time be humbled.   A greater perfection is nothing but not to appear in a strange shape; yet holiness must have a covering.

23.   If you are in suffering and are sorrowful in your soul, then take care not to burden your neighbour with it, neither in words, nor deeds, nor gestures, or else you rob your own crown.   In as much as you unburden yourself from suffering, you deprive yourself of the crown of life eternal.   And when you trouble your neighbour with this, and he bears it willingly, he will gain that which you lose.

24.   If you pray, be free from all images, and empty yourself of all created things.   You shall not pray for any thing which you can comprehend with your own thoughts, or else you adore the creature, and not the Creator.   But if you truly pray, then you shall penetrate with your will outside of the world and time; you shall also come to the Godly Magia, where you will find all for which you have prayed.   And if you have attained to the will of God, then your petition is granted.

25.   If you would find the way to Wisdom, then meddle only with such things which you do not understand.   And from what you do not understand, you shall not speak.   And if you understand it, yet esteem the matter itself higher than that

which you understand of it.

26.   If you please God, dis-please yourself in all your activities and level all your designs against your own inclination; and believe of God only such things which are against you. What you like, on that you shall die, lest you might change death into life, and life into death. Doubt your own activities even if right, and your neighbour's activities, even if wrong, and you shall please God.

27.   Do not build your house with sins, nor your apartments with unrighteousness. Do not paint yourself white with another man's blackness, nor clothe yourself in another's beauty. In all things let your soul be satiated with your own works, whether they are good or bad, and according to them you shall be rewarded.

28.   In all your adversities be easy, and have no thoughts, lest you might sin against God. If you fare well, remember God, and be careful not to forget Him. Do not esteem anything for your best, unless you suffer sorrow of your soul from it, nor hold anything evil unless you have suffered damage in your salvation, or in the hope to God, from it.

29.   Have no other thoughts of your own self except that you are against God; neither have any other thoughts of God except that He is against you. Yet think nothing of God except what is good, and suspect of your own self all evil, and therefore have a dislike of yourself, and esteem greatly what comes from God. Thus you shall please God, and have fought a good battle.

30.   Do not be envious or uncharitable against your neighbour, brother, or friend, for an envious heart is bound with ropes of hell, and can not reach future comfort, and an uncharitable heart is separated from God and His communion. Therefore take care that your light be not extinguished, and you must travel in darkness.

31.   Be friendly to all mankind, without assimilating

yourself to the world, and do not communicate with the sins of others. Wrong nobody from your side with your activities, neither trouble anyone with your burdens. Him who wrongs you, recompense with kindness, and pray for him who angers you; and therefore in your whole life be edifying both to friends and enemies.

32. Fight against nothing which proves too mighty for you; nor oppose that which is lesser than you; but prefer to be the least. Act in nothing as you think to be right, but observe what is right before God, even though you have a different notion of it, for it is written, that the imaginations of the thoughts of man's heart are evil continually (Gen. 6:5).

33. Whoever watches well over himself ought to be praised; and whoever can leave himself is honourable. Whoever forgets himself is rich; and whoever will lose himself shall be found again in God.

34. With all your heart be concerned for your everlasting salvation, and do not let the days of the visitation of God pass by in vain. O! what a treasure you can gather when you lay hold on life eternal, and discharge all cares and sorrows of this world.

35. Do not be a backbiter among your people, or else you shall not ascend to the mountain of God. Before all things love sincerity and truth from your heart, and do not have a two-forked tongue, for thus you shall be assimilated to God and His image. Neither talk nor think an evil against another, or else you are what you talk or think of. For whoever is evil, thinks evil; and whoever is good, thinks good.

36. Love all men without difference, but let the saints, which are acceptable before God, bestow upon you as much love as they have. Be acceptable before God, and men shall honour you. And take good care not to refuse the love of the saints, or by hurting them to make them cry to God

CARL A. RUDISILL LIBRARY
LENOIR-RHYNE COLLEGE

because of their love. But love the wicked and refractory.

37. Carry no burdens on the sabbath-day, but when God rests within you, rest within Him. And when God works within you, work within Him.

38. A solitary life, which is separated from the world and creatures, ought to be your greatest treasure, for we can easily forfeit our fortune in this world. Whoever acts as he is from his nativity is already in his place. Therefore shall man learn to know himself and his Creator, and what the grace of the new covenant is.

39. Take heed not to allow your own productions a free course to bring you to their intended end, or you shall gather a great heap of fire-wood, which will make you hot at that great day. But if you want to be sure, be suffering and dying in all your activities, so that of your activities nothing might remain of which you cannot take advantage at the Day of Eternity; for all that we gather here we must spend there, be it good or bad.

40. Do not have a quick anger, and be zealous for nothing but what can again atone your zeal, i.e. the love to the holy Being of God. Whoever has separated himself from you, maintain, and wait for him, under the patience of God, to his own reconciliation, that he might not perish on the Day of Judgment. For love has the shield of everlasting salvation.

41. Say nothing without faith, in order to bring forth fruits on that great harvest-day; for it is written, that men must give an account of every vain word [Matt. 12:36]. Do not hear what you dare not say; and what you do not like to hear, do not tell to another. In all your activities regulate yourself towards your neighbour's temporal and eternal welfare, and you shall live.

42. Be merciful and have compassion with the distressed. Remember in all your activities what a reward you have to expect for your labour. Judge no man before you

know his thoughts. Perhaps he has a good intention; therefore take care not to condemn an innocent.

43. Do not hate your neighbour, brother, or friend, and take care not to wrong the Elect of God, for they are his orphans, and their supplications ascend through the clouds before Him, who helps them. Therefore despise them not.

44. Whoever acts prudently with his tongue is a wise man; but he who follows his own thoughts is a fool. Whoever takes too much care for himself, shall lose his soul, but whoever neglects himself shall find himself again in God.

45. In all your life concern yourself for a good end, because all our works shall be brought before the Judgment of God, be they good or bad. Therefore love only such things from which you can expect a benefit at the Day of Judgment. And let all that does not increase your harvest on the Day of Eternity pass by; then you are safe.

46. In affliction of your soul let your heart rejoice, but when you have gladness, then be sorrowful for the life to come. You shall neither want nor know nor desire anything of God; but shall always think: I do not understand, nor do I know, what is good, because I am not yet a child. For those alone know what the Father wanted; and when they, being hungry, ask bread from Him, He will not give them a stone.

47. Do not be wise with yourself, and have no other thoughts of yourself but such as you are yourself, so that you do not sustain a loss. In welfare, and when you have a good cause, think little of yourself, but when you are low and despised, then boast upon your greatness.

48. Be careful and solicitous in all things, and meditate only about such matters which pertain to your salvation and peace. Forget all things and yourself; then you shall get clear from vain transitory things, and shall be taken up from God and the incomprehensible Eternity. All

that we do and work out is deficient; but what does not work is of great value and remains forever.

49. Do neither good nor evil for your own ease, but die, that with a clear conscience you might live, and live, that with a clear conscience you might die. For whoever does anything for his own ease, is in that which he does not in the communion of the Son of God.

50. Never reprimand your neighbour, friend, or brother about anything, unless you can answer for his defects, and atone for him before God; or else instead of reforming him you load him with heavier burdens, so that his debts and burdens grow heavier than his defects. Therefore be careful never to talk or think anything concerning your neighbour, brother, or friend without love and mercy.

51. Do not love sleep, lest you impoverish yourself, nor be too quick in running, lest you neglect anything. In all things which you take in hand, make the beginning so, as you wish to have the end. Happy is he who in all his activities does not have to expect a bad end. Therefore take care in all things not to make a bad beginning; then you shall come to a good end.

52. You shall not leave the right way for the sake of others; nor shall you because of the great multitude of them which are wicked let the love of God grow cool within yourself. Nothing shall disturb you, to go from the true way. And if the sins and iniquities of others overwhelm you, do not be disturbed, but make advantage of it for your own reformation.

53. Let no one reprove you, but your own evil, and reprove nobody except your own folly. Fly both from the praising of the wicked and from the reproach of the pious. Do no thing either for temporal honours or profits' sake, but study only to please God, so that you live forever.

54. Happy is the man who in his Calling soon becomes poor both in body and spirit. In all things which we do

besides this, the image of God does not appear, but our own. But by poverty and nakedness a man is freed from all adherence to himself, for every man has within himself a selfishness, from which, if he is not freed, he cannot see the face of God.

55.   There is no other sin, but to live without the nature of God. It is written of Abraham, he kept my laws and statutes [Gen. 26:5]. God is long-suffering, merciful, and friendly, and does not possess Himself, and neither shall you possess yourself, nor have any property, if you want to be found within Him. God is righteous, and therefore he never enters where we have yet something to lose.

56.   Whoever possesses earthly things cannot possess himself, and whoever possesses himself cannot possess God; and whoever possesses God has found his true property. O how happy is he who comes home, and rests on his mother's bosom. He has travelled well who left his own ugly seat; and he sits well who has feasted at all times that which is the most bitter.

57.   Value yourself neither too high nor too low. Neither exact too much in your judgment nor suppress your neighbour, so that (to his character) both something better or lesser might be added without perceptible alteration. If you appear to yourself much despised then have great regard for yourself, and if you seem to yourself to be honourable, then humiliate yourself.

58.   I know for the future no other labour but to rest and to bear the work of God. If in former times I had not paid too much regard for myself, and instead of that exercised myself more in leaving myself, I might have obtained that peace which my heart sought. But now my nothingness is publicly revealed; God have mercy upon me, that I may succeed.

AMEN.

THE CHURCH OF GOD

by

Johann Conrad Beissel

The Church of God

Ephrata, March 20, 1756
To Peter Becker

Since there appears to be no hope that we shall see each other again, I wish to say this: my spirit embraces you and your beloved [N.N.] together with and in the whole Church of God and the general awakening in Germany, the spiritual children of which we are.

But this is to be observed: the Church of God has its twelve tribes under the new covenant as well as under the old. Now the tribes in Germany could not spring from the unfruitful Rachel because of the rage of the Dragon and the carnal Antichrist. Because of this the number of servants multiplied and when the time was fulfilled Leah brought forth Judah from whom Christ came according to the flesh. During this time Rachel remained barren and although many a beautiful branch grew forth from the tribe of Judah under the dominion of the Kings, nevertheless, there was only one stem in which the fruitfulness of the new world remained because the unfruitful woman had yet to bring forth this seed.

In the meantime God remembered Rachel and caused the Church to wander toward the setting of the sun. I must be brief for I could easily write a book on this matter. At length it has come to pass that Rachel has begotten a son in these lands by the name of Joseph and God will add to this (as is implied in the name). This son was quite different from the other sons of Jacob and yet they were all sons of Jacob as were the twelve apostles and disciples of Jesus. All were apostles but only one leaned on his breast.

FIRST SERMON

from

DELICIAE EPHRATENSES

by
Johann Conrad Beissel

First Sermon

A profound concern of my spirit moved me to put down this wondrous writing, and to disclose some of the indescribable circumstances which led me to it. And although the text commends itself to full satisfaction, I want to introduce the subject by some preliminary remarks.

In the days of my godly youth, I sincerely believed that it would be sufficient if I made every effort to reach the utmost purity in a life of sacred love and divine enlightenment. But this caused so many severe and difficult conflicts within me that I was often frightened and horrified. Yet at the same time I was hoping for final victory and continued my sacred love relationship. But the harder I tried, the more vigorous grew the rebellion within myself. This tortured and strained me so much that often the very stones would have been moved to tears, if only they had any sensitivity, especially since my great industry and the purest passion of love continuously rekindled the fire of my enthusiasm.[1] All this made me meditate deeply, since my very desire to do good caused the evil in me to be so active. Therefore I had to investigate where the power of evil originated, since it did not only prove impossible to get rid of it by striving after the good, but my efforts even fed the fire of evil within me. As long as I relaxed in my quest for goodness, I found that I experienced peace and did not encounter any evil. All this made me go to the root of Evil and I began to investigate the abyss of Goodness to discover the mode of its existence from all eternity[2] before any evil appeared in it.

Now let me open the treatise and explain how I investigated the origin of the existence and life of all beings, in order to discover how the eternal God could produce something evil and how the apostate archangel could break the unity into duality and the duality into multiplicity.[3] For my faded heavenly magical power (magia) was deeply influenced by the fact that the heavenly femininity could not

manifest herself because of the fall of Lucifer. But I was
not aware that it was she who had made me so love-sick from
the very beginning; however, I did not know my Adam's nature
then, and thought it was already sufficient to take the
straight road to come to the Mother of eternity or the
eternal Virgin. It is hard to describe how much and for how
many days and even years I suffered, because of my love for
this Virgin. But since I did not know my own nature in the
times and days of my godly youth,[4] I sincerely believed that
my whole human nature could be transformed into the cleanest
and purest form of heavenly life. At that time I was not
yet aware of the true nature of my fiery masculinity, for it
is totally opposed to the attraction of my holy amorousness
by the eternal Virgin. My fiery masculinity had lost all
its temper because it was separated from the celestial
femininity. Good God! What tribulations did I have to go
through because my love was so heavenly and chaste: my
fiery male will was in constant rebellion against the
heavenly femininity, since he has to lose his dominion to
her. Of course, he would have preferred to embrace Eve,[5] the
mistress who was created out of his own side, whom he might
have ruled as a despotic lord.

I had spent a number of years trying to bring the will
of the Virgin and the fiery will of my masculinity to an
agreement, but I accomplished nothing in spite of the great
distress and misery I went through. At last, God, who is
the eternal Love Himself, had compassion on me and revealed
the way to the secret of the cross. I was shown that the
Virgin Sophia would never consent to an engagement or an
agreement with the masculinity of Adam; he has to be put to
the cross like Jesus, the second Adam, because the flesh of
his side which is closed has to be opened once again, so
that the eternal Mother can find an open gate to her
rightful inheritance. Now the way to true holiness is
prepared. Now the true priesthood is re-established which

entails eternal salvation. Now the eternal Virgin is looking for a groom again, for she can marry only men of the priestly lineage, who join Christ in his sacrifice of the cross. In the old covenant, when the man had dominion, the high priest was not permitted to take any wife but a virgin; therefore, in the new covenant, when the heavenly femininity has ascended her throne again, she will marry no one but a priest. Here begins the restoration of all things: for as every corruption has come into the world through the rule of man's exalted will, everything will be restored (again) when Mary's song of praise will be fulfilled (Luke 1:52):

> and the mighty ones will be put down from their thrones and exalted those of low degree

(i.e., God's femininity, or meekness, which was rejected for such a long time).

O how blessed I am! My exalted self-will has been put to the cross with Christ and its fiery male power has humbled itself after the manner of women; thus the fountain of mercy flows out into the whole world to bring salvation. Now we find our true life, in which we are saved and free from all suffering, conflict, and pain.

But now I want to come back to the subject: in the times and days of my godly youth the heavenly Venus touched me with the beams of her light and caused me to fall in love with Sophia's heavenly femininity or virginity. I experienced, however, that this femininity wanted by no means to come to terms with my fiery male will. Every day this caused many violent conflicts within me. Of course, it made me ponder deeply, whether the separation of the sexes (tinctures) into male and female, roughness and softness, or fire and light in the whole creation was not based on a wrong footing, since the fiery masculinity rules with severe harshness in the whole creation, etc. After I had spent much time in this labyrinth without finding a way out, I arrived suddenly at the secret of the fall of the first man.

For he desired to be sexually separated like the animals and therefore his spiritual eye became blind, whereby he lost the true sight and enlightenment. Thus he became incapable of having insight into his own being. The lustful staring at the animals led him to early adultery, whereupon his heavenly femininity left him and at the very moment when he was supposed to lie down in the bridal bed, he fell down and died.

Of course many thoughts passed through my mind concerning this affair. The fact that it was the contemplation of the animals which aroused such a harmful desire in Adam, raised an important question: had there not already been something wrong with the animals, since their sexes (tinctures) were separated and Adam's spiritual eye was poisoned so rapidly at their very sight? I could not neglect this question, especially since in the old covenant the blood of so many animals had to be shed in order to atone for the bodies of men. If it was not true that they contributed in some way to Adam's transgression, the animals would have been treated unjustly, which is impossible, because God is just.

The main reason why I was moved to write this, is that my sacred love for the heavenly Sophia put my Adam's body to so many trials. Therefore, it is no wonder that I asked myself about the reason for her total disinterest in my enamoured activity. Yet it is the case that the archangel in his passionate rebellion against the Goodness of God, attacked God's eternal fortress when he abandoned his meekness by arousing the hidden abyss within himself: thus God had to leave His fortress, give up His oneness, and awaken His latent masculinity, even though this is against His nature. For since the rebellious archangel had stirred up the fiery abyss within himself and had exalted himself above the meekness of the divine femininity, God could no more operate with the same femininity (i.e., goodness –

P. Miller p. 7). And if God did not step out of His fortress at this point, He would have suffered the fallen
archangel to become His husband, and God's goodness would
have been made subject unto him, which the angel had always
desired.

Now God was forced to divide the whole creation into
male and female and to subordinate femininity, which is the
gentle part, to the rule of masculinity. The purpose for
this division was to have nothing female in the whole
creation which was not subordinate to the male magistrate,
for this would have made it impossible for the fallen prince
of the angels to find in God Himself or among the creatures
any femininity which was free and ready to be dominated by
his aroused male fury. Therefore, when God awakened His
masculinity and abandoned His stronghold, He left behind His
femininity, which is His gentle nature,[6] and relegated, cast
out, and excluded the fallen archangel for all eternity.
After all this had transpired, and the whole creation (especially the animal kingdom) was under male dominion, even God
had to sacrifice His own desire to be eternally good and had
to begin to enforce authoritative order. Then it was once
again time for God to look out for His desolate femininity,
who already lamented deeply because she was abandoned and
had lost her husband. Therefore, He said to her: "Let us
make men, in our image, and let them have dominion over the
fish in the sea," etc.

Adam could have truly supported God's providence if he
had kept his principality and had not fallen into sexual
separation himself, for he was created perfectly in the
image of God, male and female. There in the cradle lay the
beautiful child which was still very young; if only Adam did
not violate the probation in this state of his creation, his
rule might have restored all the subordinated creatures from
their state of division back to divine harmony and unity,
for Adam's character was balanced and in harmony.

But it seems that he was already at that time attracted
by the separation of the sexes in God to conduct his
dominion in a masculine way. At this point everything broke
down, for Adam was neither an uncreated God, nor was he a
God begotten from God:[7] therefore, he was not found capable
to maintain his great freedom. Therefore it says in Gen.
2:5 (this is how a number of scholars translate the original
text): "And Adam was forbidden to cultivate the adamah,"
although God had made him the lord over everything in Gen.
chapter I. Now God was forced to think of a different way
and had to make a dwelling for His weakened image and create
for it a body out of the quintessence of all created things.[8]
It should serve on the one hand as a stronghold for the
weakened humanity and, on the other hand, by overcoming this
body, man was to become a princely conqueror. This is what
Christ later accomplished when he assumed the body of our
humanity. In the same way Adam was supposed to dissipate,
disperse and abolish all the venom which the fall of Lucifer
had introduced into the whole creation. In due time he
could have put away his body again if he had been victorious, and the image of God could have reappeared in the open;
yet, alas, the opposite happened.

Now we come to the deplorable fall which was caused by
Adam's lust after the separation of the sexes (tinctures)
into male and female form. Now the above mentioned beautiful child lost the nobility of paradise because it forsook
the wife of its youth. Now God's heavenly femininity had
lost her position and had to leave her royal throne until
Mary sang her hymn of praise. O wonder! What happened at
this sad event? As soon as the wife of his youth had left
him and her home, and after an animal wife had been made for
him agreeable to his magical desire, the spirit of deceit-
fulness and slyness came over him. This woman is a daughter
of Lucifer, begotten by his magical will and, therefore, she
tried to corrupt the last remnants of femininity completely,

in order to transform everything into the fiery male exalta-
tion. But the nobility of this woman is as much greater
than an animal's as the nobility of Adam's body is superior
to the body of animals. Therefore, it is hard to express
what a simple and innocent child she was before she meddled
with the serpent, although she was corrupted by the serpent's magic more than by its words. Had the woman been
able to pass the trial of the discourse with the serpent,
she might have been Adam's throne princess and his paradisical rosary. Thus, at least a slight shadow of God's
original purpose would have remained.

However, this could not happen, because Eve was weakened by Adam's will and had received the stigma of lust from
his body. But if Eve had been faithful they might have united again at a higher level of the celestial life without
having to die. At least they might have lived in this innocent childlike life for one day of God; i.e., for a thousand
years in human terms.[9] During that time, the great prince
Lucifer would have been bound once again with chains of
darkness, and the whole earth would have been filled with
innocent childlike people. Then Eve, filled with meekness
and light, would have absorbed within herself the fiery abyss, i.e., the excited masculinity, until finally God would
have found the opportunity to lead His femininity, which had
been sitting in the dust for a long time, out of the wilderness, beautiful like the dawn, lovely as the sunshine and
terrible as a host of war with banners (Cant. 6-10). After
that the widow would have brought the whole race of Adam
under her wings and affected it until her divine femininity
would have absorbed all the awakened male will and in this
way the restoration of all things would have come.

O how great would have been such a shortening of days
if the male will had not advanced that far in his rule! But
even God had to borrow the same will, and conduct His
government in magisterial robes. For the great prince

Lucifer was very eager to bring the divine femininity under his dominion, which would, of course, have brought the eternal damnation of all. For if his access to the femininity which was taken from Adam had already so many miserable consequences, what would have happened if he had touched the heavenly femininity?

Here I remember that I have to caution all Christian women, not to oppose the magistracy of man until they are adorned with the body of light in paradise.[10] For the more they liberate themselves from man's dominion, the more they are in danger that the ancient serpent will climb the tree of temptation and become their preacher. And you men, do not be proud of your office, but remember that it has its origin in your lust after the separation of the sexes (tinctures) and that you lost your princely diadem because of it. Instead, you have been appointed rulers and guardians of the animal nature of woman. Learn, seek, and strive that your excited and fiery male will may be appeased by the heavenly femininity, who will clothe you, instead of with fire, with a new raiment of light.

And you virgins, do not be arrogant. Do not hunger after the separation of the sexes (tinctures) or after the fiery seed of man; do not try to raise your dead water with the awakened fire of man. Seek rather the water of life, which inspires the fertility or the seed of the godly generation. Exert, therefore, all your industry to retrieve the lost divine femininity, for the water of meekness springs from her, as a bright flame of light from sacred oil. Therefore be careful not to excite the passionate fire in order not to defile your race. Whenever you feel the burning within yourself, hasten and run to the water of life. There you will receive your inheritance and attain the divine harmony or the holy unity of character, when you will neither immerse yourself too deeply into the dead water of the ungodly femininity nor exalt yourself too much in the fiery abyss of the aroused masculine will. Therefore be spirited, quiet, and upright in all you are doing and always moderate and modest within yourself and toward others. Likewise, the male virgins shall not be too passionate to cool their male fire in the waters of the godless femininity, for this action does not produce children of promise. But try to make the fire of your aroused abyss decrease as much as possible that you may participate to some extent in the feminine nature. Of course, this female water, which originated in the aroused male fire, is still rather "salty," since true femininity is missing.[11] But in this case you ought not soothe this male severity and harshness with the terrestrial femininity, because her water received from the serpent a propensity not only to allay the bitterness, but also to incense it with fiery wrath. This occurs frequently when the tinctures are mixed. If it happens to you, you have to hasten to the source, i.e., the Mother of eternity, whose femininity has remained immaculate.

Even though we have treated several subjects concerning the relationship between man and woman, and between male and female virgins, we can no less pass by the spiritual builders of the house of God* in silence. I would have indeed much to say about them which I can hardly trust to my pen, but since I have a strong support from the eternal Mother, the heavenly femininity, through whom all things will be restored, so that God may become again all in all, let us touch briefly on the subject. How are you doing, you spiritual builders of the house of God? What foundation do you build on? Did you communicate the eternal Mother through the word of your speech, and did this decrease the fire of your male self-will, who fervently insists on his

---

*Clergy

own right? Did it make your will meek, gentle, and feminine? Indeed you may proclaim words, but not that Word
which became flesh in the original femininity. In your
office, you are therefore only the builders of an edifice,
which the wrath of the Almighty will break down in good
time.[12]   For nothing will remain forever, which is not born
in the holy temper out of fire, light, and water. This
water does not extinguish the fire completely, but it allays
its severity and makes it agreeable to the light, which
detects and reproves all things. O how much does the
eternal Mother, or heavenly femininity long to be in us, in
order to reduce and abolish our ascending will, and to put
on us once again the female raiment of light.

It is apparent that any magistracy, ecclesiastical as
well as civil, has its high rank only because it has to rule
over the femininity which has been poisoned by the serpent,
for which Mother Eve was responsible. Therefore, an office
in itself has no dignity to attain paradise. Thus, all
offices can exist only until all the femininity, which was
poisoned by the serpent, will be restored under the pure
Godmanhood of Jesus, who was begotten immaculate from the
heavenly femininity and then suffered himself to be nailed
to the cross in his male office, in order to atone fully for
the tear which Adam's sexual division had caused. No saint
of whatever stature, not even someone like an apostle, can
achieve through his office greater dignity than the cross of
Christ, for on the cross his office ceases because Adam's
division is expiated. If during his life he has put on much
of the heavenly femininity, constantly mortifying his fiery
masculinity, he will awake in the resurrection in a male and
female body of light according to his achievements. It is
remarkable that the Apostles throughout the time of their
office never called themselves anything but servants of
Jesus Christ. Consequently this office did not make them
children, but only servants, because a servant does not stay

in the house forever. Their office lasted only until they
were martyred. But in a noble, purely spiritual sense, the
apostles were the twelve spiritual sons or the tribes of
Jacob, of whom the twelve spiritual generations were born.
Out of this race the number of 144,000 virgins was chosen
and sealed. For by the spirit of the new covenant they had
the word of heavenly impregnation within themselves, in
order to multiply the divine race. Outwardly, with their
bodies, they were under the law as was their office; but
inwardly they were clothed with heavenly nature. The promise that a woman should compass a man was continuously
expressed in their words, so that they diligently sowed the
seed of the new world. Outwardly, their male image was
ruling the Word which was dwelling within them. Although
the heavenly femininity was dominant in the Word, and had
the precedence, she still had to stand under the external
masculinity of the Apostles as under a male guardian,
comparable to the guardianship of Joseph over the Virgin
Mary and her child.

This explains what it means, whether a man in his
office becomes a servant of the new covenant, or whether he
is only a steward over the animal nature of the earthly
separated tinctures. If he is among the latter, death will
reap all his fruits, for together with his works he is
within those limits where the will of man governs. Therefore his awakened fiery self-will is exalted above others
and consequently at a very great distance from the meekness
of the Son of God. Of course, only a few know about this
matter, because people are ignorant about spiritual things.
For almost all men remain within the realm of separation and
division, where one tincture dominates the other. All this
began with the fall of Lucifer, which has even broken
up God's oneness,[13] to the extent that His male property was
separated from His female property. Although God had intended to remedy this later with the first Adam, Adam ruined

this plan completely, which grieved the heavenly femininity
so much, that she had to remain a widow for a long time.

Then how can this conflict come to a good end? How can
the most pitiable femininity of God be reunited to her true
husband, who does not dominate her in his wrath? How can
God's masculinity be discharged from the office of the judge
and put on again the female habit, thus resolving all the
divisions and pacifying the whole world again? If this
shall happen, the heavenly femininity has to give birth to
her own husband out of the eternal womb. He must have male
and female chracteristics, like God, and upon his shoulder
the government will rest. Now a virgin is pregnant from the
seed of the heavenly woman, and all the exalted selfishness
begins to be abolished and must return to the bosom of the
eternal Mother. Of course, Jesus filled his office in the
figure of a man, but his character was not male, but female,
for he lived in humility and obedience even to the death on
the cross. The arrogant masculinity, who rules in the fiery
abyss, could not tolerate the sight of this feminine or
rather heavenly character in Jesus' masculine likeness.
This is why he had to be crucified. If Jesus did not have
within himself the fount of heavenly water, i.e., the
heavenly femininity, he could not have performed the
priestly function of sacrificing himself and praying for his
enemies. This most humble man broke the seal and opened,
once again, the gate of life which had been shut, and he
appeased and silenced the awakened wrath. Because of him,
the pure fount of the meekness of God has begun to flow
again. No man from Adam to Christ could have consented to
this humble subordination, because the revengeful abyss of
fire in all men made them unable to sacrifice themselves and
then to pray for their enemies.

If Christ, although he had been crucified, had not made
atonement for his enemies, he could not have become the husband of the eternal Virgin, for, the one, whom she is sup-

posed to marry, has to be a priest, since the Virgin <u>Sophia</u>
will not embrace any man in whom the fiery abyss is still
burning. Thus, if anyone wants to be called bridegroom of
the Virgin, let him first become a priest who is sealed for
the atonement of the whole world. And if a virgin wants to
be married to the priest Jesus, let her be a virgin both in
body and spirit, or else the priest will not receive her
into his side. For the eternal virginity has to end all
division and make the lost union of God flourish again.
From the beginning of the world this was the foundation and
the aim of all existence.

Now Adam's masculinity is avenged and atoned for at the
same time. This could not have happened if Christ did not
have within himself the fountain of heavenly water, which is
the divine femininity. The fury of the fiery wrath pressed
him very hard when he sweated blood in the garden. Therefore, the judgment of fiery anger would have incensed him so
much that he might have revenged himself, if only there had
been a single spark of the fiery masculinity within him.
This happened to many martyrs, who during their martyrdom
were so inflamed with anger and vengeance, that they did not
offer themselves freely on the altar. They are still lying
under the altar and expect that the judgment and the revenge
of their enemies will make them happy. Such men have no
part in the blood of atonement, but only in Abel's blood,
which cried for vengeance against his brother.

In Christ, the fire and the light have finally been
reconciled and both have been made one. But the division,
which the rebellious archangel forced even upon God, had
spread throughout all the creation, even down to the
animals. In all things the fiery masculinity was separated
from the gentle femininity and given dominion over it, which
divided the pure heavenly element and destroyed the meek
wholeness of God. This made it necessary for God to make a
last dance in order to cleanse the holy dwellings again and

separate the strange chaotic mixture which had resulted in this visible world. Thus, this earth is the excrement or the refuse of the holy dwellings and therefore the spirit, who governs this element, harbours an eternal vengeance and hostility against godly men and tries to revenge himself upon them by depriving them first of everything that is his, e.g., temporal goods, etc. And if this is not enough, he even takes their bodies and kills them, although he should be their nurse and mother, because they grew to some extent in his own garden. But it will not be different until the fountain of water which was in Christ will finally mitigate and unite everything. The last purgation, however, when God will judge this world, will not be based on His forebearance.

When I consider how close we have come to the eternal Goodness through Christ Jesus, I am comforted as one is comforted by his mother. For although the loving Virgin Sophia embraces us most kindly, our natural masculinity suffers from the severest passion towards her, as from a spring of fire, because in her meekness she tries to embrace it in order to make it subject to her will. But the fiery masculinity still searches for a tempering fountain, which it can rule in order to remain exalted and to maintain the throne. But if I consider Christ, the son of the Virgin, I find that he has both tinctures, the male as well as the female in the exact balance of temper. This means that his fiery masculinity is clothed in water and light and that all that is not mitigated therein, has been crucified. The reason why even the Apostles fled when Christ was arrested, was that they were afraid that the fiery source of their masculinity would be appeased by the judgment while their self-will was still exalted. Therefore, fearing to lose it, they fled, but did not really know what they did. The holy women, however, followed him to the cross, for not only had they nothing to lose, but they came to regain their lost possession.[14] This is why they looked so diligently for the grave, but they also did not know why they did it. It was the greatest miracle then, that Christ's resurrection made a holy woman the first apostle, who brought the message of the resurrection to the other Apostles. Of course, there was still a certain weakness in the male constitution of the Apostles, which caused them to flee and which lasted until the Holy Spirit was poured out on them and they regained their even temper. This Spirit in the form of the holy dove will not cease to hover above the fiery faces, until they are all mitigated and the fire is extinguished by the fountain of paradisical water. In the same way the Spirit of God had been moving over the face of the water at the fall of Lucifer. This explains why everything has to be restored by the heavenly femininity, and why Christ in his office is only called a servant (Is. 53), even though everything exists through him. For, although Christ would have been crucified and resurrected and would have made atonement for the burning fire of wrath, no children of heaven and paradise could have been born if the Spirit had not descended.

Now we know exactly what kind of community the Christian Church here on earth is, for it always emphasizes the dying and dead body of Christ. But everything which dies with Christ on the cross is delivered into the womb of the eternal Spirit, i.e., the heavenly Mother, and flourishes greatly. Under her service the whole work of restoration makes a glorious progress. And as the number of those who are delivered into her bosom increases, the offices which men hold will cease to be. For as in Adam all die, so in Christ shall all be made alive, both Christ, who is the first fruit, and then all those that are with Christ at his coming. The end will come when he will have transferred the kingdom to God and the Father, and when all authority, violence and power will be abolished. But he must rule as a

king until he has laid all His enemies under His feet, and
the last enemy to be destroyed is death. But, if all things
will be subjugated to Him, then even the Son will be subjugated to Him who has given him all authority, so that God
may be all in all (I Cor. 15:22-28).

Now we can see that even the royal office of Jesus
Christ will end and he will abandon his past masculinity and
relinquish himself to the eternal Goodness, surrendering
everything up to her rule. Then it will once more be as it
has been before the ages, and the righteousness of God will
resign its office, for all unrighteousness will be brought
to an end and abolished forever. The masculine property
which was born in wrath had been the appointed ruler over
the femininity which the serpent had poisoned. But then it
will have to resign its office and surrender it to the
eternal Mother who is the overlord of all. Thus the whole
creation will return to its original etheral state as it was
intended. For as the restorer himself will finally be the
first to lay down his masculinity, his office, and his
kingdom, likewise those things will of course be abolished
throughout all the realms of creation. Now we understand
how the fallen archangel used the enflamed abyss of fire to
provoke God's supreme masculinity, and caused a separation
in it, which pervaded afterwards the whole creation. Adam
was created as a harmonious being in order to restore the
unity in the world. Of course, there was not little damage,
when he himself lusted for the separation of the sexes.
This was the occasion for the command not to eat of the tree
of separation.* But after he had eaten, the femininity,
which was taken from him against her own nature and character, was poisoned by the serpent. All this has caused God
great difficulties, for the will of man was already so
corrupted that God could not be pleased with it any more,

---

*here male and female are equalled to evil and good.

especially since the pure Virgin had abandoned Him.   But if
Eve had withstood the temptation, at least she might have
passed for Hagar, the Egyptian maid servant, and even that
only to a certain extent. But nothing like that prefigures
in the wonders of eternity.

Now let us go on and examine briefly the order of restoration. There was no small damage done when the innocent
femininity defiled herself completely; therefore God subordinated her will to the will of man, who had caused all this
through his lust for the separation of the tinctures. And,
since the will of man through his lust had corrupted everything, God gave the word of promise to his female partner
and said that the seed of the woman could bruise the head of
the serpent (Gen. 3:15). Consequently, after Adam's will
had corrupted everything through his lust for a fleshly
wife, the word of promise was given to a virgin, and in her
we regain everything that was lost in Adam. This virgin was
determined to love no man of beastly sexuality. O wonder!
What happened? Soon the virginity awoke. She had sat in
the dust for a long time and had been longing for the right
man to be born, who would end her long widowhood. Thus, the
will of the Virgin Mary not to know a man sanctified human
virginity, and by the conception and birth of Christ the
heavenly Virgin has been liberated from her house of mourning. Adam's will and rupture was atoned on the cross. O how
holy is the magic power of heaven! Through Jesus and Mary[15]
it was introduced once again into the divided tinctures of
the human race. This precious will of the Virgin Mary not
to know any man, and the crucifixion of Christ, who by
immersing himself into the gentle fountain of water, became
female again and like the Virgin, atoned for and abolished
the fiery will of Adam, who had lusted for the separation of
the sexes. Now a temper is restored which is pure and godly
enough to produce heavenly offspring. As Lucifer and Adam
separated everything when they exalted themselves in their

will of fire, so Jesus' immersion into the water of gentleness and the purity of the Virgin Mary's will, everything, including the very least, will be restored to unity. And this will conclude this treatise.

I pray that everyone may bear the depth of my thought in this discourse, for if I unravelled the whole matter fully, it would consume my humanity. My masculinity, which is salty with fire, has been soaking already for a number of years in these divine waters of God's lost virginity or femininity. But up till now, I found it not yet possible to rinse off this salt and fire, for wrath must be atoned by wrath. For however godly the female fountain of water may be, it is unable to mitigate the fire which in its wrath is exalted above itself. This is the reason why the Virgin Mary could not give birth to a female image of her own sex to bruise the serpent. Of course the fiery abyss of my masculinity would have loved to immerse itself into the gentle spring of water flowing from the heavenly femininity or Virgin Sophia, if only the sweating of blood in the garden of Gethsemane could have been avoided. For the Virgin Sophia cannot offer her watery femininity to be impregnated in anyone whose fire is not revenged by the fire of revenge, and this is the mystery of the cross of Jesus. For even though he was the meekness itself, righteousness required that he offer his male image as food to the woeful judgment of fire. After this the holy women could attend to his body without shame. In the same way, I want to be united to the Virgin Sophia to bring heavenly fruit. But first I have to suffer outside the gate dressed in Jesus' body. There the reproach of Christ is my honorable gown and his death my life.

All this tortured me so hard for a number of years, for on the one hand I carried within me the heavenly Venus and was so much in love with the celestial purity that I cannot pronounce it; but on the other hand I carried with me the

tedious image which is incapable of heavenly endeavors.
Therefore, I must constantly remember that Christ said about
himself: I must yet be baptized and I am so fearful until
it is accomplished. This is the pendulum of the clock in my
life of faith: as often as my industry brings forth a
flower of paradise, a sword is drawn against me, as if I had
committed the greatest crime. This has been going on for
many years already and it will continue until my sinful body
will perish. Vale!

Peter Miller's Footnotes

1. The meaning of these words is the following: The
more we are inclined towards the Good, the more the Evil
within us becomes active.   This is a truth which is confirmed by a long experience; therefore, if we do good, and
do not come into the judgment for it, it is a proof that our
goodness was hypocrisy.   For, since the two principles of
love and of wrath contend strongly for the over-lordship, if
one of them is moved, the other one is also set in motion,
in order to maintain the equilibrium.   And certainly one
principle is changed into the other if an alien mover
enters.   The Evil is the power of the Good and supplements
it, and vice versa.   One serves the manifestation of the
other.   This is why the Fall resulted in so much evil, because so much goodness was corrupted.   And if the angel of
jealousy was not checked, he would have transformed all the
Good into Evil.   The initiated in nature also know that all
sweetness is transformed by a sour agent, called "mother,"
(Mutter) into vinegar.   This sheds light on Paul's letter to
the Romans, for it is certain that he referred in it to
nobody but himself.   And since the author has been used by
God in His holy laboratory, where Evil is changed again into
Good, it is not surprising that he also had to pass through
such fervent ordeals of fire with his Adam's body until his
own evil was turned into good again.   Otherwise, only very
few people reach this toil through their conversion.   Most
attain no more than a sound morality, which can make you a
good Jew.   But if one does not follow Jesus Christ to the
cross, the enmity against God is not abolished.   Consequently such men are the first to side with those Pharisees
when they crucify Christ.   This is the origin of the doctrine of salvation by grace, for on the way to God nothing
remains but the dust of our vanity; it is dangerous and may
easily lead to heresy if one arbitrarily presumes to be

saved even before one has come to dust.

2. After the pattern of the good master John (17:5),
the author had sought in his prayers for that period in
eternity when Evil was not yet manifest and the Goodness of
God ruled. He asserted then that that period would reoccur
after many ages, when Evil will be sealed up and the whole
creation will have returned to its ethereal state. Here he
called this Goodness of God various names, such as the
femininity of God, the Mother of eternity, or the Virgin
Sophia; he also points out that the angel of jealousy pursued her fervently in order to subjugate her. Therefore,
God was forced to take her into holy custody and to relegate
the fallen angel from her forever. Thus, even though we
grant him restoration to a degree, access to the Virgin will
be cut off to him for eternity because of the outrage which
he has committed against her. At the Creation she was
intended to be the woman whose seed would crush the head of
the serpent, and who was to be Adam's wife; but she left
him, when he, after his too ardent inquiry into the
propagation of the animals became desirous to have such a
helper too. Therefore in the Old Testament, especially in
Isaiah she is called an abandoned wife and a sorrowful
widow. But she has found her proper husband in the manifestation of Christ in the flesh in the New Testament and is
called the Holy Spirit.

3. I want to attempt to show the author's view of how
Good could become Evil. In the first place, it is certain
that both the fallen angel and man had been created with the
highest degree of freedom. Secondly, God's omnipotence was
not manifest when the Fall was contrived, or else it could
not have happened. Thirdly, the darkness from which evil
originated existed indeed from eternity, not in a manifest,
but in a hidden way; therefore it was not evil then, because
it was in harmony with the Good, which is very different
from the teaching of the Manicheans. Fourthly, when the

hidden God moved to reveal Himself through nature and creature, a desire arose in the darkness to make its wonders
manifest, too, and this desire caught the prince of angels.
Since the abyss of darkness was in him, this desire took
hold of his free will so that he broke away from the whole
to exist on his own. He had the ability to do so, because
according to the first proposition, he had been created with
unlimited freedom. If he had been ruled by the law, the
Evil may have been prevented, but then he could have accused
God of guarding him and of not giving him any responsibility. This is the reason why the law does not better anybody but only the gospel, because it calls forth what is in
man through freedom. But it is improbable that the Fall
could have been controlled either by the love or by the
omnipotence of God, for love was the cause for which the
angel became the devil and if God had loved him even more
this would have only increased his wickedness. Besides, if
God had used His omnipotence, the fallen angel would have
been justified by this very action, because God Himself
would have restored His equilibrium, and would have demonstrated that He was an arbitrary despot. Since, according
to the second proposition, the omnipotence of God was still
hidden in the depth and God was only manifest in His smallness, the fallen angel was deceived. Therefore he allowed
himself to desire rebellion against God. We need to assume
this, or else we could not find any reason why a cunning
spirit who knew about God's omnipotence could commit the
foolishness of rebelling against the omnipotence of God.
And from this point, he derives his accusation against God,
namely that he was deceived. He argues that he should have
been ruled instead by the law and that so much responsibility should not have been given into his hands. But as the
smallness of God was the occasion for the devil to come into
existence, the same smallness in Christ Jesus will be again
the cause of the destruction of his kingdom. In other

places the author often used to talk about the Fall briefly, mentioning that darkness is the root of the wondrous tree of the paradise and also that wrath is the root of love, and doubt the root of faith. But the fallen angel had desired to tempt the source of all things, and therefore pulled out the tree with the root, so that it wilted.

4. When God first revealed Himself to the author, and he was made drunk by the vine of the new world, he did not yet know anything about Christ's cross and thought that all his humanity would change to celestial purity. But, when he reached by severe penitence an innocent life, it finally happened that he was, like his master, counted among the evildoers. Then he got to know the cross of Christ for the first time. In Christ's school he studied an advanced course about the Fall of man and about restoration. He also talked about this subject at another place, saying that the right-eousness of our lives and the righteousness of our faith are very different. The former makes us a good Jew, but it can-not take away sin and its root. If you meet Christ in this state, you can still crucify him in the flesh. But the lat-ter does not lead us to accomplish works, for, when we have done what we can, we have still a more important debt, which we cannot repay by our deeds but only by suffering that which others do to us. Thus, the path of faith puts an end to our best works. Through penitence, we have been placed under the law together with Jesus. But soon we will follow him to the cross, be liberated from the law of righteous-ness, and be put under the law of faith. Here the law of fear ends and the law of love and faith begins, which leads us from the path of righteousness to the path of salvation. This is the new way of life which Christ has opened.

5. In the author's opinion, Adam was appointed by God to be priest over the creation in order to lead it back to Him again. For this purpose the Virgin was joined to the

man and they were to fill the earth with a priestly race. Therefore, the spirit of Solomon, who was a passionate wooer of the Virgin, revealed the Song of Songs, which records the conversation of a loving couple. Since, however, Adam inquired too deeply into the procreation of the animals when he named them, the same lust arose within him, which in Christ's words already constitutes adultery: "who looks at a woman", etc. Thus, the Virgin withdrew from him and a concubine had to be created for him, as he wished. In his 18th Theosophical Epistle the author comments on this subject: if the grandfather Adam had not stimulated the external principle when he used his male will, the visible world would have remained closed forever, for he did not need to know the wonders which were in it, because they were all perishable and evanescent. From this it seems to follow that the Fall happened before the creation of woman, which is also said in Romans 5:15, where the Fall is attributed to the one Adam. Since I Timothy 2:14 seems to contradict this, the author distinguished between sin and transgression and said that sin was committed before the law was given and was the cause of the same. Transgression followed later and Eve was guilty only of the latter, but not of the former, because she first ate of the fruit, disobeying God's prohibition. In his wife Adam received a helper for the erection of his kingdom on earth, and now I want to use the author's own words from his spiritual talks. The mystery of the self-will, he says, is very deeply hidden within man, and God took many pains to bring it to the light. Then, when He failed to accomplish His purpose with the fallen angel and had to use man, He created him according to His holy idea without any will of his own, as for a divine comedy. Even though it is said that Adam had a will, he really had none before the Fall. Therefore, when he was supposed to pass God's trial during his temptation, he was not able to succeed. When he desired the comforts of the creatures, he revealed that he was ruled by his selfishness and made himself incapable of being a priest of God. To make him reveal the deepest roots of this self-righteousness, God created a woman for man and gave her into his dominion. Soon it was manifest everywhere that man was a tyrannical ruler, whom God had to limit through the law in the old covenant, since he was no more able to live freely. Besides, God had him circumcised to prove that there was nothing good to be expected from the seed of man. And, even though God could have destroyed this kingdom of man's will at once, it would not have served His glory. Therefore, He preferred to use His forbearance. Thus He had to assume humanity Himself and start where Adam had left off. Therefore He said: "See, I have come to do my Father's will, etc."

6. The meaning of these words is very deep. In the first place, we can be certain that the fallen angel had no other intention than to bring God under his control. He thought he knew an easy road to this end, since (according to note 3) the goodness of God or the Virgin at that time was still ruling and God's omnipotence which he had to fear was still hidden in the depth. Because of our earthly reasoning let us not discuss here, how far he reached his goal and whether he subdued the Virgin. Nevertheless, the serpent which he used in order to tempt man, is a child of this relationship. The author calls her a daughter of Lucifer, a child of a whore, who consisted of good and evil and had inherited from her mother all the beauty and from her father, the jealousy toward God. This violent intrusion broke the temper of the deity and the gentle feminine part of light was separated from the harsh and fiery male part. If God had not interfered, the fallen angel would have brought everything under his control and kept everything from flourishing forever. In order to prevent this, God had to guard the Virgin in the fortress of eternity and to exclude from it forever the fallen angel and all who are

affected by his lust. From this Virgin, who is the heavenly
Venus, all awakenings originate and she also made the author
very passionate in his spiritual youth. But soon he recognized that, because Lucifer and Adam had violated her, she
would hardly engage in any intimacy with him before he had
passed the obligatory education. Therefore, his spirit moved
him to join through holy baptism the household of the humiliated humanity of Jesus Christ, as the first Christians had
done. So he finally developed a Christian character, which
trained him so much, that in the end he reached the temper.
His ascending male fire was transformed into a gentle flame
of light, as Scripture says. The author learned from his
own experience that the Virgin does not welcome anybody into
her holy tent who has not yet passed his obligatory education in the struggling church and who has not broken with
his own self. In the following, the author will cover how
this holy broodhen will keep the infernal birds of prey away
from her chicks, even though she has not gotten any claws to
defined them and how she, who is the honour of the house,
will finally distribute the spoil. After the Virgin was in
safety, God began, to the terror of His enemies and against
His own nature, to conduct a magisterial office and thence-
forth was called an angry God.

7. We can see that Adam could not take responsibility
for the great dignity which God gave to him, for instead of
letting himself be crucified for the fallen creation, which
Christ Jesus did later, he lusted to exist for himself and
to have male dominion. Therefore, he lost his chosen
position, which passed to the second Adam, for he was better
qualified for this task, being not created, but a God
begotten from God.

8. Two reasons are given why the weakened image of God
had to be shaped in earth: In the first place it was done
in order to check the ignited fountain of fire, and to prevent man from becoming a complete devil; secondly, man

received his body in order to regain his lost glory in the flesh through penitence and conversion. Therefore, although the author granted to all the fallen creatures a final conversion, he also maintained firmly that after this time of grace, no more children of promise would be born. To be such a child can be understood as the privilege of the firstborn. The fallen angels and the unrepentent people are completely excluded from this privilege; otherwise it would have to be proven that they can assume bodies even in eternity.

9.   Here the author begins to talk about the origin of the millennial church on earth. In his view this was the last attempt to restore Adam without the cross of Jesus Christ. Great glory was intended for him when God had created Eve, but he could not enjoy it because the woman meddled with the serpent. Thus they had to flee too early and this glory, taken from Adam, will not manifest itself until the millennium. The reason why the church of this time will only last a mystical day is that it is not built on the foundation of the cross. Therefore, at the end of this period, the church will face a most severe trial, for the released dragon will have the remaining heathens surround the camp of the Saints, causing the greatest misery ever on earth. But in this great emergency the upper church, which has gathered in the meantime in the air, has to lead the way. If it were not for this church, the trial would not even be set up. And because of these things Revelation (20:9) says: ... and fire came down from God out of heaven, and devoured them.

10.   It seems strange that woman was subjected to man with such severity, since man has as little right to have his will as woman. But it was necessary because of the spirits of betrayal. But in the first world this law was not in use, the Holy Ghost was in charge of the court of justice and man could not yet prevail in his office. This

was the reason for the Flood because as long as the holy women, who were supposed to propagate the seed of promise, were under no dominion, they were in danger interbreeding with Cain's line. After the flood, God could establish a relationship with Abraham and make him lord over Sarah. Therefore, in the old covenant, woman had to be under a strict guardianship until Christ finally ended the rule of man on the cross at once.

11. These are the waters of misery or the sea of anguish, in which all will have to bathe who want to regain the lost glory. Through this water all the awakened male will has to be abolished again and therefore it has a salty quality. Many indeed have tried to allay its bitterness through the earthly femininity and thought they could serve God better if Eve was at their side, but through this they lighted the fiery wrath within themselves even more, because this relationship was not separated from the being of the serpent.

12. From this we can conclude that no worker in the house of God is allowed to multiply Adam's lineage, for, while Adam should have helped to further unity, he made the tear only larger and brought forth fruits of death, which increased the sufferings which waited for Jesus Christ. It is impossible to prove this law in Scripture, since the marital state belongs to the Old Testament and is justified in the new covenant by God's toleration.

13. It seems to be a new idea, contradictory to the immutability of God, to maintain that the Fall caused a change in God Himself and broke the balance of fire and light. But we have to agree that the wrath which awoke in God, was not manifest from the beginning. This serves to increase the dignity of the mediating office of Jesus Christ, because he stepped into the tear and restored the temper in the deity. Therefore, after this, God abandoned His quarrel with men and made His messengers offer His Goodness with entreaties and supplication (see 2 Cor. 5:20). The same view

was also maintained by the enlightened J. Böhme who said that Lucifer was a large portion of the deity. All this can only be understood from God's revelation in nature and the creatures, for what else God is, we cannot and must not know because the finite does not comprehend the infinite.

14. If Eve did not fornicate with the serpent, she would not have been put under the dominion of man, but would have been his princely crown. But now Adam's selfish rule was supposed to be broken on the cross and women liberated from their position as maidservants. Therefore, the holy women were always leading the procession to the cross. This only speaks about the spiritual state, but externally the law will not be revoked as long as the old world stands, because women still carry the likeness of the serpent with them.

15. According to these talks, the will of the Virgin Mary not to know any man is an essential part of the work of salvation, because it was a start towards the abolishment of the separation of the tinctures. Throughout the period of the old covenant, the divine providence was waiting for her, and in her the lineage of the covenant, as well as the lists of generations of the evangelists, were ended, even though they conclude with the male sex. It is also her alone through whom the Savior of the world assumed the fallen human nature, for since the will of man was weakened by the angel of jealousy, he was not allowed to assume anything of the masculine nature. She was also the first of her race to discover through the Spirit, that God takes pleasure in virginity. This led to her resolution not to know any man. And in this she was wiser than all the holy women before her for since they sought in vain to conceive the promised destroyer of the serpent through man, she did the opposite and sought him in abstinence from man. In short, God found more in the female sex than in the male sex after the Fall.

REFLECTIONS

by

Johann Conrad Beissel

An Echo

O abyss! I cry into you, to be covered all over with the spirit of eternity, that I may be transported into your tent where they rest securely. You have indeed taken away peace from the earth, and yet you have not made known unto me how long the time of this warfare shall endure; but your height, depth and breadth shall earn the last victory, when the time of contention has arrived in its fullness. Why should I not long after the consummation of your work, great God! The turbulent season has lasted long enough for me, and I fear [the time] when the floor shall be thoroughly swept, for the tedious wars have produced many defilements, which in the time of peace might have been avoided. And this is what presses me very sore, because even in the time of war such causes were augmented which retard perfect peace and dispute its approach. Therefore I have a fearful solicitation and cry into your abyss in order to be by it entirely clothed, by which mortality is swallowed up in eternal life so that the consoling days may appear in the presence of God.

We read in diverse places that just and pious men have obtained the greatest victories more through the weapons of prayer than by carnal instruments, and in this is my whole transmuted, so that I cry incessantly to the seat of mercy: Lord! help your people, the remnant of Israel, and hasten the collection of the dispersed in Jacob, that they may honour you. We all wait on you with vehement desire, for the time of war and tribulation has continued long enough, and therefore we all thirst after the times of refreshment in your countenance. O God of eternity! hasten the end of that heavy conflict. Your own creation cries unto you for her deliverance, for she is involuntarily put to such hard trials, because the time of her travail is come, and her redemption is nigh at hand. It is your honour, O dispenser of all things, that the pomp of your kingdom may be revealed under the whole heaven and the ignominy of the children of your people taken away! For this they now all aspire under your patience. O that you would soon disrobe heaven and earth of their old garments. Then surely the children of the adulterer would be stripped of the raiment in which they are now dressed. In the meanwhile I shall not cease, O abyss of eternity, to invoke you, that you through your efficacy diminish and disable the power and business of time in order that your unity may appear in each of us. We will wait on you, for you have enamoured us by the spirit of eternity which had so far prevailed that we despised all perishable things. But we meet with an endless struggle, for we are only impregnated by the spirit of eternity, but eternity itself or the child is not yet born. Therefore we sigh and groan incessantly for deliverance from all things that encumber us.

O that God, the everlasting love, might recover his possession among us that all vanity might end in destruction. And truly his magia operates effectually with his relatives that the child of eternity might be born by which the ruin of vanity is accelerated. But the terrestial and infernal womb is equally busy to bring forth its firstborn to the sore affliction of the spark of eternity which lies concealed in the temporal womb in no small measure.

For when the child of eternity is born, three worlds lay claim to it, to bring it into their bosom. But the first impregnation was performed under a great aversion of both the infernal and terrestial womb, and with it was combined an inclination for the womb of the blessed eternity. I do not doubt that when the time of wars is accomplished, King Solomon will restore the child undivided to his true mother, because she is a mother of mercy and will not press her children to death as that parent did, who first dispatched her own infant, and then requested that the babe of the innocent mother be divided.

O therefore eternal mother lay hold of your child; receive it into your own lap, nourish it tenderly; then the time of war will cease. For she, who overlaid and killed her own offspring, strenuously desired the living child to be divided, which belonged to the mother of mercy; but the king's sentence is that it live. Therefore we all cry in you, mother of eternity and lover of mercy: receive your children and help them, for that hostile mother always has the knife keen, and insists that the child be cut in two because the whole will not be her portion. O how often must the infant of the true parent endure stabbing to the effusion of blood from her, who had destroyed her own son. And for this cause the children of the sterile groan and agonize for the completion of the seasons of sorrow and conflict, when the cruel mother with her dead child shall be doomed to everlasting banishment. For the Lord loves righteousness and delights in mercy; moreover he is not a God of the dead but of the living. Therefore he will help the poor to their right, so that they shall rejoice and be glad when the oppressor is exiled and the envious destroyed.

O how sweetly will they rest in the bosom of that mother, who tenderly nourished her children. O mother of all things! We cry to you incessantly; help us in our distress so that we all may be delivered from that cruel parent who has pressed to death her own child, and requires part of the innocent. Hasten the time of her banishment, that the just be oppressed no longer. Then the seed of the unfruitful shall receive their lot and portion, and the reproach of the maid-servant shall be taken away forever.

Now I rejoice in my God, for the Lord has comforted his people and showed compassion on the poor. He helps them gloriously, and maintains their cause unto the posterity of his holy inheritance. No more shall any one raise up against them, for the envious one with her children are come to an end, and the bond-woman is cast out with her son.

Therefore they of the barren shall now dwell in the house. Now is the whole earth full of the knowledge of Jehova, the Lord our God, and every nation is filled with his praises.

* * * * * * *

A Resonance

prophetically describing the last wars of the militant Church, together with the greatest and last Victory, obtained by the hand of the Woman.

My heart is inditing a fine manner. I will bring to light a Divine discourse. I will relate the wonders of eternity. My thoughts shall devise heavenly speeches. I will speak of things that were hidden from all ages: that the mother has crowned the son on the day of espousals; the bride has encompassed him with the glory of heaven, for he was stripped of his dishonourable and ignominious coat on the cross; now he is exalted in glory and power, and the bride, as the daughter of the mother, stands at his right hand. They who saw it marvelled greatly, and were quite astonished. Now come the children of the mother, rejoicing in her beautiful attire. Their clothing is angelic purity, and their ornament chaste, celestial, virginal and spousal love. There are mere children of the solitary and sterile in whom, after the days of tribulation are ended, the eternal Word shall move and utter his voice, saying: be fruitful and increase and replenish the earth, that you may become great multitudes.

These shall be the days of the joy of the Lord which shall break forth from the Almighty. They shall be the seed of the desolate, begotten within the term of her divorcement and sterility and brought up with much anguish and sorrow under many and diverse tribulations because they are or- phans, and their mother has no husband to comfort her at the

season when her children were so distressed and rejected.
In this circumstance she was often afflicted with storms and
tempests, when she was reproached by her adversary for her
widowhood, and her children must bear the shame of their
virginity. O who could survive in the afflicted seasons of
the rejected widow and her offspring? But now she is
brought home by him who made her, and crowned by her dispenser, and clothed with glory and honour. The garments
that she wears are made white in the blood of the lamb, and
the diadems of her children are embossed with gold. And now
she appears in beautiful pomp, far outdoing the sun in
glory. Who can attain to her beauty? Or who can come to
her brightness? Here the oppressed in the vale of misery
behold it, and rejoice that the bride of God will be manifested again. Therefore they forget their affliction and
days of mourning and are so attracted in the vision that
they are clothed therein.

And we will extend our desires towards her. O eternal
brightness stretch forth your wings over us and make our
steps to drop with holy oil, that we may have our joy in the
Lord our God. We will wait for your goodness in hope, until
the days of tribulation and sorrow of heart are ended. In
the meanwhile we will praise the mercies of the Lord and
exalt his goodness and magnify him who has formed us, for
his deeds are praise-worthy among his people, and he causes
his saints to rejoice; he creates deliverance for them in
the time of their misery and distress. He casts down the
mighty from their seats, and lifted up the poor out of the
dust [cf. Luke 1:52], for he has said that from henceforth
he will not rebuke the children of his people, but turn to
them and accept them, for he has heard the cry of the poor,
and he has remembered that for his sake they were derided
all the day long, and the cup that they have drunk of shall
be put into the hand of them who have reproached them.

Now although the spirit signifies great things to us,

yet we will not venture ourselves into such a battle, where the mighty are laid down by the auxiliary of great hosts, but we will abide within the borders where she, that tarried at home, will divide the spoil (Ps. 68:12). Therefore the time is now come that the wars of the Mother shall be carried on in the church of God. This war shall deliver to the spirit of eternity all the spoil into its bosom, whereby even God himself will obtain his lot and inheritance. On the contrary, in all the battles that are sought by men, they divide the spoil among themselves, and although a hen cannot preserve her brood from the talons of the hawk, nevertheless we are told that the mother of eternity's first born child is a son, who is born not of the will of man, nor of the will of the flesh, but of God [John 1:3]. This youth is of another generation, which is not so much as mentioned on earth. Because of this, his wars are not carried out with carnal weapons, but are mighty through God. For he judges and contends in righteousness, not for the treasures of the earth nor precious things of this visible world, but for those of heaven, or the goods of eternity. Therefore people and nations will come to worship him and prostrate themselves before this wonderful victorious prince over all the kings of the earth, because he will not wage war for the earth, but rather give cause to make faint the hearts of the inhabitants of it.

And because the intent of this war is not to contend for gold or silver or any of the earthly treasures, therefore will the hearts of the dwellers on this globe be daunted, for neither silver nor gold or any precious terrestial thing will be of any value to deliver them from the warlike force of this mighty youth. Then they will begin to cast into the streets their silver and gold and also their other treasures which they have gathered, and loathe them as mire and dirt.

And the remnant who do not have them shall then begin

to cry and say: O ye mountains, fall on us, and ye hills, cover us from the wrath of the judge, who sits on the throne [Rev. 6:16]. In this consternation the mother's children will be gathered into her chamber and dandled upon her knees until this severe war be accomplished in victory. Then will this youth come together with all his heroes, and offer to the mother and her children all the spoil which they have gained. Then they shall all salute him by the name of their first born brother and prostrating themselves will worship him.

And now, his wars being ended, he comes home to his relations in the house of his mother, being now of maturity to wed; and since he is the first born son of the virginal generation, it would be improper for him to marry one of a foreign blood. Because all his kindred have but one mother, he was necessitated to take to wife his first born spiritual sister, or first to give her his hand, to lead her as a bride.

But this was contrary to the seat of the Pharisees, although it was no more on earth but in hell, for no sooner was the contract of the spousal course celebrated, but the chief prince of infernals arose and marshalled his whole army, and encompassed about the whole camp of the saints. But because the king had ended his battles, he appointed this last victory for the bride. Now arises in her that male-fire, obtained by his conquest, to the utter extirpation of the very last foe of God and Christ. Now this occasioned a joyful wedding-day. O how shall we rejoice at these our nuptials!

These contain immeasurable great mysteries, as mentioned above, namely that the king should leave the last victory to be obtained by the action of the bride, for it is written that she, which tarried at home, shall divide the spoil (Pf. 68:12). These are heavenly depths, for when the bride of God has obtained the last victory, then shall

appear the last structure, namely the temple of the holy
spirit, which shall never be destroyed nor broken. The new
Jerusalem shall descend from God out of heaven, as a bride
adorned for her husband. Rejoice O heaven! rejoice, O
earth! Let the thrones, authorities and dominions rejoice!
Let all pure ministerial spirits rejoice over the bride-
grooms and bride! Let all the companions of the bridegroom
and bride rejoice, for the marriage of the Lamb is come.

Now the sorrowful have ended their days of mourning,
and the afflicted and miserable are lifted up out of the
dust. The marriage-feast will continue for many days, but
the last day will be the most glorious. Then shall they
drink of the richest wine of the best vineyard, and the
maidens will go forth to conduct and attend the bride into
the king's bed-chamber. O peace! O rest! O safety for
ever and ever! Now the king awakes from his last sleep, and
immediately gives orders for the last trumpet to be blown to
proclaim the everlasting day for night shall be no more,
Halleluia.

SPIRITUAL SERMONS

by

Johann Conrad Beissel

The Thirteenth Sermon

I see the trees blooming in the garden of my God and therefore I say, "Be at ease, oh maiden Israel, for your salvation is closer at hand than in earlier times and the period of sorrow and misery is now totally behind you. Therefore you ought to seek comfort in your God. You will no longer be referred to as grievous or as spiritually intoxicated, for your salvation is upon you as you wish and desire. Soon you will be led into liberty and jubilation. Your depression and bitter complaining will have been ended. Your great suffering and afflictions will have passed. The bitterness of your tormenting anguish will no longer be heard. You will be blessed and progress, for your many prayers have reached God. Your great suffering has ended and disappeared. Your great salvation and its many blessings approaches you. The clouds are giving way (after such unbearable misery) to an honoured rain which will refresh the languished inheritance of God's favoured. In what a fine state your dwellings will be when you bring in your plentiful harvest, when generation after generation genuflects before you and realizes that you are beloved of your God. All your persecuters will then be disgraced including those who rejoiced and found happiness in your miserable condition. They will be adoring at your feet, realizing that you represent the seat of all justice and that their salvation is contained within you. You will be astonished and your heart will rejoice. Instead of being compelled to remain in misery, you are exalted and raised into a state of honour and glory. Heaven and earth rejoice and shout for joy and all green forests flourish! For your Lord has comforted his heirs and pitied them in their misery.

So be at ease, you holy word, you beloved heir of God, for your stature has never been more lovely than now, you must make a new appearance. You will be rooted and raised. Your love wishes to nurture you when it says, "I am aware of the suffering and anguish of my beloved, and therefore I have become moved with pity for you and I will reunite us with intentions of recreating your youth by raising, supporting and caring for you. I will absolve you with sacred oils in order that you may regain the former strength of your legs and find happiness therein. Your teacher will never again flee from you, but instead he will accompany you, care for you, and preserve you. Your God who loves you will endure the burden of your sorrows so that you will not be lacking any possessions. Therefore, be at ease, mournful daughter of Zion, in your misery. Forget your complaints, the burdens of your heart and your many tears. Observe your contented sons who are progressing much better in comparison to the meager and gaunt conditions of your times because the merciful rain has replenished your strength. Oh to what a great extent you will thrive after the rain, and the lovely sun warms you. Oh highly praised beauty of God and his love! How you lead those beloved from their youth, caring for them and ending their lamentations at middle-age and raising them to the point that they become aware of your gifts. You support them to the late years of your life and times of great anguish, fear, poverty and scarcity. Old age becomes youthful with the spring-like replenishing of strength. Oh happy days! Oh sacred time of renewal, the ascent into the heavens was revealed to us. We must replenish our lost strength and regain our productivity. The generation of Melchisedech will arise and govern the kingdom which has lain in rubble for a long time and the formerly disgraced maidenhood will be revealed in honour and glory, for the shame of their sterility has passed and Melchisedech will expose his people. The successors of faithful Abraham

denounced the custom of circumcision and then conformed to
the old traditions like Hagar and her children. Melchisedech
who for a long period belonged to the relinquished priesthood of God now managed both political and religious
offices. The long concealed and rejected Virgin now made
her appearance, seeking her first and last inheritance from
her king, priest and husband, unaware that the sceptre of
grace and mercy had long been calculated and that the
high-priest's blood of the long rejected Virgin was
acquired, for she remained chaste in her state of widowhood
and she sought no strange sources of comfort, committing
herself to no man. Though he was exposed to many dangers
throughout his life, Melchisedech declared his sovereignty
over endangered widows and barren maidens whose fears,
anxieties and apprehensions were suddenly removed. The
might and power of the Virgin will conquer all her enemies
and her entire generation will be spared from all anxieties.
She is no longer afraid or contemptible, but will be
honoured and glorified. The preparations for the glorious
wedding day will be arranged for the spiritual marriage.
Melchisedech's people will be made known to the entire
world, for his children will number as many as the dews of
sunrise. The Queen of the priestly office will tend to all
remaining peoples. The solitary will bear many children
while those with husbands will become barren. Those who for
a long time have lived in misery and embraced the dust of
the earth will be seen seated at the right hand of the king
and will be honoured and glorified. Near and far the
miracle that the lowly were exalted and honoured will be
acclaimed. The choirs of heaven rejoice and exalt over this
salvation; all the saints have been lifted toward this
light, for all the betrothed have been reunited with their
beloved and their treasures, including the priest and his
rejected, misery-imprisoned Virgin. Now the bright peoples
will expand and develop so that all people and kingdoms will

appear and inherit the gifts. Amen.

Melchisedech lives in and among the entire generation of maidens and has committed himself to the stength of the eternal life.

The Fifteenth Sermon

I have had this task for a long time and desire once more to present a teaching which concerns high graces. For slightly more than one year, God has strictly disciplined me to regard my services as divine. Oh God! how one is degraded by coming closer to doing so each day in one's occupation. In contrast, how great and glorified one is upon limiting oneself within one's own boundaries. What great deeds can be accomplished. One cannot count the steeples of God's city or measure the temple or sanctuary with the assessments of one's own vain conceits. One desires to ignore all the valuables of God by attempting to constrain them and by acquiring estimations about their limits so that they do not surpass the boundaries and measures of the reasonable. Oh misery! Oh great distress! All your advice originates from your detachment with God. Therefore, I repeat, "Oh how one is humiliated when one comes close to God". I can admit that in my state of humility and nothingness, I could not arrive at my foundation on my own. If I desire to be successful in reaching God, it is necessary to be knowledgable of something. To wander in humility and not to appear in arrogance is to touch God who is of a natural quality. We want to accept all the godly characteristics and qualities, including being humble of heart but not being arrogant of one's belongings for this would conflict with the God-like qualities. According to the doctrine of humility, the more roles one assumes, the more evil one is responsible for. However, pride may be considered the opposite, for the more one becomes involved with the self, the more one realizes one's justness. God delivers us from ourselves and leads us beyond our own confinements so that we become detached from selfishness during good times as well as evil; otherwise we will not be accepted into the community of God's son or into the union of the perfect righteous beings of the next world.

Oh what narrow paths we encounter on our pilgrimage!
Oh what bitter deaths we embrace as we hope to earn the good
of the heavenly kingdom but we once more evaluate the advantages of following the evil-doer. What actions can be taken
in such a case? If one directs oneself toward the right in
order to expand the good, the angel strikes with his exposed
sword to stop the extended hand which is then compelled to
search with the self for fulfillment. If one seizes the
left in order to scrape a living for oneself, the abyss
opens revealing the presence of the judge of the living and
the dead.

Though the path is narrow, it still remains the holiest
transaction of the expansion of eternal glory, for in being
subjected to it we become purified, angelic and heavenly so
that when the heavenly song of the murder or the new tune is
sung no misleading tones will be heard. Oh what a glorious
strewn path which again brings about heavenly beauty! Oh
eternal knowledge! how you have advised us while recog-
nizing the concealed cross over us, for one escapes from the
anger and is again portrayed in a God-like image. Should we
then not be content with our holy wanderings, for the gates
of the city of the living God welcome us and the rewards of
the spirit will be accessable in the heavenly eternity.

If we hope to attain this high state of nobility, we
must remove our touchstone from the harmony or concord of
the godly things, for as long as we are in this position of
difference, we remain sinful since we are continuing to
carry our cross. In such cases, the opposition governs over
the entangled tongues while God's anger arouses the perpetual course and as a result will remember his burning in
future eternities, for all will become as had been expected
and in this manner all will organize as is fair. How much
time must pass before every man rejects his individual

opinion and renounces his will in order to gain more knowledge of God. In order to escape this misfortune, one must
passionately call to the spirit who tells us to flee from
Babel where our great fancy lies so that we will not participate in her sinfulness or be subjected to her torments.
Therefore, rejoice, you holy and highly favoured generation,
for you have entered into a union with God and have been
accepted into a harmony with the next world. You will
encounter no misfortune during the time when God judges your
souls. Honour, praise, gratitude, strength, integrity and
glory characterize God, the eternal king who delivered us
from future anger through the crucifixion, resurrecting the
first abandoned glorification. This has been presented in
such a manner that I and others may learn from this
teaching. The highest retribution which extended my life be
eternally thanked that the clarity of the light can be shone
from underneath Christ's cross.

The Twenty-Fifth Sermon

As we read Jeremiah, 20, we hear the prophet complaining and saying, "Lord! you have convinced me and I have allowed you to persuade me. You have been too powerful for me and have won; but I have been mocked because of it and everyone laughs at me. Even my friends are interested if I will stumble. However, the Lord is at my side like a mighty hero, causing my persecuters to fall."

In general, one wonders why the prophets dealt with evil since they are regarded as being so holy, and since they were killed, the acts they are to perform are again presented by God to the human children. In my opinion, there is no position more difficult under the sun than when God instils strength into a person who is required to serve that which causes him to be brought again to his origins. However, when man has temporarily been spared by God from straying sinful life, he must then fear neither disgrace nor danger of death. Therefore, a learned prophet could rightly say, "If I were a false god and a preacher of lies and if I would evangelize like them, I would be the preacher for these people." For my intentions, these words will be transmitted as a text and will take into consideration the sovereignty of life or the new world which would be less maintained than by another prophet so that he would not be throttled because of his holy teachings. All miracles which he performed were gloriously received but he could not claim that he was heaven-sent or that he was God's son. Had he been such a person, one would have said to him, as to the Pharisees, that he was the devil's son, and as a result he would have been a brother to the Pharisees and scribes and consequently the envious death would never have occurred. Thereafter, no witness of God who preached the truth in order to gain eternal life could present the truth to the people without having his life endangered. When he is not

being condemned, the witness is subjected to various vexa-
tions, disgraces, and slanders, etc. which oppose the holy
and healing teachings. Therefore, it is not surprising that
the first-born of the human family tree laid the foundation
stone of this murderous temple. The second person laid the
stone of the temple of the living God. It appears as though
the first created person caused by his propagation the beginning of the creation of a murderous generation which
carries within itself the witness of the lost glorification
and can not suffer as a result, although Cain's action of
murdering his brother was sufficiently publicized. Abel
would never have been killed had he not stirred the justness
of God. It is no better in our time, for whoever is raised
with the truth of eternal life in mind must see to it that
his house is large enough to hide from his disgrace. However, if he only speaks elegantly without becoming involved,
he will be followed by hundreds of people. But this must not
be done, for as soon as an encroachment is made on Adam's
murderous generation or in his family-line, anger, evil conjectures and various spiritual difficulties will appear as a
result. All this was caused by the birth of the first Adam,
and the existing justice and messages of paradise were
seriously being questioned, for in the meantime, the leader
of the evil generation who, along with his wife, was diso-
bedient and rebellious was thrust out. Therefore, revenge to
this day can still be found in this same generation of which
the brother murderer was the first born. If a preacher
appears who does not belong to the existing truths or family
line of Adam which has been expanding for many generations,
he will not be accepted. He can say what he wants, no one
will care. The tree must not be affected when its roots are
disturbed, for the trunk always produces new branches even
when some have been broken off. Oh how many of those who
pursued heavenly trivialites were tired out before the time
and encountered the present before the future which is

realized without having been pursued. Thus, instead of participating in the spiritual struggle like Jacob and the angel of the Old Testament, one first sufficiently prepares oneself as by expanding Cain's family line so that one will not be caught off guard as happened to Jacob in his struggle. Then certainly, the sterile should give birth to her seven while she who has bore many children must discontinue to do so and grant the domestic authority to the solitary. Just as the world filled with injustices was created by the founder of the evil generation, who was not lacking in evil qualities, so will the founding father of the New Testament not be in need especially when the Lord wipes away his tears and weeds the wheat. Consequently, this generation will begin to call and say, "Oh mountains fall upon us! Hills cover us from the judge's face! Oh what sorrowful products of this evil generation! One would freely admit that blessed is the body which has remained chaste and the breast which has stayed pure."

Christ did not treat the Pharisees harshly because they were Jews or because they carried the despised titles of Pharisees, for according to Christ they were children of the New Testament and founders of Israel. The reason for it was that they claimed to be among the first-born of Adam whose son killed his brother whom God had favoured. Therefore, he refers to them as children of the devil who was a murderer and liar from the beginning and had rejected the truth.

According to this, one should not be a Pharisee in order to carry out the sentence; one should only act on the basis of what one is. Our father will eventually teach us his ways which he acquired from his father telling us not to accept the witness sent from heaven. All of this is in our day an all-encompassing fraudulent matter, for though we are closer to being healed than at any other time in the past, the secret of evil is closer to being revealed. I now wish

to discontinue my discussion of the generation whose founder
was a murderer and wish to turn my focus on another
generation which has a different father. Whatever caused
him to take a wife or a bride from the evil generation was
successful, for he found a reason for her, like Samson had
among the Philistines, whose father and mother freely
responded to with the question, "Could you not choose a wife
from your own generation?" However, he sought purpose in
Adam's body where he set himself up in his father's home,
upsetting the privileges of the first born, tainting the
pure virgin and becoming a murderer. According to God, the
feminine generation is more at fault than that of the male,
since he eventually was compelled to seek out a virgin who
then refused to become acquainted with a man of Adam's
generation. Through this, she became worthy to receive him
who was heaven-sent in order to restore the lost splendor to
the day and place a curse on the sins of the flesh committed
by Adam so that the murderous and evil generation may be
eliminated. Now even the elect of John according to Adam's
body is also being mocked and cursed and drawn out of the
breast of Jesus, the son of the Virgin who, because of this
is made worthy of being the first-born son of this mother of
the generation of maidens. This one established laws
different from those of other peoples and taught that those
who simply hate their brothers are already guilty of murder.
Now Adam's entire generation alone with all its hellish fury
will be disinherited by God whose favour rests on John the
first-born of another people who are opposed to Cain.

Though the Philistines believed they were victorious
because they not only blinded Samson but also choked him,
they actually strangled one of their own, their grand-father
Adam who without it, carried death within him, and the
spirit of life and immortality was lost. Although they
believed they were only mocking him and thought this would

prevent him from causing them further harm, they did not
realize that he would be purified and cleansed from the
torture they imposed upon him. Therefore, he went to the
lowest part of the country where houses were supported on
columns. In such a dwelling, all the princes of the
Philistines and all the authorities of Edom and Ammon were
gathered and celebrating a joyous festival commemorating the
supposed falling of a beautiful star from the heavens. While
they celebrated and acted out their victories, he grasped
the two columns symbolizing death and hell, and caused them
to bend. The entire building collapsed, trapping them all
inside. Those who attempted an escape were caught,
unclothed and glorified; the remainder, however, who did not
possess the strength to flee were eternally disgraced.

These are the gallant deeds which the other person
(whose immortality was not endangered since he had not
tasted death) had exercised in his degraded state while he
was single and was, therefore, compelled to confront even
the coldness alone. Having accomplished such glorious deeds
while he was still single and in a low state, what will be
the result of the expansion of the new generation of virgins
from people to people as they force their way from death
into life? In this transition, the many spiritual heroes of
faith were born, with whom he will move forth and engage in
great battles, and, as a result, that which is discussed in
other regions will occur. However, those of my enemies who
did not wish me to govern over them should be brought forth
and strangled before my eyes. Miracles will be performed on
that day when the Lord appears with his many thousands of
saints and proclaims judgement over all godless creatures
and people of Adam's generation who attempted to suppress
the generation of the eternal maiden which was born from the
water and spirit. In the meantime I take pleasure in the
fact that I have been delivered from the corrupt and
murderous generation in which man hates, envies, disgraces,

defames, jeers and is indifferent toward others. Adam's generation will be prevented from further expansion by gathering its products and burning them in the eternal fire. Then all saints and followers of the Lamb will call out, saying, "Lord, holy and just, fair and true are all your judgements, just as you condemned the great whore. This is the woman of the entire earth, of Adam's people, who disgraced the blood of the Old Testament and defamed the saints of the Most High as she was situated on the many great waters, Amen."

The Thirty-Sixth Sermon

My thoughts flow toward the calm eternity. I must live and work like the old fathers who have fulfilled their existence to the extent that nothing remains to be pursued or remains undone if it happens that my final hour should approach. Therefore, I am forever occupied, directing my spiritual humanity upward toward the spirit of eternity. Nothing will remain unjudged until that day when God judges the world through fire. In the meantime, I continue to yearn for a quiet and concealed change. I must ensure that I do not construct any other temple or altar other than the one built by Melchisedech which is located in the land of Israel in the city of Salem. The animals were then sacrificed on God's grace-giving altar from which the sacred smoke rises with a pleasant odour. Where the priesthood is being maintained, there is an unending burning and offering up of the self. All rudeness is weakened, and all harshness and coarseness subdued and eliminated. During this sacrifice, God appears face to face. The barking of dogs and the shrieking of strange birds is no longer heard. Instead, there is eternal youth and submission. In an obscure manner, we discover that the throttled Lamb is constantly sacrificed upon the altar of the world as a sign of the reconciliation of the whole of creation.

In the meantime, I will spiritually glide over there as previously mentioned and will stop at the side of my altar, where I will be discretely sacrificed while all crudeness is repressed and all indolence is spiritually renewed. The most trusted community which I possess is the most secret affection of amorousness in the eternal Spirit. Wherever such confidence is maintained, no secrets will separate friends. Only one among all these is lacking for me, namely, the sacred family line has been sealed from my view. The maiden who lies by my side has been fertile to this

point, but has borne only girls who are easily misled and
conquered by the serpent. I yearn for a son, a boy who will
control the people of all generations and govern them with
an iron fist. Through this boy, my woman will acquire a
righteous marriage partner which she lacked in me for I am
incomplete since I originated from the line of the enslaved
woman and was not born of the virgin. While giving birth to
this male child, my maiden will die. Yet, she will not
encounter an eternal death, but instead will endeavour to
support me in my debasement, all the while bearing many
children over which she endures much sorrow and laments.
This misery was caused by my family line through which she
was made fertile and was exposed to mortality. By
subjecting my wife to mortality for which I am responsible
during the birth of the male child, we will undoubtedly die
as a result of our faithful devotion to our marriage vows.
Now Rachel will become barren and bear no children over
which she will lament, for the birth of the boy marks the
removal of strength from the fire-breathing dragon which
will be prevented from misleading the heathen and will
possess even less power intended for killing. Now Rachel
and all her children will become immortal, for they are the
promised children of the New Testament for whom all death
has victoriously been conquered. Through this boy, my
manhood was vanquished on the cross and my wife need no
longer fear for the danger caused by human neglect which was
conquered through the crucifixion. Both tinctures or
qualities, the super-human severity and weak or feminine
appeasement, have been united to the extent that the female
and masculine like a light flame of fire will be surrounded
and overcome. Now the line of the holy Samson no longer
requires expansion from the fiery will of man since it has
acquired the sacred moderation through which the heavenly
and knowledgable femininity is highly honoured, for it
steers the helm toward the authority of the blessed word's

transplantation. The Lord has aided me; Zion can bear her children without grief and without bodily harm. Now his chldren will be born like the dews of sunrise. Now the people belonging to the priest Melchisedech will be made known, for by his blaze 144,000 and all those of the earth and Adam's generation have been carried off. Now I have my most beloved in my arms and I am in hers, for my righteous one has come into my acquisition. In my difficult service for God, during which time my sterility prevented the sacrifice of any people, a maiden was eventually presented to me, permanently terminating the shame of my widowhood. Oh what a soft, concealed and totally meaningful bridal bed! Through this marriage the Enochian change will develop through God automatically at the peak hour, for he will be transferred outside of the world and time without encountering death. Though the wise wedding day belongs to the period of the Enochian Church, the secret bridal bed is still a dominating symbol of that time when the fertility of the new world commenced and during which time a totally different church period originated which favoured not only the number seven, but eight, nine and ten as well. The conclusion is again reversed, for the sacred number one exposes the unity of all other things and as a result, all divisions, separations, and differences are eliminated. Access is gained to the calm eternity through the number zero.

Oh sweet life of contentment in which all times are united and days made one! Now Adam's bridal bed and his created chamber are burnt in the fire. A different generation which knows nothing of Adam's miracles will develop, just as there arose a new people previously who had no knowledge of the Lord or his miracles. In the meantime I am content and rejoice in the Lord my God who permits its success and does not abandon those who genuinely trust in him. Oh how many years have I served my beloved bride like the beautiful Rachel during which time my reward was freely altered over ten times. Heaven is also aware of the fact that she often lamented over her children. Though Herod caused much wailing, he was unable to stop the boy who along with his mother has returned to God in opposition to the followers of Herod who were completely rooted out. Because the previously mentioned male child was able to conquer and eliminate death on his own, one need no longer fear for the danger of death; therefore, Rachel and her children will be made immortal. In the meantime, I will faithfully learn during this period of great misery to cherish my bride who will not entice me to forget my honour as Samson did. Oh eternal life of God, be my protection, honour and pride forever and do not forget how bitter I have been toward you and how I have suffered for your sake! Amen.

The Forty-Ninth Sermon

May the purity of heaven always be in my heart. How delicately beautiful and comforting it rests in the spirit of the mind. If only my earthly body were entirely transferred to the amenity of paradise so that no vexation would sprout from the earthly magic of which we are composed and therefore pevent the heavenly magic from effortlessly continuing her creative works. Eventually the Scripture which states that Zion will bear her children painlessly must be fulfilled. If only it could be fulfilled once, the lingering sorrows of God's creations would come to an end in myself and others. Therefore, I call to you, oh Spirit of eternity! Inspire and stimulate me with your heavenly essence so that all combined strengths and transactions which oppose sincerity will be devoured. My moaning spirit will be brought to its completion and I will be granted the opportunity to exist in the pure and heavenly component of celestial purity of my soul's delight for which I yearn. In this heavenly state of cleanliness, the features of the bridal bed belonging to the chaste and wise love of Jesus are exposed. Out of it, the children of the New Testament, of Paradise and of the new world will be born.

Gather yourselves! gather yourselves all you who dwell in the presence of the heavenly beauty of beloved spirits so that you conform to this decree, for in this sacred bridal bed of God's cleanliness exists the possibility for the expansion of the generation of God's famed wisdom to ensure that you all may become fertile through it. Now the roses and lilies are blooming in the new world.

The Fifty-Fourth Sermon

Because I have at this time no extraordinary ideas to present, I will attempt to discover if something from the deep underground of the holy element wherein my soul is eternally suspended in a sacred state may inspire me. I am incessantly occupied with drawing strength from God's being which devours all pernicious life and brings forth the ever-lasting growth of the Spirit in the new life of Paradise. I greatly desire to fulfill all ordinary tasks under God's patience so that I may joyfully look forward to the judgement day when everyone will be judged according to his deeds. So my spirit melts away and transforms into dust in order that it may be brought before God's authority and rediscover its wealth. Because you have endured so much suffering here on earth over the years and grieviously spread the word under God's patience, you will be granted so much more happiness in the time following the judgement in the countenance of God and in the company of the saints. Apart from this, I am always sorrowful and concerned about the sterility of God's Church on earth to the extent that even Sarah, like Rachel, cries over her children and refuses to be consoled, for her time has passed. Though the consolation no longer belongs to the spirit of eternity, it is said, "Forget the voice of crying and the tears of your eyes, for your work will be rewarded." The established signs of the grave and the clear indications of sorrow are still obstacles for those who desire to exult joyfully in the heights toward Zion. In the meantime, one hears the shouts against the ascent as the watchmen call,

Arise, arise! you who are clever, be prepared
Clad yourself in the pure wedding dress
Discard the earthly burdens:
Be as pure as angels, the poor in number
Are the brides of this wedding feast
The maidens are only guests.
Observe the eyes of the bridegroom
On your course:
They desire their equals
They are simple according to the nature of the poor:
Whoever follows their example,
He will achieve his goal.

Oh true and valued souls which have been granted control over the sterility of Sarah and in the same manner over the Blessed Virgin who was unacquainted with men. You ignored the fertility of Hagar, the Egyptian maidservant, subjecting her to Ishmael's mockery. In your sterility, observe your true, righteous husband as the son of the virgin. He will remain chaste according to the example provided by his mother who refused to become acquainted with any man. Since you must bear your scorn because of your sterility as every saint also must do, (I Sam. 1:6) it is necessary to search in your grief not a man, but instead the altar of God through holy prayers, and protect your prayers for him. While Aaron's priesthood suppresses your eagerness for fertility to an intoxication for sterility, Melchisedech will honour you when the purification of such a wine to be drunk will be placed in the secret cabinet where the mysterious bridal bed will be concealed from all who voluntarily weep over their sterility. Oh what joyous songs of praise will echo when the Lord welcomes the barren into his house in order that they may become good child-bearers, and those who had so many children will no longer do so. In the meantime, Hanna must eat sorrowfully for a time because of her sterility (I Sam. 1:5) and Mary must bear the disgrace which came through her pregnancy (Matt. 1:19). Eros goes to the state of pregnancy and cries as if her maidenhood were shamed and disgraced (II Sam 13:19), though only the coloured dress of the mortal maidenhood was torn. The mother of the blessed generation will present, instead, a harmonious dress. For this reason you need not concern yourself with your maidenhood, for you are the chosen people and the beloved generation. You will forget the shame of your maidenhood and will no longer ponder your widowhood. You will be exalted from your state of inferiority and will find happiness in your God who has loved you and who will rid you of sighs, change your disgrace to honour, and your sorrow to joy, Amen.

The Sixty-Fifth Sermon

(This sermon involves a reflection concernig the solitary lifestyle)

The solitary lifestyle, through which one attains the highest and eternal good and conquers the desires and life of the conceited world, is not only a total detachment from the physical, the rejection of all unnecessary time, wasted associations with and among others, but also much more, including a shunning of the bodily spirit from all sensual qualities which consist of hearing, sight, taste, smell and feelings. Nothing in the visual world can occur without the incorporation of at least one of these five if they are revealed through us. If we wish to attain the sacred life through the renunciation of the world and its vanity, we ourselves must be in the process. Even if we conceal ourselves in the most extreme region of the world and contain, restrict or control the passions of the mind, nothing is accomplished, but rather the opposite occurs and instead of acquiring violation, a sea of unrest is aroused within the self.

The outward loneliness, according to this ought to be employed purposefully. Firstly, the mind must beware of the beasts' affections which claim that the essential sustenance of life is eating and drinking, for in this concern thousands of other desires are united. Secondly, it is also important that when this has been achieved one does not reflect on the total number of possessions abandoned in the kingdoms of this world or become attracted to magical or objective aspects (which under assumed titles are obscured causes of conversion and also of praise) or attempt to visit one's former friends and acquaintances which in general will cause much damage for you since you have unintentionally strayed from God and have sought comfort in the Beast.

When reflections on father and mother occur, one finds oneself regretting what one has abandoned, and one is confronted with an untimely sympathy for one's parents as if one had not endured sufficient services for them. However, if one strays, one will again abandon something, for though one believes that one has plenty to contribute, one finds one has reasons for the opposite upon acquiring great self-pity and mercy and upon discovering that one's parents are lacking in comfort.

Thirdly, spiritual pride which is also present in the solitary life is also partly responsible, for it corrupts all. It brings fulfillment into the human mind and exceeds beyond all additions of the beast and, therefore, can play no role in the solitary lifestyle.

The attempt to escape from all such misguidance serves as communication of it. If this single deception is not arrested, all others will at once become entangled. This illusion is referred to by name as infatuation. In all which one does involving this name, one becomes subjected to all remaining vices. However, in contrast, all acts and intentions one has which are seemingly innocent are actual signs of rejection against the power of the greatest deception. Nothing but the word of the Virgin and her example ought to be understood.

Such are the circumstances of the solitary life, namely, a life which is intended to be isolated and detached from the world has no need for the maiden, and, therefore, can never prosper. No matter to what extent one becomes entangled with the sacred life, one will never overcome the dilemma of the Virgin. If one involves oneself in modesty, the ever present Virgin will be waiting to offer a reward. If one becomes obsessed in the search, the Virgin will be at one's side. If one seeks chastity, one imitates the Maiden. Beside those who strive to attain moderation and restraint stands the virgin who rejoices. In being awake and vigilant, one is simply imitating past qualities of the Maiden.

Such is the portrait and character of the solitary life which is believed would mislead its followers. Under these circumstances wisdom and knowledge of God are the most difficult to attain in a solitary life, for one must reject the comfort and the Beast before God's everlasting love can again restore the last good and inheritance of the people. When God has reunited his people, the Virgin can again claim the people and the people will have God restored to them through the lost Maiden. The Eternal Wisdom is once more present and will become our Sister and Bride as God's Son is our first-born brother. Again we are children of God and his love and that which Adam abandoned by committing himself to a woman over a virgin is rediscovered.

THEOSOPHICAL EPISTLES

by

Johann Conrad Beissel

The First Epistle

(On the authority of an ever-trusted friend in Germany who took it upon himself to seek out and then restore the lost spiritual glitter of life in a sympathetic manner and to re-establish the immortal life through love. No fewer important documents concerning the great article about the justification of faith and no less concerning the chaste Bride of love, the saintly Sophia, must be submitted through this authority.)

May the spiritual life force and Jesus Christ, the spirit of love, greatly flourish in your soul so that you may live, and may the healing power, acquired through the blood of Christ, be what you desire, Amen.

My dear and worthy brother in the Lord,

As we make our way toward God, nothing but the dust of our deprived state will remain. So it is with God. It occurs through a strange but marvelous and righteous seed, and we realize we must attain it in this state because it is not possible finally to see God in any other manner. The selfish life can take root to such an extent that it becomes impossible to free oneself if one has not been acquainted with God. Though we may be eager, our eventual goal and aim is still always directed toward the self. This however is significant because God could otherwise not counsel us to perform to our best ability. It now depends upon whether we lose and then present ourselves to that which we seek. This could never have occurred had God not demanded so much of us. Jesus' cross will remain concealed from us until all justice is established in the heavens on the altars through which the lion's anger will be stirred by the service of Moses, causing the first tablets of the Testament to break. Through this, one will unknowingly become subjected to different statutes, causing one to change under the broken tablets as the House of Israel did. It is totally clear that this was the result of the worshipping of false gods, for 500 years thereafter, Jerobou who originated in the House of Israel established not one but two periods during which this blasphemy against God occurred. Thereafter this caused so many sins throughout time that God severely reprimanded the ten tribes and allowed his anger to direct them out of the Promised Land, causing great turmoil. This was brought about because the people of the Old Testament and the broken tablet sinned even more by not attempting to discover the reason for the broken tablets, but continued instead their false and sinful religion.

Oh, what immeasurable miracles of the Almighty have developed through this transaction! Oh, how few souls survive such ordeals as the worshipping of false gods because they refused to be led any further by the four living things but instead halted at a standstill and degraded themselves.

What more need be said in this transaction concerning our entire Christian Church? Do we not exist under the law of the broken tablet of the Testament of Jesus Christ? They were broken during that time when the banner of blood of the holy martyrs was painted another colour and thereafter the portraits of earthly monarchies were drawn upon them and represented by various types of animals. As the lion was beginning the process of conversion, it could not progress further than a calf in its active life. Because the calf is a pure animal of sacrifice, one would assume one would ascend to the highest heavens; however, the human countenance remained behind. This was the reason why no one could any longer be dissuaded by the king of Israel from false worship, and thought he was quite pious.

Now we are progressing somewhat with our work. It was threatened and avoided to the point that these spirits always took advantage of the work of each other in their employment. The service of the spirit which is false must be honoured because the great forces of idolatry occur as a result and because it is difficult to create a diversion away from it, for man desires to worship or be worshipped. This presents to me a very profound mystery, especially when I observe the fall of mankind and consider that it did not oppose God's justice when in Moses's household so many innocent animals were slaughtered. Therefore, it is noteworthy that God employed such great spirits for the pictures of the animals, promoting the return of mankind in order to produce his own picture. One could freely contribute something of one's own experiences and fulfill the law by judging such strange sacred relics according to his conversion or be at first condemned to death as wrongdoers. Mark my words, this death involves much more suffering than the death which one must endure for having sinned where there is still hope for reward; here, however, one must surrender oneself hopelessly, and it hurts to have to give up that for which one has worked. Here one is required to trust God or have faith in him. Here one seizes the sacrifice of reconciliation in Jesus Christ and is judged by God as a righteous man. When one can progress no further, one must humble oneself, and whoever dies thus, is absolved of sins.

My dear and worthy brother! I understand the condition of your soul quite well and compassionately sympathize with you not because you are in the worst position, but because I am aware of your spiritual weaknesses and I cannot find anyone who would be willing to lend a hand in times of need, for the cordial embrace of love seems to have died out and the community of saints was debased. If only the injured arms were not wounded more through secret beatings which is realized to a large extent by my spirit. I have frequently wished that you could be here. The condition of your soul has been realized for a long time through the eyes of the Spirit and you have been assured that he will not remove his hidden hand of grace in which he secretly carries you and from which he will not abandon you. If he did not secretly watch over you, the spark of the will would have been extinguished and you would have fallen into a life of pride. Therefore, my brother, hold on tightly. Do you not realize that you are closer to him in your unconscious state than in the peak of your strength when you possess the power to move mountains? We will not be judged according to our strength, but according to the extent of our graces and the gifts of Jesus Christ which are presented even to the faithless. As a result, his praise will increase the joy of God's children when their spirits are renewed and raised out of the dust after a long period of suffering.

Now to consider that person of whom you are reporting; the one abandoned Sophia and committed himself to a woman of this world. It would have been to his advantage had he followed Jesus. I must confess that the daughters of Eve possess a great burning and fiery desire for the sons of Adam. Still the hidden desires are much more powerful in their burning state where the center of life with its rays of light impregnates the heavenly Sophia. For this reason, the maiden Sophia remembers so few true wooers and lovers, for as soon as her special disposition is in view, attention is focused on Eve's daughters from whom the best are sought. From there the powerful unity of mind from both generations originate; each seeks its lost in the other but it cannot be discovered because of the aroused vanity. Very few will become sober through this until they experience the undetermined losses of the blending [of the two] encountered through an addiction to the devil by which they are betrayed by false imagination. The chaste life of God withdraws back into its centre and seeks the arms of the soul and therefore cannot be present. Because the soul becomes irreproachable desiring the ardour of a blessed burning of love, it is always led further into the mortal woman until body and soul are weakened and the woman's betrayal must be experienced with suffering. One finds oneself conquered by and bound tightly to the earthly spirit to the extent that one excuses oneself for not attending the communion of the great God by saying, "I have taken a wife and therefore cannot attend."

We cannot understand why marriage is disadvantageous for him, since there is a certain arrangement in the natural kingdom for the creature, like man, who lives according to the course of the world in an impure state of desire. Such a state, however, is satisfactory since there is a goal to be achieved in the marriage state preventing the people from wasting their lives. When we discuss people who have greater control and participate more, it hurts us deeply when one disregards them in order not to lose the sensuality of life. I will realize that reason will find me at fault especially by those who exist in the heaven of love. I also know that without the healing no one will see the Lord. No one will be honoured before having struggled for this good cause; therefore, of what advantage is it for someone to serve Christ in battle for five, ten, or fifteen years and thereafter stone oneself before one's enemies and become a slave after having fought so eagerly? We have no witness as to who has been promised the victory of the struggle and the battle without being conquered.

I am quite aware of the effort one must exert in order

to renounce the woman of this world. He who knows all realizes all the painful and fatal struggles which I have encountered in the many years of wandering through the desert of temptation. I still remember how throughout the years the devil tempted body and soul and did not secretly support the merciful love against my will without my becoming corrupt, for the weakest powers of the will in the false imagination are stronger than the greatest desires of the spirit which result in a state of unconsciousness, causing almost everything to be subjected to death. For a long time I could not differentiate between left and right since I did not wish to surrender to the falsity of the powers of temp- tation or be conquered by any other such force. In the end, I became exhausted and took refuge in him who had called me, and I earnestly urged him to save my soul from my enemies. I also persisted to illuminate a light of God's happiness within me while arousing and stirring my weak spirit of life to motion; this heavenly strength to live has not possessed me until this time. From this point on I have been firm in my attitude toward my enemies and have been so to this hour, but further persistence requires a guilt-free, unmaterialistic, chaste, and sober lifestyle so that the enemy may not claim any part of man as his own. For as soon as this occurs, God can and will not protect us, but allows one to become aware of one's weaknesses and become always purer as one appears before God.

I could add much more, but I am not permitted to elaborate in writing or orally so that I do not lose my strength. Nevertheless, I do wish to recall some issues in order to discover if your disposition can be elevated to the heavenly happiness. It is advantageous that we are subjected to our own state of nothingness which devalues all the powers of particulars, including those of the great multitude. We must regard the fact that upon remaining in this state we will eventually be raised by great forces so that we will not fall into a false unconsciousness in our weakened condition and become a mockery of the devil. For when he can no longer mislead us with worldly pride and its fluctuations, he looks toward the body (which, after abandoning pride becomes even more inclined to it), attempting to lead it to the unchanging house of affliction, and he hopes to gain people desirous of God's own community by this method. It is certainly true that all defeat and submission of the spirit is not caused to a great extent by the hidden heavenly powers of the grace of God, but also by the devil's deception which originates and will cause us to turn our suppression and behaviour against our neighbors; it will exert pressure through humility and destruction even though one may be intolerant, impatient, and spiteful in one's attitude toward one's neighbour. True destruction is known by this sign: if one is naturally calm, still, quiet and generous but imprudent toward one's enemies like the devil, a hidden force will be led, causing even our neighbour to receive the good intentions according to his needs and because of the suffering, agreement and inner peace, quietness and gentleness will result. I have, frequently, wished to tell you orally, hoping that it would benefit your soul, that the will and stratagem of the enemy are experienced, and therefore he has no longer access to my own soul even though he continues to shout at me from outside like a dog through the children of evil or through false brothers.

I will expand upon the remaining without any omissions about my healing and its fulfillment in this time so that I may remain in a state of blessed anticipation until the day of Jesus Christ's coming when I wish to expose myself before him. Though I have fought my way through bitter battles and am compelled to continue my meagre ways, I will not be discouraged, for I am sure of him in whom I believe, and have faith in the knowledge that he will guard that which I have enclosed until judgement day. Therefore I live in great hope and appreciate the gifts of God, thanking him also that he made me worthy of enduring his ways and accepting his will. I must admit that grace has led me through great suffering and dejection and has converted me as a Christian.

For these reasons, I also held fast to the life-spirit, Jesus, in this land of many powerful oppositions. My male and female companions with whom I wandered have remained on their part quite optimistic, and I continually hope that a small sign of the first Christians is represented in us. We wander in as Apostles, arranged as some of the thousands of the breakers of bread. We are, however, no longer in contact with the persons who enter from the outside world, the majority of which are corrupt people, exposed to disbelief and the sorrows of satisfying earthly livelihoods. They therefore are bound to the business of the outside world (which causes the greatest separation between those who enter from the outside). The majority of the people have no spirit and have valued earthly things over your law and have become Christians in name only. I hope you will wish to have these letters which I have directed to you in this country. The person Yohom Iopohe is a repulsive mortal being who continually peers into the secrets of evil where he sees nothing but waste and depravity. This is not surprising if one considers that he is looking into the devil's kingdom. Could he, however, see God's love, he would realize that God's Church on earth has become invincible through the tribulation of Christ's crucifixion.

The Forty-Third Epistle

On account of our apathetic humanity the sacred heavens of God have been sealed through the fall, but will be opened following a lengthy course of time.

Greatly honoured sister,

I hope that your mind will have cause to be revealed, for in all actual opportunities, the authority of the heavenly enlightenment is quite unrevealed as is my opinion of the fact that a certain alienation always remains. Diligence was by yourself and others continually altered, and, therefore, there remained no means by which it could be promoted. I believe you ought to strive to attain total unity and submission of the spirit and body, and that you ought to attempt to discover if the grace of God's sacred fire revealed through his love is contained in yourself.

Then certainly, when nothing totally unique is revealed in the heart, one assumes that all was done in vain. One must strive to maintain a totally simple heart and be humble in spirit, for self-love and pleasure is an atrocity against God. So no part of us is deserving of any honour, but it may be this worthlessness of ourselves which will be referred to as the lost goodness. As soon as some of this is discovered within ourselves, the unfamiliarity for God and his love will disappear. The heavenly enlightenment does not instruct our people to regard themselves highly, but rather reveals the contents of the heart and mind which expose the humility within the self, causing great displeasure. God's satisfaction begins to be aroused within us, removing the detachment and revealing his love.

I could mention much concerning the advantages God and his love present to the open-minded person and especially where God's favour and his love lie. Everything expected in such instances in return is provided by the Lord of happiness, especially when favours for others are involved so mutual expressions of gratitude. Taking pleasure in the self results in the offence of God and one's neighbour while finding gratification in God and one's neighbour glorifies God and others. All that is determined outside of that is worthless and vain. Therefore, it would be ideal if some progress were made on the part of various hearts. God has, to this point, ignored and allowed much folly in various manners, but unfortunately very few of God's own virtues have been perceived which like a lovely dew expanded over one another, especially where the hidden agreement and association with God are concerned. One must grow to know God as he is and maintain one's love for him as is done between friends so that one never attends to oneself or any other beings.

Up to a time I lingered in a state of human weakness and in many imperfections. This totally contradicts the law of the spirit and of my own conscience. I realize that certain time periods are terminating and that the path for a different period is being prepared. The turtle dove is heard on earth and announces to us the advent of the new world. Day lingers and nights grow short. The open door of the Philadelphian period of the church welcomes us into the city of the living God where citizens and inhabitants are granted endless liberties. And you, most worthy of people who are followers of the maidens, disciples of the Lamb, preserve the nobility of the spiritual and lovely maidenhood beyond the value of all priceless pearls. For you represent all of

God's eternal wisdom and love. If the citizens of God's city are considered worthy of honour, the inhabitants of the king's palace must be even more highly valued. If the attendants and servants of the king are glorified, how much more are they who are attended to.

Therefore, my beloved, you are not subjugated to the king's servitude and are not counted solely among the maidens' numbers, but instead are considered as the chosen ones of God. Therefore, have no regard for the triviality of the noble's great reputation; abandon all unnecessary concerns and cares of life, and do not consider the way of our God in terms of spiritual or comely poverty for this is unworthy of your king. Do not be two-faced or unfaithful, but rather treasure your spiritual wealth with your whole heart. Carry gladly the yoke of your imposed burden which is the love for your groom. Take heed that you diligently secure his love within you more every day, for it is your maidenly bridal ornament. The contract between you is based on glory and pure love. The love which I bring to you is worthless in comparison to the most pure spirit of the godly cleanliness. My arrangement did not become heavenly of its own accord, but rather through various changes which were introduced. Death was upon us and grew more powerful in our just state and as we aged, we acknowledged grace, mercy and the pleasantness of God. I am and will remain indebted to God and will continue to be the subject of your thoughts.

P.S. It was not my intention to allow my subject to have strayed to the topic of sisterhood, however important it may be. As long as there are no misunderstandings, I am satisfied. I greet and love you. Vale.

F.G. I who am nobody.

MYSTIC CHURCH DOCUMENT

Mystic Church Document

A printed document of the so-called Sabbatarians of Pennsylvania was issued at the request of the Moravians under the following title:

The mystic and theological document of the Brotherhood of Zion, concerning the most significant facts of Christian doctrine, including a supplement in which is published the same impartial considerations of the conversion of the so-called Moravian community and the reason that the establishment of churches could not be permitted. Germantown, C. Sauer, 1743.

Preface

Dear Reader,

We were moved for important reasons to publicize this doctrine and witness the most significant facts of Christianity and God's ways how he lived among us. This is, however, in contrast to our lifestyle since the role we have chosen is silence. For some time, men have come to these regions with many false pretences about serious and eager services to God and interests in the Church. After we endeavoured to help where possible with our love and favours, we were compelled to make the acquaintance of these people if we were to be considered in God's favour and display no doubt or uncertainties. In the meantime, we were granted the opportunity to study and familiarize ourselves with their teachings, to determine the type of effect they had and to observe how they led the people astray from the true religion.

By God's will and because of our conscience, we have been compelled to separate ourselves from them. We then published this present document wherein the most significant statements of Christianity are stated, concerning the fall of mankind from the Old Testament, the Priesthood of Aaron,

Christ and the Church of the New Testament, the reign of the Church and its submission, penance, faith, law, gospel teachings, etc. We were impartial in our thoughts concerning these people as we debated whether it was proper to permit the establishment of a church community. We were determined to notify all interested people, with whom we were united in a bond of brotherly love and friendship, so that the purpose of this doctrine may be clarified.

The first statement.
Concerning God and the fall of mankind.

God is unique, an incomprehensible entity, an unreachable and unseen being, who does not desire to be known, understood or imagined. In this one, perpetual, unattainable being lie concealed all secret powers, including wisdom and knowledge which were hidden for eternities and which were finally revealed by the Son at the end of time. Despite the fact that God expressed himself through his first creation, our forefather Adam failed the test and crumbled in God's hands. Therefore he fell into a life of vulnerability and was subjected to penance and suffering yielded up by the earth. These reasons were made noteworthy so that God could better reveal his being of the most profound nature and existence. We acknowledge that Adam has been created for the purpose of a heirarchy and heavenly kingdom in which he was introduced to the company of knowledge. However, Prince Lucifer infiltrated the creation and therefore, when Adam attempted to discover the mysteries of essence and the environment, his great imagination was contaminated. The ability to reason left him and chastity became stained. Since man could not exist without human company, God created an earthly Eve to satisfy man's great yearning. Because we are, however, speaking of knowledge as the first companion of Adam, one must not become separated from her since she appears complaining in the Old Testament as an abandoned widow who must remain barren, for her husband Adam is unfaithful and had committed himself to a stranger. She carried nothing less within her than the pure seed of the word to her righteous chosen husband until the time of the victory when God's intentions would be revealed with the transformation of the Virgin Mary and the proclamation of Jesus through whom all the sinning daughters and sons of Adam would be absolved.

Had Adam only remained with his Eve in that pure state, none of the ensuing events would have occurred. God would not have had to make quite so many covenants with mankind. However, because of the seriousness of the roguish activities, during which the devil and man conspired behind God's back, the fall and the shame and nakedness of man became inevitable. Because of this, God allowed the growth of good and evil in that apple tree containing the damning fruit. Since Adam was an incomplete person, actually vulnerable, who had experimented with evil, the result of the sin of entering into the forbidden is exposure and eventual death. Moses clearly describes how the woman was betrayed by the serpent when she held Adam's heart and life in her hands. Though Adam fell, it was through her action. For this reason, we blame Adam, but the revelation of the sin occurred through the breaking of the commandment on the part of Eve. According to the witness of the document, Adam was not tempted; the woman, however, was led astray and was the initiator of the breaking of the law. (I Tim. 11:14). Because of its occurrence, the victory wreath of Paradise was lost even though they were at first in an angelic state. There was no alternative: they were compelled to leave and the angel with the crude sword guarded the entrance. What a profound secret which confines our understanding to a time beyond death! It was written; if only he had not tasted! Had he not penetrated the evil of the fallen man, the possibility of redemption would not have been considered and he would have lived forever, the good having prevented him from residing eternally with God. Oh how often we have no other purpose in mind than to extend our hands toward the tree of life and with it to attempt to avoid the bitter death upon the cross. To consider ourselves sinless is the greatest evil.

The second statement,
Concerning the extent of the Family Tree and the Church of
the Old Testament

Adam and Eve lost their nobility and the world's burden would have to be carried on their shoulders. God, however, became merciful and comforted them when they encountered evil. During the six days, the people were subjected to slavery and as a result, God added the seventh day which became blessed. Therefore, we make an example of the seventh through holy celebrations and prayer of great thanksgiving to God which is continued until the feared birth of the six week days of God's children is solved and the Sabbath is transformed. Following this, the family line of man was expanded on earth and a government was formed under circumstances which sought power against God. This occurred under the rule of Nimrod whose earthly reign began with bitter opposition against God and his holy word. It is noteworthy that the first born man was his brother's murderer because his brother's sacrifice pleased God, for a conspiracy with the devil could only result in evil deeds.

Apart from the murder, the family tree brought forth contact with God. Then God spoke, promising the appearance of a hidden redeemer whose words would be passed from generation to generation until the contract arrived at its goal and became incarnate through the Virgin Mary. Here one could report the intensity of the search for the promise on the part of the patriarchs of the Old Testament as seen by the example of Abraham, Judah and David who were driven about and finally became the fathers of nations. The devil attempted to persecute them through Bileam and they were often in a state of need and deprivation - (see II Chron. 9). Israel frightened their enemies, causing even the Canaanites to fear them. Thereafter, as the population multiplied - even under Egyptian slavery - God finally led them away by the hand of Moses who brought them to Mt. Sinai in order to engrave God's law into their hearts.

But what a calamity! They sinned and failed to obey God. For this reason, God carved his laws on to stone tablets and they placed them into the Ark of the Covenant. For the people, however, he established totally different rules by which to abide which were best suited to them. Through this, one may discover the purpose of God's law and come to know that God had not yet achieved his goal. The Jewish Church fell since it had established laws which were in direct opposition to the Ten Commandments. Christ was the first who dissolved and fulfilled them; but after him, they were ignored once more since the Christian, as well as the Jewish Church, could not face up to the truth. However, because God's law must be fulfilled, we continue to wait for the time when the law and all God's witnesses, which are presently being ignored and covered with shame, will be, according to his most profound spiritual purpose, proclaimed and fulfilled.

At this point, additional information concerning the priesthood of Aaron should be mentioned. Man would have fallen into the burning pit of fire and would have been destroyed had he not been redeemed. Because Jesus Christ and his holy sacrifice of reconciliation had not yet appeared, God was compelled to find satisfaction in the sacrifice of animals. Since Adam's downfall was caused by a serpent, many thousands of animals in Adam's community were to be sacrificed yearly during Jewish Temple services. It is remarkable that the first who held that position, a slaughterer of calves, created a scandal among the people of the time by describing God's great intention. One could see how poorly the priesthood of Aaron was considered and how the people blamed him as the cause of their sinfulness. There was no other alternative and the sinful nature could not be rooted out because of the people's ignorance.

We must continue to describe how such a priesthood in the early Christian Church is established. After Christ and the first martyrs departed from the world, it was proclaimed that it was not known what happened to the priesthood. It was difficult for the people to live their lives under the witness and judgement of God. Because they hungered for a god or an equal in order that they might perform better, they were presented with priests as they desired. They clothed themselves as images of Christ, preached gospels concerning the immortality of man until they believed themselves to be immune from all evil, allowing themselves total freedom. Every religious sect, no matter now small, desired a priesthood in order to falsely quiet the conscience. This much has been reported about the priesthood of Aaron.

The third statement

Concerning Jesus Christ, the mediator of the New Testament. Having discussed the background of Christ in the Old Testament, we now turn to Christ in his role as reconciler. We are familiar with the common methods employed by Christ to restore peace which are imperfect since we can easily accept his teachings, but they have no effect when Christ's name is not taken to heart. Before Christ resurrects within us spiritually, we must first realize that he is literally crucified within us. From here on, one has important and emphatic reasons. Whenever experience was lacking, the

Evangelists claim that his holy teachings were understood as so paradoxical that not only did his friends leave his company, but also his disciples departed. No one remained by him of the twelve who were most affected by the word of life. John 6 - Whoever accepts Christ in order to gain hope and life has done nothing greater than those Jews who followed Christ in the desert because of the miracles he performed. However, when he expressed his beliefs to them, they were prepared to stone him. Those who love Jesus Christ, even though his teachings contradict their attitudes, have nothing to fear.

Even for those who take great pains to understand God's ways, difficulties present themselves. Oh holy secret of our restoration! How you are concealed from our senses! Oh how your paths are covered with folly and your ways with disgrace. How often you sway toward the path of danger and murder which in flesh and blood attracts mockery and fills the senses. Why is Christ called a "stone of offense" and a "rock of annoyance"? Why must he alone claim that "he who is not vexed by me is blessed"? In conclusion, had we not betrayed him at that time, it would not have been necessary for him to betray us.

Now we will continue to discuss him according to the biblical passages. He is called the Son of the living God, the reflection of his magnificence and the image of his being, the first born who makes all other first born holy. He appeared as a mortal, using our humanness to disguise his heavenliness and after spending 30 years under the guardianship of his parents, he began his public life of preaching. Through his baptism, he was sanctified and confirmed. Thereafter, he was tested and during a period of temptation lasting 40 days, he conquered the god of this world and the earthly kingdoms. During that process, he achieved such great efficiency that he conquered the prince of rage. The spirit of betrayal and the might of darkness which imprisoned human generations were conquered in the Garden of Gethsemane. Having sacrificed himself on the cross, he descended with his new powers to preach to the imprisoned souls. After rising from the dead, he ascended to heaven, dissolved the Church of the Old Testament, and took the fathers, who were waiting for their completion, into glory. They became known as the foundation stones to be used in the creation of the church of the New Testament. The pouring out of the Holy Spirit ensued, forming the god-like creations in a special manner which could occur only now. Adam's error was eventually corrected and the knowledge flowed openly back into Jesus, born of a Virgin.

Oh what an all-encompassing, important secret which even angels long to uncover! This is the first-born who received the living word and presented it to the sons of Adam who were his brothers. Through him, God spoke with the ancestors. Through him, he communicated with Moses in the burning bush. The community was able to eat and drink in the desert because of him, for he was the rock and their constant companion. David referred to him as Lord, etc., and we value reconciliation so greatly because through it all sinful sons and daughters of Adam will be healed at various degrees. We also recognize that by abiding by his heavenly teaching the sole manner of achieving sanctification is made possible. Idols and figures play no role in our lives since they lead us away from the truth.

The fourth statement
Concerning the Christian Church

A distinction must be made between the church and a sect. A sect is established by the will of man and is maintained and controlled by human intelligence. The Church, however, may be compared to a woman; a woman is representative of submission just as a man is an image of strength. Not that the

Church is definable in terms of men, women, youths and elderly people, since the Church cannot be described according to human aspects, but it becomes part of their lives after they have been tested by the cross. The Church remains a virgin, her husband being Christ who exposed her through his crucifixion. Through him, she is granted fertility and given the ability to bear children as the dew brings forth the dawn. As the Old Testament states, her God-sent ability to reproduce was not exposed; she remained chaste. No one wished to lie by her, for everything depended on earthly Eve. Upon finding her Virgin-conceived Jesus, her widowhood concluded and she submitted for the first time to her strength to conceive at Pentecost in Jerusalem.

There is a wide variety of households in this quarrelsome world, but the undivided Church consists only of one. She roams about upon the earth from one people to the next and searches for persons with whom she can feel at ease and with whom she may continue to indulge her heavenly pleasures. It would be desirable if people did not treasure their own earthly existence to such an extent, for the Church would then acquire more worshipers. But the rage of the devil is so overwhelming that she must conceal herself in the desert and not dare to establish a dwelling place. Now that we are willing to accept God's discipline and confinements and refer to ourselves as members, we participate in all the activities even though the devil who obstructs the ways of the Church continually attempts to accuse us of creating sects.

From afar, we realize that the Church is invincible and that the powers of hell cannot defeat her. She does not value a good earthly impression, since to be a flower of the time does not allow for the possibility of eternity. Her strength lies on the proclamation of the cross; the more she appears defeated, the more unconquerable she becomes, just as her leader, Christ, was an invincible king when he hung between two murderers on the cross. All communities which were constructed in the Far East by the apostles did not come to an end by being defeated, but simply ceased to exist on earth. This was inevitable since it is not possible for any one Church to flourish permanently on earth.

While this creation is being described, it is essential to elaborate further on it. The creation consists of two parts: the heavenly and the earthly. Both are in conflict with the other, and the place which one chooses to inhabit must be abandoned by the other. The latter controlled the government up to the time of Christ through whose revelation it was humbled. When Christ appeared, a great intrusion entered where Adam and Eve were united, causing the great discord among Adam's children against God's doctrine. The rights of this creation of the Christian Church were lost and given to the Pagans. In that time, sin gained strength, defeating the creation of God and filling the Church with thieves and murderers who opposed God. Concerning the first, namely the creation of paradise, it is certain that wisdom is entrusted to our male - limbo in sorrow, since she will lose her maidenhood to it. She does not need our driving human will for fertilization, since she already possesses the human fire and seed within herself. It is stated here that in order to die, the governing human will must be nailed to the cross and in its humiliation, sink into itself, checking its heated resurrection within ourselves. In such a manner, the chaste marriage bed is prepared for her and we participate in the mystic pregnancy during which time our sunken human will becomes feminine and receives the seed of the Virgin. At that point, Eve completed her services; her hidden femininity was no longer in demand since one's own fruit and agriculture sufficed. This much has been mentioned about the Church.

The fifth statement
Concerning the two positions of the Church

We now continue, having positively established the existence
of one creation which possesses the power to govern the
Church, namely that of Paradise. One reaches the conclusion
that only one leadership is present and that all states of
life are connected to it. The deficiency found among these
states of life cannot be taken seriously. At this point, it
is important to record the most significant teachings of
Jesus Christ but avoiding trivia. All states of life have
their limitations as they teach us to disown our earthly
possessions and to freely choose poverty. After this is completed, they continue and attack us in that area which
unites us in a natural relationship of flesh and blood with
this earth and teach us to despise father, mother, etc.
Though these are important processes, they are only necessary preparations for the eventual attainment of Jesus
Christ's teachings. Having displayed unfragmented confidence in these statements, the personal life, though it
appears innocent in its arrogance, divine glamour and many
virtues, remains to be condemned to death by the teaching of
Christ. Here appear various exercises and Christian doctrines and different lections which require many years of
suffering and faith to which no further reference will be
made. Just as the body's limbs differ, so are there various
positions in the household of the Church. Two states of
life are recognized above the others: the house state and
the solitary state. In the Old Testament, no differences
among these states of life are indicated; all remained
united despite the role which the spirit played in the services of God of separating men and women. In contrast to
that of the Old Testament, the Christian Church dismembered
the states of life in advance, causing divisions. Here one
discovers the many holy men and fighters for Christ who

rejected worldly splendors and chose for their part the disgrace of Christ as did many devout women and girls by whose examples angelic exercises and purification became the final rituals before death.

The solitary state is important because, it firstly has not become entangled in the business of the world and secondly because it is central to Christ and his holy teaching. Therefore, it is extremely tragic when the souls abandon this state and choose another. How much pain and suffering is required until that time when they return to their original state and discover no eternal reward has yet been gained. Happy is the man who waits patiently while God eliminates his deficiency. It occurs frequently that we restore ourselves in an incorrect manner, following a common trend or at least attempting to regulate ourselves with good appearances of transient things in our souls of burning fire. Oh great folly! When we again require God, the half of the healed wound must be reopened and we must again be made sensitive to our deficiencies and helplessness. Therefore, great caution is imperative or the desired end will not be attained. As long as a part of the outside world exists in which the soul finds comfort and nourishment, God will remain aloof, not acknowledging the solitary life. The people's blindness is tremendous, and no one is aware of this all-important fact. Everyone avoids the position of voluntary poverty and scorn of the world from which true salvation is acquired. It must be made known that the state of marriage was established for important reasons including a disciplinary action for fallen mankind. When the state office acquires a burden, God will aid with the carrying of the load since all which humiliates man in his state is controlled according to God's will. It is God's plan for mankind that each person carry his burden. He who is referred to as a slave is already being subjected to the carrying of a load. However, he is a free man before

God who will inflict no other difficulties upon him. He who is free and has not yet acquired an earthly state must become a servant of Jesus Christ since his unbound state allows for so many more freedoms according to the teachings of Paul, I Cor. 7,21. In the Church we are able to recognize a confined and restricted marriage. It would not be wise to reject such a state of life since we are only human and not properly disciplined. We must first be trained in this state in order that suspicion may be eliminated on its own and forbidden to enter the marrige. Should this state of life be instituted within the Church as something which cannot be dissolved in this life, God's plan would not have been fulfilled. There are various schools in the Church and it has been proven that the state of marriage is such a disciplinary school. God controls the people through the cross which is contained in the marriage state. It would be quite ignorant to confine one's soul simply to one school for a lifetime, for the fact is, the soul could be promoted to a higher class in which the changes for profit would prove greater. Therefore, not only do we insist that this state in the Church must be forfeited and dissolved, but we also claim that blessed marriage partners, even after faithfully having committed themselves to each other, will find it imperative to dissolve this state. If one becomes earnestly involved in this state, it is an actual sign that God had never manifested himself in the heart or that infidelity is part of the marriage. Certainly, it was inevitable that such occurrences happened frequently in the early Church. The experienced apostle Paul was compelled to teach the men to cherish their wives. This would not have been necessary had changes been imposed upon the state through Christianity as could only be natural.

The sixth statement
Concerning the rule of the Church

As previously mentioned, the preisthood of Levi could not suppress the sins and, therefore, Christ appeared and introduced a completely different priesthood into the Church, not according to Aaron, but according to the ways of Melchisedech. The priestly system introduced by Melchisedech was continued in the New Testament under the command of the High Priest Jesus Christ who ordained others worthy enough to accept the vocation. Because it has been discovered that this statement was not taken seriously enough, it became necessary to elaborate further. This office may not be governed by man since human government does not belong in the Church, for it stems from the dark world. There is a much greater demand placed upon a person who has been prepared through great amounts of suffering and testing, since temptations from the devil increase with the importance of the occupation one has. One must be able to differentiate between what one is and how one presents oneself in order that one may not be recognized by the devil. It should not be necessary for one to acquire nourishment and support for his spirit from an occupation, since these would have been earned previously throughout his life with God so that he may spend his time in the peace of eternity with God. Through his love for God and his neighbour, he was willing to become equal to mankind in order to bring them salvation. He was driven by the greatest urgency, it was forced by the greatest need and his work was his greatest priority. Then the time came that God was revealed to him and he could prostrate himself before God's feet and raise his hands in his innocent state, proclaiming, "Lord! You know I have not come on my own." Furthermore, he must have remained just, so that righteousness became his companion and his defender in emergencies. In conclusion, it became necessary for him to lose and rediscover his soul before it could be presented to his brothers.

It would be proper to mention some facts concerning baptism and other Church rituals. Baptism is demanded by God according to the law of the first installment, for we are committed to him and can never be set free. A stagnant community is only an enslaved wife to God and can only bear illegitimate children. Baptism is not simply a ceremony which can be altered or dissolved, for God has included his grace in the ritual. A baptized person is given more privileges from God than an unbaptized person and God may claim him. God will bring a baptized person into his confidence while an unbaptized person is less eligible to be taken into God's trust. Baptism is the seal of the covenant and whoever has been baptized is united with God and acquires strength through him alone. The same importance is given to the establishment of communion and foot washing. Certainly, there must be more to it than one believes, for it is written, "Whoever drinks or eats unworthily will be held responsible for breaking God's laws." Because man can be put on trial for this offense, it stands to reason that God has presented himself in a certain manner; otherwise it would be illogical to charge someone. If someone has gone too far in atributing such importance to visible objects, one should be reminded that the Ark of the Covenant was also a visible object, but nonetheless, many thousands of people were killed by it and in contrast, many souls were saved by it also.

The seventh statement
cncerning the submission

The most significant duty which confronts us on our way toward God is the submission of our outer and inner humanity, all that we are and possess for God. In the church, this is greatly emphasized. The entire existing monarchy must be destroyed and the great powers and command, which are situated in the flesh and blood, along with it. Whoever believes he is in control of himself and the creator and master of his actions has not yet accepted Christianity. Something which occupies him does not belong to him and it becomes uncertain when the day will appear when he must trade the freedom he has taken for granted for the lowest level of slavery. It is necessary to question the manner in which submission and Christian freedom can exist together. The answer is that freedom is not a question of authority, but consists of acting out of free love to God as to oneself. Whoever searches for freedom within freedom, will never discover true liberty. When he loses the freedom wherein he sought his freedom, there is no future in store except that of the lowest form of servantship. If he, however, chooses, out of love, to follow God and enslave himself to following the road to eternal life, he becomes a free man, though he be a slave since his servitude becomes his shield of freedom of which no enemy can rob him.

Oh noble soul which is rediscovered through the act of submission! It had shamed God to the point that he himself desired to be put under submission. His righteous majesty will allow him to be submitted to the point that nothing smaller, nothing lower, and not anything slighter than God himself may be found. Since the beginning of time, no greater miracle than the incarnation of Jesus Christ has ever occurred. For God placed himself in the state of a servant. Oh most profound secret of Jesus Christ's incarnation! How great and how low are you? Who was ever lower than you since you permitted your arms to be stretched out on the cross in your state of abandonment and humbled yourself before the commandments of God. Who was ever greater than you since you ascended into heaven and set prisoners free? Oh immeasurable greatness which is acquired through the submission and humility of oneself to the will and purpose of God. It would be desirable if we could communicate to the heart of those souls in this state who desire to be saved. Here it is necessary to solve the question concerning the reason for the undertaking of servitude on the part of Jacob and Rachel and circumstances which caused him not to be frightened away even though he had experienced disgrace at the side of Leah. Here we find that the Church of the New Testament has been presented according to the image of a woman whose greatness consists in degradation and submission. Whoever insists upon existing in his own state of greatness may not live under the rule of the Church of the New Testament, for Christ appeared in order to humble all the rich. However, his kingdom, because it is situated at the lowest level, will not fall, but exist throughout eternity. Whoever makes it his spiritual duty to become the lowest member of the Church community will be given the opportunity to become a teacher and commander since he has lowered himself in order to give others advantages. When Christ wished to present an example of his humility, he prostrated himself before the feet of his disciples and washed their feet as an example of the submission of his total self.

To be glorified by God is to submit oneself as a servant and bound man out of love for him. Even though he is capable of employing his might to control all, it would be contradictory to his majesty and the freedom of mankind to do so. We acknowledge the priviledge and great nobility of the first-born Lamb of God whose original heir and privilege have given freely to something which can neither be seen nor heard, neither tasted nor received. When the period of their bondage is over, they, along with their righteous nobility, will be pardoned by God. Whoever is lacking in faith and love for God to the point that he trades in his supposed freedom with the burden of Christ,

cannot be assured that his liberty will end in eternal
servitude. If anyone, at the end of time, was known to have
concerns about possessions which were then given priority
over God other than those for God and finds after the
bondage that the desire to obtain freedom is weak, he will
have been born into slavery and his liberty will be
forfeited. Though we have obtained it through compulsion
and force, this man will be disqualified from the game since
he has nothing more to offer. As we realize by the
character of Abraham who is followed by Isaac, the promised
son, the concept of freedom is very significant, for Abraham
witnessed the freedom of Sara who represented the bondage of
grace, and though he later lay at Kethura's side, Isaac
still received the inheritance and the children born of the
woman were sent off with gifts.

Here we find it necessary to include additions concerning the spiritual engagement of the Church. As previously
mentioned, children were born and raised in a heavenly
manner in the Church. However, the establishment of father-
hood and maternity was imperative if man was to be cared for
and protected. All which is required is discovered by us
here, namely that man laboured and became clothed in the
simplicity of Christ, involving the lowered state of Jesus
Christ's humanity, the doctrine of God and the word of life
or, in conclusion, the strength of God in a state of human
frailty and the wrapping of the Christ child in swaddling
clothes. Whoever escapes from such confinements simply
because he has no desire to commit himself to the burdens of
this holy state of marriage or because he would rather live
according to his own ideas, is guilty of breaking the sacred
marriage vows which are difficult to reconstruct. Because
his anger was again aroused, the disposition will be
spiritual boldness. It will observe all happenings vexa-
tiously and attempt to destroy all that is superior to it

and all which is God-sent. Much could still be reported concerning the reason why God's people were not permitted to intermix with foreign women and why Phineas joined the priesthood, having rejected such whores. Whoever discovers this insight, wherein God is located, in the best-appearing things when demanded, granted and renounced by the circumstances, is fortunate, and God will favour him because all his actions are sincere and without fault. Nothing obstructs our path more than wrong understanding, for when it is aroused in us, it seizes the mystery of starry magic as occurring through the simplicity of Christ and we will become fortune-tellers and sign interpreters, viewing all through vexed eyes, interpreting good in evil, aware of the explanation of this and that and how the stars affect all. It is noteworthy that all soothsayers must be punished with death by the Jews and that the Church stands always in opposition to these people who included Janes and Jambres and Simon who was accused of being a magician.

The final statement.
Concerning the first awakening of penance, faith etc. and
the final judgement of God over fallen mankind.

We have been informed that flesh and blood may never obtain eternal life in God's kingdom, and that in God's faultless purity established by the cross this state is the root of all evil and hatred of God, and that although it bears the law of God's love within it, it has no intention to act by the law. Therefore, no one possessing the purpose and the will of the flesh may enter into God's kingdom. We are also aware of no other bliss than the one acquired by Jesus on the cross for which his successors await. Christ did not offer strange gifts to preserve his life, but instead offered his life as a sacrifice. In the same way, we must offer our lives out of love to him if we are ever to appear as his images. In the Church, therefore, we recognize a peaceful government, for no privilege of the right can control anything on earth including the life of an individual since the sacrifice was offered in order to make almost all righteous. Had everything been righted, there would be nothing else to achieve and all disputes and envy would have been conquered.

Furthermore, we are aware of the future of Christ in the Church through the flesh in the first awakening which occurred in angelic purity as angels sang, "Praised be God in the highest and peace to his people on earth and if Christ in his assumed humanity must again be crucified, he should first resurrect and ascend into heaven." If the summons from heaven is brought to the heart through the first awakening, man will tread immediately into the state of repentance within the Father's household according to the law and will attempt to discover if he has the ability, obtained by conforming to the law, to flee from the powerful death sentence. The law states, "To do so is to live." Justice acquired, thereafter, her claim to the people and the law controlled them with its requirements until that time when a serious change in penance caused the law to be satisfactory and its requirements to be dropped. Man was freed from the restrictions in order than he could commit himself to God (see Rom. 7:23). However, if atonement passes and justice remains uncontrolled, there will be no progress on the way to God, the heart will not be separated from the earth, and man becomes an adulterer since he subdues himself and commits himself to another even though the first establisher of the law still exists and rules by his controls.

When justice complies with the law and man becomes a perfect being of fairness, he will at first be condemned to death as an evil-doer because the right of his strange appearance and that of the evil root of enmity desires, against God's will and all lawful deeds, to continue uncontrolled and unjudged. This is the mystic and spiritual death which is far more grievous than that for which one suffers when one sins, for in the latter there is always time to consider hope and reward, but in the former, one must be hopelessly sacrificed, requiring one to trust God or to believe him. The household of Jesus Christ will be revealed and one will acquire one's holy sacrifice of redemption, and faith will burst forth. When one can proceed no further, it becomes necessary to submit to death if one is to be freed from sin. It is imperative to possess faith, love, hope, humility and patience, for the path is narrow and few are they who change in order to conform to it.

ON THE STATE OF ADAM

by

Johannes Hildebrand

On The State Of Adam

According to this document, the heavenly and virginal creation was physically obstructed by the first Adam but was again revealed through the almightiness of Christ's crucifixion. It was revealed by Johannes Hildebrand, a prominant member of the community of Jesus Christ in Ephrata.

Beloved Reader,

Motivated by my thoughts of the injury inflicted upon the occupied spiritual soul of Joseph, I decided to record Adam's innocent condition and his state following the fall. Before the fall, Adam was the complete Godly image in virginal male and female quality and reflected God's likeness, heeding the words, "Remain fertile and expand your numbers." This clarifies the fall as the text plainly indicates (Gen. 1:27, 28). It also relates further how he discovered a great difference while considering the animals of two separate generations which were divided according to their slightly differing expansions. Through the fascination of his observations a magical desire arose in him to possess such a manner of expansion which, however, he could not locate anywhere. For the crude human being, it remains unrevealed and secret; however, for those possessing the eyes of the spirit it is exposed. For important reasons, the Bible juxtaposes the passage concerning the naming of the animals with that of the creation of woman (Gen. 2:20).

Adam became feeble and weak in will while searching for his heavenly created pure origins so that he could be reunited with them and expand his numbers. Since the extraordinary contemplation of the desires of his will and the insight of the spirit were detached from God's observation for too long a time and separated from the inspiration of the sacred words, his heavenly image could not be fostered or maintain the strength to govern mightily. The spirit of his mind became obsessed with the notion of acquiring such aid as previously mentioned. And this was the reason according to God why Adam acquired misconceptions through his imagination and was no longer in a position to multiply. God spoke, "It is not recommended that man be alone." However, Genesis 1:31 states the opposite, namely, "God observed all which he created and was convinced of its goodness." It is crystal clear that a great change arose from the time of the first creation when he appeared as a masculine and feminine image until that time when it was no longer recommended that he remain in such a state, but instead was divided into two parts as the Bible indicates. Thereafter, God caused Adam to fall into a deep sleep as the Bible indicates in Genesis 2:21. One must note that the sleep is a distinct weakness of the spiritual life which is subjected to a state of unconsciousness. As long as Adam remained in complete heavenly might, no sleep could conquer him, for the total likeness of God is reflected by the spirit and great extraordinary life force as revealed through Christ. Upon destroying the powers of death through the crucifixion and completely reestablishing the lost image through his newly acquired humanity in the resurrection of body and soul in Adam, no one can deny that he had conquered his drowsiness. Through this the great transformation was revealed, which is unattainable for the crude worldly human who lives solely for his earthly desires. Therefore, he has acquired the great and true perception of the error and recognizes the fall in the most crude sense as Adam and Eve who were completely oppressed in their disobedience as recorded in the sermon involving the serpent. However, since they are unfamiliar with people in a complete state of innocence, they cannot be expected to judge them in any other manner.

However, in the present a spirit of confusion assumed the appearance, form, and stature of the murdered Lamb in order to preach a gospel which contradicts the teaching of both Christ and his apostles. People are misled into believing that the experience of suffering and death must not necessarily be encountered in order that one be considered blessed, and that penance is needless, for the chosen people could then be misguided as is indicated in the final portion of Revelation where witness was given to the local meeting. To the question of friend Gruber, "What is this falsity through which the selected can be misled?" the following response was given by Count Zinzendorf, "Firstly, the teaching of the serious struggle for penance led by God; secondly, to reach grace by the earnest striving for atonement." Through certain teachings, many minds were inspired by God especially those which had already begun an earnest life of penance and trodden onto the path of suffering and death. However, some teachings contradicted the clear testimony of scripture as proclaimed by John in his words, "Perform the true works of atonement," and by Christ in his plea, "Since the time of John the Baptist, the heavenly kingdom has come into authority and those who have access to power seize it. Furthermore, endevour to enter through the narrow gateway." Even Paul stated, "I perish daily." Therefore, if we suffer with him, we will be glorified along with him and give witness to many testimonies which one had previously ignored. For this reason, my mind was preoccupied with the thoughts of Joseph's injury for a time, since I was involved in [Count Zinzendorf's] conference [on the union of the Churches] for the third time during which I contemplated the aspects of the Count's teachings which were written in accordance with Christ's true testimony and were considered of great significance to me, especially at the third meeting in Oly, Pa. Therefore, it was clarified that Adam in his first state of innocence was concealed from the complete heavenly image of the people and for that reason the secret of the crucifixion remained disclosed.

Therefore, I express a spiritual longing for God that he may be among us in these troubled times and ever more reveal the communion of the Lamb based on the secret of the cross. Through it they are protected by Jesus' way of the cross and are not misled into directions of corruption which only appear pleasing. After being sufficiently acquainted for a time following the conferences with the actual evidence established by Christ's successors, we as members of the body find it appropriate to tread in the ways he left behind and to find fulfillment in his past suffering. The spiritual will seized me as I became more conscious of my aim to endure it to the last. Thereupon, on the first day of February of this year, it happened that a brother and sister from Zion and Kedar who also were members of our community gathered to carry off and bury a widow and deceased sister of their house. Our general supervisors and managers were also present and they held a constructive and important sermon which movingly emphasized how greatly they were affected by the mortality of mankind to which man was subjected after the fall, for there was no other medium through which God could be discovered which would liberate him from mortality except the painful and vulnerable power of death. God subjected the sacred humanity of Jesus Christ to the most bitter grief so that when mankind experienced it, it would be more endurable. It is noteworthy to prepare many other solemn expressions in order to cover short paths. In other sermons, the following ideas were expressed: No one knows the reason for the revelation of Christ's features, for it was not made explicit. While speaking these words, an astonishing and remarkable disclosure was momentarily revealed to my heart and mind and it made such a great impression upon me that I was inspired to record it. Oh what an amazing secret! which is concealed, unreachable and unattainable through all human reasoning and concerns, namely the reason that the sacred aspect of the godliness and humanity of Jesus Christ had to be exposed in such an unpleasant manner. How spiritually content and comforted through love are all true successors of Jesus Christ who follow the example of his actual suffering and death and those who willingly submit to the daily sacrifice as pure, patient lambs until the process of arresting the crude animal-like humanness is accomplished. As expressed by the sacrifices offered twice daily, in the mornings and evenings, the successors of Christ who endured the suffering upon the cross and mortality followed his example according to his words, " He who wishes to follow me must take up his cross daily." The Lamb of Easter which was sacrificed once in the year represented such an image of which Paul commented, "We too have a Lamb of Easter," Praised be the Lord who has presented us with actual knowledge, purpose and will. Amen, alleluia! Amen.

One is compelled not only to record this very considerable secret and this knowledge revealed through grace but also to allow our directors to read them, for this information is especially relevant to those who gladly accepted the fact that God required them to adhere to the principle regarding knowledge as a testimony which was already published. They also were contented to know that all selected souls were cautioned and aroused in being reminded that they should not follow any other path but that which involved the pain and death experienced by their master Jesus Christ who walked and prepared this way which is the sole possible access to God. Therefore, I find myself dutifully obligated to report the manner in which various speculations were presented and revealed to me.

Having sacrificed itself, the heavenly, virginal womb was again opened and unsealed for Jesus Christ, the second Adam, the son of the Virgin conceived through the Holy

Spirit. It was first made inaccessible by the actions of the first Adam since the rib was removed from his side from which a woman was formed causing the maidenly creation of the spirit to cease and to be revealed in the image of a woman characterized by mortal, unchaste, crude desires. In contrast, when the side of Christ was pierced, conception and parturition were spiritually instilled into the virginal strength which prepared the way for the spiritual maidenly humanity to again be born from the burning love contained in the heart of Jesus Christ. We now notice that Christ possesses a manner of creating in his side, while Adam's side was actually sealed by flesh, submitting him to a position where he sought a form and likeness to that of animals and then became the most debased, earthly and crude part of humanity. Therefore, the first Adam no longer had the ability to create contained in his side, but the most degraded form of humanity from which all impurity is expelled. We realize now why this creation was a blasphemy before the untainted eyes of God and why in the Old Testament it had to be united with an offering and involved in a purification process.

Oh great misery! The first Adam obtained physical strength from Eve just as Christ acquired it through his resurrection. His legs were not bones as hard as stone with which one seals and bars doors and locks, but instead they were bondages of the spirit, namely, strong magical powers which could successfully penetrate all without being obstructed. These strengths were transformed by a powerful magical impression into hard bones. While Christ lay in the tomb, these bones again materialized through the power of God into the magical strength of love and into actual human stature, form and image of flesh and leg to the extent that he could present himself before human eyes fundamentally in the strong extraordinary power of his body, allowing his hands to grope and then moments later be concealed again although closed doors could be penetrated. Here it would be fitting to record the words of Scripture which state that he died through the flesh but was revived by the spirit, the presence of which he acknowledged namely through the spiritual strength of his body which granted him access to all and lectured to the imprisoned spirits (1 Peter 3:18-19). Paul also claims that the true believers will be transformed amid trumpet blasts during future times in Christ. Also according to Paul, Christ had completely restored all in his assumed human body which was lost through Adam, the spiritual creation as well as incarnation. For what was born of flesh is flesh and what is conceived by the spirit is spirit.

Moses' words state that a rib was removed from Adam's side and it was shaped into a woman. This rib represented the powerful magical and feminine strength in Adam which could be rephrased as his implanted and created maidenly womb which he obtained during his creation in his side. It consisted of one-half of Adam's humanity, Adam's rose-garden and femininity through which he became capable of creating without external aid just as God is undivided within himself. In this harmonious manner he created a son from himself as well as all the worlds and everything imaginable. The other half, however, was the human portion and in both of these attributes Adam became a chaste man and kept the power to procreate within himself, not unlike Christ, the second Adam through whom all who wished to appear before God must without fail be reborn as he himself clearly explained to Nicodemus.

Because of the following reasons, the womb in Adam's side which received and created a powerful, magical strength became referred to as a rib. All the great extraordinary might of the spirit when united by restraining influences becomes solidified when the strength of the influence endures until the spirit of the bodily essence is converted and transformed into an earthy substance. All this is caused by the influence of Spiritus Mundi who acquired his power through the fall. Since the strong, magical, creative force was at first incorporated into Adam's side, the fall caused the embodiment of bodily essential strength in the rib of the side. Therefore, one is justified in referring to it as a rib, for it has been one in the side. God's creation is a spiritual formation of love extending from the heart through the side which is situated next to the heart unlike the low, earthly, foul, decayed stomach of the animals. Therefore, such crude births are, totally without grace and mercy, predestined and condemned to a death of pain and suffering. Through them, God's image was exterminated and destroyed and presented itself in the likeness of an animal in a terrifying form and structure on the site of the heavenly image. It is necessary that it be sacrificed as in the Old Testament where the sacrificial animals had to be purified in compensation for the sins of mankind.

As stated earlier, after regarding the inner markings of the animals in order to name them according to their natural forms and the qualities of their characteristics, Adam desired that he also have an assistant to accompany him. God then created two divisions from a second formation source and was again compelled to penetrate with a strong magical power in order that both became complete images. However, when the decline caused by the consumption of good and evil was terminated, their great magical spiritual bodily strength became solidified through the influence to such an extent that their delicate corporeality's strengths were transformed in their sides into ribs as in their total humanity. This power also caused other formations. The state of the entire heart was brought to an abrupt ending and their virginal womb was tightly sealed. Rather they adhered to such a creation as Adam's mind, altered through the observation of the animals, which was then ashamed since

it was modelled according to that of the animals and was
blasphemous before God's holiness, although it will indul-
gently and patiently be tolerated by him until the time of
the restoration. Such a creation finally embodied itself in
the second Adam, Christ, and lost in him all its privileges,
for it has been revealed that he, according to the natural
process, became incarnate through a woman. More
importantly, he subjected himself to the piercing of his
side from which Eve was created from Adam and which was the
source of the spiritual birth. During his insensibility his
heavenly, virginal womb was again constructed and restored
to him upon waking.

Praised be the Lord of Hosts who has revealed to us
this honoured and noble heavenly Virgin as a spiritual
mother in the heart of Jesus! As a gate in the side of
Jesus, she is open to us. The magical will of our soul can
again gain access and in faith can enter the virginal womb
of Jesus in whom we receive the Spirit and are again reborn.
Our natural creation also reaches its destination and is
fulfilled through an image, and therefore the High Priest of
the Old Testament could only take a virgin for a wife. It
would be proper to include Paul's statement here, "I have
entrusted to you a man who will be born of a chaste virgin."
(II Cor. 11:2). Likewise the bride of the High Priest had
to be in all aspects a pure maiden just as as Mary was
externally an untainted pure Virgin and also contained
within the depths of her soul this heavenly innocence which
was passed on through the promise until it eventually
reached the generation of Mary and there achieved its goal.
From her, Christ obtained his humanity and was then
crucified. Through him we gained access to the heavenly
womb so that we may, through the strength he acquired for
us, follow his example and be reborn by his sacred humanity.
Therefore he claims, "When I am glorified I want you to
accompany me." The heart of his love located in his pierced

side is greatly exposed and draws us toward him through the entire love of the complete strength in our hearts, for he hopes to unite us with himself and that we be reborn in him according to God's likeness. Whoever desires to follow in his abandoned way of suffering and death and to submit the crude inherited life to one of sacrifice must enter into the spirit of the mind with a pure heart and penetrate Jesus' pierced side leading to his heart of love from which his blood flowed that we may be ransomed. He demands without fail the return of the likeness lost by Adam during the fall so that calmness and peace may be restored to his soul and every soul. Amen.

It is disturbing that in these final unsettling days such a multitude of spirits who rejected the strength appeared in order to mislead even those who have begun to answer the cry of Jesus' voice. However, they had not yet totally arrived at a resolution to endure the process of following until its completion. They thought otherwise and entered another door in order to escape the great suffering. In this manner, the host of spirits was strengthened, gaining access to the Lamb's form and calling, "Walk down this path which the Lamb has prepared and is now so leisurely and smooth. Upon it one can travel without discomfort. Accept his earnings, for you have been redeemed and liberated through the shedding of his blood. Believe and accept it. You need not strain yourselves with difficult undertakings and self-inflicted suffering since the Lamb has already accomplished these tasks for you. You have been declared holy for believing in the blood he shed for us. Yes, even your children who are witnesses of the faith are saved through your holiness. Because you have accepted the image of God through Christ's merits faithfully, the likeness can physically be transplanted and passed on to your successors. God in the beginning created man and woman in his image that they might extend the likeness. It is fulfilled by the creation of a child within the body of its mother, conceived through the Holy Spirit, for marriage is a holy sacrament established by God in the name of Jesus Christ and in the service of Redeemer we alone are holy, for works and individual righteousness are of no value.

Many of these same reasons are acquired by these spirits partly from scriptures and partly from reason and are used to mislead and attract even those with good intentions.

One can be easily tempted to abandon the way leading to Christ, for it is difficult to follow his example and impossible to ignore one's natural desires. Little knowledge remains of the first created people, of their innocence and pure heavenly and virginal likenesses. Therefore one is easily attracted to the pleasant and comforting but injurious images in nature, in which suffering is unnecessary. However, upon departing, one seeks repentance humbly since one had received the potential for rebirth during the first revival as well as a privilege of priesthood where one serves God day and night, and since one had devalued all this for a pleasant appearance and submitted to one's desires for materialism.

I cannot avoid relating something published in a document from Frankfurt by a certain A.G. On page 36 the following was written, "The human potential of the believer is regarded as a sacred tincture and is intended to be transplanted to produce a spiritual union of the glorified, to be a testimony in an orderly manner of holy children and to extend God's image. When one sleeps with one's wife, one must conduct oneself as if one were in Christ's presence or as if one were attending the sacred supper." It remains as he desired. This much can I, Johannes Hildebrand judge concerning it: I and four other directors of our community namely Heinrich Kalckgläser, Friedrich Foltz, Ludwig Plum and Jacob Keller were attending the third conference in Oly and we delivered a publication to the Count in which we conveyed the differences between the single and married life and described marriage in terms of its three varying degrees according to the testimony of scripture in order to emphasize the fact that we do not simply reject the state of matrimony. The Count answered us in this manner, "Our married state is much more honoured than your holy position of matrimony. I state publicly, If I happened to die while in bed with my wife, I could say to the Saviour, "I was in the process of performing my duty (which is to say I was doing it in your name)". We replied to his statement by claiming he was mistaken and should be publicly known as a heretic and because we discussed this matter privately with him, he angrily departed from us saying, "I do not wish to associate with you" although we spoke modestly with him. When we repeated this during the conference he bade us remain silent saying, "I cannot bear to listen," and when we continued to speak, he became angered and wished to leave the room. From his earlier words we were certain that he regarded this sleep with another as a most holy work performed in the name of the Redeemer. By stating that even the mother of Jesus had to be cleansed according to the law proves that the external birth through which flesh and blood are created cannot be a pure heavenly image although the spiritual humanity contained in this assumed bodily humanity has remained completely chaste and even the external mortal humanity is fulfilled through suffering and death. Therefore, Scripture records that the Redeemer, like a child, adopted a body of flesh and blood, but he was not conceived from a human, but from a virgin which however did not ease the pains of his bitter death. Had Christ to die such a shameful death? Could not his Father have excused him from it since he only, so to speak, embraced our humanity as one who subjected himself to the preaching and correcting of sinful expansion of the gospel? The Scriptures state, "That which is born of flesh must decay." It is surprising to realize this if one insists on asserting that a grave error exists in the evidence of Scriptures. Even more disturbing is the fact that people who are recognized for their religious fervour have become involved in this issue. But what can be said? If one possesses an unjustified purpose and does not totally wish to follow Jesus' way leading toward death, one will righteously find oneself abandoning the guidance provided by such a spirit. During the pursuit of Jesus Christ, the eyes of our spirit will be opened to the recognition of the first created Adam in his innocence and to the realization that Christ, by preparing the way by his death upon the cross, again attained this state of innocence.

To again analyze the main concern, it is necessary to mention that the physical birth of the lowest portion of the body and the rebirth in the top part as in the heart are united through the spirit which Paul refers to as the new birth of the hidden people of the heart. Whoever recognizes the obscure reason concerning the sacrificial burning of the kidneys along with the fat during the Jewish offering clearly realizes the difference between these two types of births. The kidneys are the second heart from which the power of the incarnation flows. Therefore, two kidneys exist, one of masculine and the other of feminine characteristics of which the strength is greatest in its seed form, composing the being in a masculine or feminine manifestation. A hidden strength is situated in the human heart at the centre of the soul where the heavenly source of the new humanity is formed and created through the eternal word of virginal male and female qualities into a single human image. Therefore, rather than two hearts, only one is necessary and it is located in the side of Christ which was pierced by the spear directly under the chest. Oh great miracle of which a mark remains imprinted upon the human body! The milk-producing breasts are found on the top section of the body in front of the heart, indicating that the true nourishment which man requires from the chest of Jesus may be acquired through his wonderful love. Oh how my soul rejoices upon discovering access to the Spirit wherein it can embrace certain confidence and union of hearts through the faith and Jesus Christ's gift of grace, and can leisurely obtain nourishment for the renewed humanity from the love contained in Jesus' heart. While the physical mother attempts to employ her powerful influence in order to choke the small boy during the birth, the strength of the spiritual mother will eventually conquer the other so that the new humanity can again be conceived by the immortal body of God. Alleluia, Amen.

In reference to the previously mentioned kidneys, God spoke, "I the Lord have come to determine the worth of both heart and kidneys," (Ps. 7:20) and David claimed that his kidney caused him to suffer nights (Ps. 16:7). David pleads to the Lord with the words, "Cleanse my kidneys," (Ps. 26:2). Faith will harness the kidneys, (Is. 11:5). Isaiah spiritually discusses Christ and his true followers and successors. That does not suggest that one ought to live sensually, for those with common sense realize what is intended by this statement. Lastly but also of significance is Paul's statement (I Cor. 6:13), "The nourishment of the stomach and the appetite for nourishment exists, but God will destroy these and those." It is noteworthy that neither desires nor that related to desires were formed during the first creation of Adam; rather he acquired them through his fall. For all which God through his judgement must suppress was not present during the first creation, but originated through the defection. Out of reason one must ask, "If Adam possessed no stomach, to where did the nourishment which he consumed go?" Answer: It went into the body and not the stomach, for he had an immortal body force and a unending and continuous flow of nourishment to eat as Christ acquired following his resurrection. Reason will question further, "Following his resurrection, Christ consumed food in the company of his disciples. Did his manner of eating differ from ours?" Answer: Yes, it is undeniable, but did not the three angels who accompanied Abraham also partake in food as stated in Genesis 18:1-2 and in Tobias 12:19. "It appears as though I eat and drink among you, but I consume a type of nourishment invisible to man."

Thereafter it is written of Adam's innocent state before Eve's appearance, his condition after the fall, and the new humanity which he will again acquire through the second Adam of Jesus Christ. Out of love for the truth of all God's beloved souls who consider the completion of sanctifying spirit, soul and body earnestly, the information was established. Those who disagree with this meaning ignore it. Yet he should be made aware of the evidence who opposes false presumptions of an intended bliss. He who longs for truth must search and plead for the ability to see correctly and long for a pure heart in order to understand properly. Amen! Amen!

Furthermore, I have been reminded of one small additional comment concerning Paul's words in Timothy 2:7. "Not Adam but rather his wife was misled and initiated the transgression." From this statement one can draw a reasonable conclusion concerning the fact that the entire fall was caused by the woman because of her disobedience and the tasting of the good and of the forbidden fruit. This is true, for desire originated within the woman who tasted and tempted Adam through which they became angered and repented that they were originally sinless but not as entirely pure as Adam was before encountering Eve. Note that Adam was at first extremely good (Genesis 1:31). However, thereafter he was no longer in the highest position of glory but descended to a lower state in which he was required to sleep whole nights before he found sleep unnecessary. Yet he was still not in the degraded position and stature as we ourselves are, for Adam and Eve were still in a good state of Paradise in which they will increase their numbers through the virginal force and quality. Both contained the heavenly Virgin within themselves, but they were divided into two likenesses, one masculine and the other feminine and they were not yet as human as thereafter, although their bodies were becoming more solidified and they began to require sleep in their weakening state. They were no longer of a spiritual essence, but of Paradise qualities, and therefore could expand through the power of the Spirit in a maidenly manner just as the Virgin Mary was able to conceive through the power of the living word who assumed a mortal body and appeared after the fall. Because this was a possibility, it was certainly possible for Adam and Eve also, for the heavenly light image had not yet left them, but rather was still located in the center of their souls penetrating their bodies with the glory of Paradise which enveloped them, for clothing was unnecessary until after the fall when they acquired naked and crude bodies, foul stomachs and reproductive organs. Were they not overcome by the temptation of tasting from the forbidden and the good of the tree, Adam could have inseminated Eve in a heavenly manner through the power of God's Spirit and his own masculine, heavenly and virginal strength. Had Eve received the seed of Adam in a heavenly mode as Mary the mother of Jesus had, the fall would never have occurred, death and curses would never have been encountered on earth, and they would have experienced their first most complete state without suffering and death. Oh misery that it occurred as it did! One hoped that God would have pardoned him and allowed the wandering souls to appear before God and his kingdom so that God's image cannot be transplanted through flesh and blood. The teaching concerning the transplanting of God's likeness in a physical

sense is false, for the seed determines the eventual creation from it.

According to Christ's words in John 3:5, is impossible
to reach God's kingdom without first being reborn of the
Spirit and the heavenly water which provides the potential
for the heavenly incarnation in which the life spirit is
found in the soul. No physical likeness is implanted into
the heavenly image, but rather a spiritual seed in the
hearts of the true believers is sown by the sacred word.
The Holy Spirit is the sower who writes Christ's followers
and kindles true faith in the soul so that Christ can redeem
and liberate them through the shedding of his own blood. He
presents his soul to his Saviour as a living sacrifice so
that body, soul, and spirit may be healed as Christ guides
them through the suffering process, destroying an old crude
life. The amount of life which is destroyed determines the
extent of the heavenly life which is born in the soul, not
in empty conceits, but instead the flaming love of Christ is
powerfully and sensitively kindled as a bride in relation to
her groom. By accepting the position as a bride, she eventually obtains what was lost through Adam, namely, the
feminine generation is again reunited with its masculine
component and the male generation acquires his lost counter-
part again and the injury caused by Adam is again healed.
Those who are capable of it, seize this!

While it is possible to clarify the whole issue in all
its considerations from the least to the most significant so
that all would be accepted, it would be sensible to be well
disposed toward each truth-seeking reader in the state of a
servant as contained in this document. One wishes to present
a reason and he demanded of one or another point further
elaborations concerning the issuing of this document.
However the conflict between the mocker, quarreller, and
disputer of words is cancelled in order that all be accepted
no matter what one's opinion is. Whether in criticizing or
publishing one must write in honour of God.

THE NAKED TRUTH
STANDING AGAINST ALL PAINTED AND DISGUISED LIES, DECEIT AND FALSEHOOD, OR, THE SEVENTH-DAY SABBATH STANDING AS A MOUNTAIN IMMOVEABLE FOREVER.

by

Michael Wohlfahrt

The Naked Truth [of the Seventh-Day Sabbath]

Proved by Three Witnesses, Which Cannot Lie

The First Witness

The first witness is the eternal God himself, who after the creation rested on the Seventh-Day, and did also bless and sanctify that same Seventh-Day (Gen. 2, ver. 2,3) and when he gave his holy moral law, did earnestly command it in the Fourth Commandment (Exod. 20, ver. 8 to 10).

Remember the Sabbath-day (not a Sabbath-day) to keep it holy.

The Seventh-day (not a Seventh-day) is the Sabbath of the Lord, thy God; and not a Jewish, or any other man's sabbath, but the Sabbath of the Lord thy God.

This witness is truth, and changeth not, neither can the Scripture be broke.

The Second Witness

The second witness is our Lord Jesus Christ, who did confirm and establish the same with his holy example, in going on the Sabbath-days in the synagogues, teaching and preaching to the people, speaking to them the Words which he had received from his Father, telling them that he was that Messenger from the Lord, of whom the Prophets had foretold, and especially the Prophet, Isaiah 61. That the Spirit of the Lord shall be upon him. And this he did on the Sabbath-days, as we read Mark 1:21; 6:2; Luc. 4:16, and other

places, where we may read that he went into the synagogues
on the Sabbath-days; but never told the people that that was
not the right Seventh-day which God had commanded to be kept,
as some witlings of our age will argue: Nay, nor never told
them of any other day to be the Sabbath; neither then, nor
the times after. But rather showing with his own example,
that he delighted in the same Sabbath, doing right Sabbati-
cal works upon it, curing and making whole the sick; for
which reason he also was counted a Sabbath-breaker by the
blind Scribes and Pharisees (Matt. 12; Mark 3; Luke 6). But
Jesus looking on them with anger, being grieved for their
hardness of heart, reproved them, showing them that they did
not judge a righteous judgment, seeing they themselves did
circumcise a man on the Sabbath, and yet the Sabbath was not
profaned by it, and they would be angry with him that he
had made a Man every whit whole on the Sabbath-day (John
7:23). And at other times he showed them, that they did not
understand the mind of God in the holy law; for he himself,
being the Lord of the Sabbath, knew that it was lawful to
do good and to save Man's life on the Sabbath (Matt. 12:12),
seeing that God appointed unto men such a blessed day on
which he should rest from his labour (which came upon him by
reason of sin) and hear or know the counsel and will of God.
Thus he may come to be made whole of his spiritual sickness,
and to be raised from the dead unto a godly life. Now Jesus
being the right and true Physician both of soul and body, he
not only told men what to do, but also showing with his holy
actions that he did rightly sanctify the Sabbath according
to the true mind of God, doing good to poor men, forgiving
them their sins, which are the real causes of their
sicknesses, and so removing the cause, he could easily and
without labour cure the sickness. Since Jesus, the Lord of
the Sabbath himself, has sanctified that blessed
Seventh-day, keeping it according to the right and true mind
of God, giving us therewith an example what we should do

also, who then dares (I say) who then dares to be so bold,
and take upon him to make void God's holy law and
everlasting covenant, and pretend to set up a day for the
honour of Christ, where there is neither command, counsel,
nor example for, in all the Scriptures, but men's notions
and imaginations inspired in them by the spirit of error, to
oppose God and to deceive people. Others count every day
alike, including also the Seventh-day Sabbath and holy rest
of the Lord among the six working days, quite contrary to
the law of the Most High, and against Christ's own example,
as also against the holy Apostles and all the first
Christians' practice, customs, and orders, which I shall
bring for a proof, as my Third Witness.

The Third Witness

It being very plainly set down in many places in the
Acts of the Apostles, I shall only mention some to prove
that the Apostles and all the first Christians did really
keep the Lord's Seventh-day Sabbath, and never knew of any
other day as we may read Acts 13:42, in plain words, thus,
And when the Jews were gone out of the Synagogue, the Gentiles besought, that these Words might be preached to them
the next Sabbath [mind here well] the next Sabbath, not the
next morning, or the next first day, but the next Sabbath,
and in the 44th verse, we see their desire fulfilled, for
the text says, "The next Sabbath-day came almost the whole
city together, to hear the Word of God." O blessed by the
great Lord for ever, that he has preserved such plain truth
for our sakes, that we may not be shaken with any wind of
false doctrine. We do also read of Paul in the 17th chapter,
ver. 2, that he went into the Synagogue, as his manner
was, on the Sabbath-day; again there is no mention made of a
first day, nor of any other but of the Sabbath: Nay the

word First-Day is not so much as mentioned in the Greek to
that purpose, in all the New Testament. We read in the 20th
chapter, ver. 7, that the disciples came together on a
Sabbath, or in one of the Sabbaths, to break bread, and not
on a First-day, which the learned know well enough. I shall
not search for more proof, seeing I have God and the whole
Scriptures on my side; and whereas Jesus himself saith
(Mat. 18), In the mouth of two or three witnesses every word
is established, especially such three ones as I have brought
to prove the Seventh-day to be the Sabbath of the Lord, and
so the Sabbath of all his true children.

Wherefore, seeing these three witnesses cannot lie, but
do stand unchangeable for ever, yea even the Rock of our
Salvation hath established it, I stand on sure ground, and
do not value all the world to fear them, or to bend under
their human inventions, or customs, or fashions; but I stand
in awe unto that great God, and Judge of all men, not to sin
against him; for that beloved Apostle of Jesus, John, tells
me that sin is the transgression of the law (I John 3, v. 4).

Many indeed have tried to show their wit, for rejecting
the Lord's Seventh-day Sabbath, but they never could bring
it to bear; nor could they ever with all their school-
learning or fine philosophy move or shake any true child of
God, that is well builded up in the love towards God, and in
the faith of Jesus Christ. I rather say, that they therewith declare that they are enemies to God, in rejecting his
holy and so well established law, and perpetual covenant,
and undertake to prove the repealing of the Lord's holy
Seventh-day Sabbath by apostolical authority, when they can
never show either command, counsel, nor example for it.
Others would fain have the first day to have been set up by
the Apostles; but all in vain; for we have proved the
contrary. Neither is it in any servant's power to change
the will and command of his master, without a plain command
so to do, which neither I nor they ever shall find; but

if they will allow the Popes of Rome to be right and true Apostles of Jesus Christ, then they may prove the repealing of the Sabbath, and the institution of the first day; for by them that first-day was erected, and was called by several names; but yet the name from the idolatrous heathen beareth the sway to this very day amongst most people, and is called Sunday. And so this was all done, that the Scripture might be fulfilled in Daniel, Chap. 7, verse 25: He shall blaspheme the Most High, and take upon him to alter and change times and laws.

It is wonderful that such a world of people, yea, of so many ages, have not, nor do yet see the mystery of wickedness, iniquity and lawlessness, whereof we read in Daniel the Prophet about the golden image of Nebuchadnezzar, unto which all people, tongues and nations, were to bow and to worship, and that at such times, when they heard the sound of the cornet, trumpet, sackbut, and the noise of the dulcimer, lute, harp, and other fine musical instruments, they were to fall down and worship that image; I say, since they do not see, or rather will not see, I shall not be fearful nor slack to tell them, that their first day of the week, instituted without God and Scripture, by the Pope of Rome is that same image, whom all people, tongues and nations in all Christendom (so called) do worship, for it is a part of the number of the beast, having 60 cubits in height, and 6 in breadth, which is 66, the last two sixes in the number of the beast; for the whole number of the Beast is 666, six hundred sixty six, under which six hundred, as the first 6, are included in the many forts of vain worship and men's doctrines, viz. infant-sprinkling, worshiping the bread and wine, adoring and worshiping the saints, and so forth; of which it is not my task now to meddle with, but only to show the last number of the Beast as 66. For indeed as it is the last number in the number of the Beast, so it was the last and the hardest work the Pope had to do, to bring people to the worship of that image (for many churches would not yield to it so soon) and so it will be the last image for all the dissenters to forsake again, seeing how hard people are set to it, and how customary it is become to them. And no wonder at all indeed, for it is made of fine gold, having so many brave and great learned men of all sects to prove the worshipping of this first-day, by their school-babbies, called man's reason and philosophy, and all the world admiring them and their learning, in explaining or rather perverting the plain will and counsel of God. It has farther so many noble kings and princes for protection, which defend his worshipers with the sword, and by their authority. Who now would not worship such a fine image, especially when it is erected in such a fair plain, or place, viz. instead of God's holy Sabbath, and is also with great authority, by great fines, and loss of people's good commanded that, as soon as they hear the noise of the fine music, viz. bells, organs, and many other sorts of musical instruments; yea, of drums and pipes, and the like, to fall down, that is, to come to worship to their great steeple-houses, to lay by all manner of work (which yet God hath commanded to be done at that day) and help to worship that image. Now this noise having filled their ears encourageth them to be more fierce in bowing unto it, adoring and admiring the finery of it. Other little sects now that are descended from the Whore, fearing yet the power and the claws of the Beast, do still bow unto that image, although not with such pomp and vain glory, yet at the same time, when the noise of the proclamation is heard, they not having light enough to see the mystery of lawlessness, and the vain worship people are serving in their pretended love towards God (whereas they are lovers of the world, and fleshly and carnally minded) not yet having faith enough, to trust in that great God of Heaven and Earth, and holy Lawgiver, they must bend, and fear them that kill the body, but afterwards can do no more, not regarding him who after he hath killed, can cast both soul and body into hell-fire. This now I would fain have people to consider.

O therefore! All ye people, tongues and nations, that hear these words, turn to the true God; worship no longer gods which are the works of man's hands, and of human invention; be no longer deceived; the light of God shineth very clear in these latter days wherein God maketh known his truth again, which has been many years hidden, viz. the low, mean, and despised doctrine of Jesus, and of his holy and world-rejected life, which has been hitherto desolate, having very few followers, it being a very narrow path to walk in, and a strait gate to enter at; therefore all the world doth despise it, as a poor widow that hath no husband, and is desolate, nor no body to defend and protect it; but the children of this world have protection enough, and are well fed and maintained, and defended in their vain worship. But let me tell you, the time is very near at hand, that God will destroy the worshipers of images, and break in pieces the strength of the Chemarims, and black money-priests, and send out true labourers into his harvest. O happy are they that take notice of the signs of these times, and draw back their ears from lying, and turn to the low and despised truth; for it begins to shine forth very bright and clear, and I hope will be enflamed more and more by the Spirit of Jesus Christ, that all Gentiles and nominal Christians shall clearly see it, and give glory to the Lord. Therefore repent truly, with all your hearts; come to the right fear of God; begin to love him, and keep his commands with all your souls, mind and strength; enter into the holy doctrine and life of Jesus Christ, follow him, and learn of him to obey God, and to do his will; forsake the world; deny your selves; take the cross of Jesus upon you, and learn of him to become meek and lowly of heart; strive and labour hard in the grace of God, to overcome your old nature, and become new men, spiritually minded, and partakers of the divine nature; for except being thus renewed, it is in vain for you to imagine that you be Christians. This I tell you as a word of truth; then you shall find rest for your souls. Now I with every one of you that is willing to forsake the vanity of this world, both spiritual and natural, and to serve God in purity of heart, grace, love, and peace from the only God, the Father of our Lord Jesus Christ, remain a lover of all mankind, desiring your welfare and happiness.

MICHAEL WELFARE,
A mean Servant of Jesus Christ,
and Pilgrim walking to Eternity.

FINIS

SELECTED LETTERS

by

Peter Miller

[To Peter Lehman]

I could not allow this opportunity to pass without renewing our intercourse in the spirit. We have for a length of time not heard anything of you, other than [that] you are still living alone. To this all encouragement is given so long as it will be acceptable to God to keep you in that way, to the time when he will place you under other instruction. Then too the high apostle Paul was three years a hermit, after his conversion, and so it was with our solitary brothers and sisters. But now this way of life has disappeared at this place, and God has given us other work to do; yet we can rejoice, if in your part of the country, this angelic way of life will again get to be common, as it was in the East; only so that the work of God may be carried forward.

But allow me to say something to you: out of three things one will fall to your lot. As for the fourth, the falling back into the world, I hope that God will guard you from it. But if the son of promise is not soon born to you in your solitude, and you, like Sarah, remain barren, do not be discouraged, much less give way to the natural mind, for the natural mind brings forth the man Ishmael; this angelic state can prove a burden to you, as for many in days that are past, who have again sought consolation in the visible world.

Let it therefore not seem strange to you, if in your solitude the good does not pour down in torrents, for we must, like Sarah, for a length of time be led to and fro, till we are brought to such a state that we are prepared to receive the mystic word. But mark! a hermit must be a hermit, and not search for his good abroad; much less spend his time uselessly among men who do not have eternity in view, as their first object. These will follow vain pursuits, and rob the traveler of his oil.

Now to proceed further. You are, in your part of the country, the first one of the solitary brothers of the order of the church of Ephrata, and you owe it, according to the teachings of Christ, to put your pound to the exchangers. But you do not know, to what purpose God intends to use you. You might be the first one of many solitary brothers on the Alleghany mountains, for that with our departure from this life, the order should become extinct, I have never believed.

I can here honestly not keep something of weight hidden from you.

We have for some time been spoken to, to appoint you a Minister on the Alleghany mountains. When you were here, I could have brought you into a strait if I would not have had too much respect for you. Therefore I would yet say this: be on your guard as to worldly-minded people, for the desires of a church awaken a prophet, and the pressure of the world will be against you.

I have now, since the death of Conrad Beissel, served the church twenty years, and have never allowed myself to be exalted by the praise of men, that I might have fallen, nor have I allowed myself to be alarmed through wickedness, and flee my post.

JAEBEZ.

Ephrata, August 26, 1788

Septr. 29th. 1774

Sir,

Your very respectable character would make me ashamed to address you with words merely of form. I hope therefore you will not suspect me of using any such, when I assure you I received the favour of your letter with great pleasure. And permit me, sir, to join the thanks I owe to those worthy women, the holy sisters at Ephrata, with those I now present to you, for the good opinion you, and they, are pleased to have of me. I claim only to respect merit, where I find it; and of wishing an increase in the world, of that piety to the Almighty, and peace to our fellow creatures, that I am convinced is in your hearts: and, therefore, do me the justice to believe, you have my wishes of prosperity here, and happiness hereafter.

I did not receive the precious stone, you were so good to send me, till yesterday. I am most extremely obliged to you for it. It deserves to be particularly distinguished on its own, as well as the giver's account. I shall keep it with a grateful remembrance of my obligations to you.

Mr. Penn, as well as myself, was much obliged to you for remarking to us, that the paper you wrote on, was the manufacture of Ephrata: It had, on that account, great merit to us; and he has desired our friend, Mr. Barton, to send him some specimens of the occupation of some of your society. He bids me say, that he rejoices to hear of your and their welfare.

It is I that should beg pardon for interrupting your quiet and profitable moments by an intercourse so little beneficial as mine; but trust your benevolence will indulge this satisfaction to one who wishes to assure, sir, that she is, with sincere regard, your obliged and faithful well-wisher,

Julianna Penn.

To the Honorable Lady Julianna Penn: Grace and peace from God the Father and his Son Jesus Christ through the influence of the Holy Ghost.

Both the extract of your Ladyship's letter to the Rev. Mr. Barton, and also the letter to the Sisters, were faithfully transmitted by the said gentleman. That your Ladyship hath honored the Sisters with your handwriting, convinced me that you are a patroness of that life which is so much against the modern taste; and herein the idea I have of your Ladyship's merits hath further confirmed me.

The Sisters are a venerable society, founded forty years ago, and have ever since not only been an honor to your sex, but also an ornament to this province, and as I have the honor to be their President it was incumbent on me to answer in their name.

Your Ladyship was well informed that they are enemies to all superfluities; and I may further say, that they are very scrupulous even in things necessary to support this life.   I will not mention here what moved them to this rigorous life, neither what cause they had to consecrate themselves to perpetual virginity, for your Ladyship is better acquainted with this way than to stand in need of any human information.   It is now near half a century elapsed, since in your province the powers of eternity exerted themselves with such a vehemency, that the foundations of all denominations began to shake and that everyone thought the Kingdom of God was nigh at hand.   At that time amongst others have enlisted under the banners of Christ many young persons of both sexes, which after they by water baptism had publicly quitted all claims to their natural prerogatives, settled here and there as hermits, in the great wilderness of Conestoga, after the manner of the fathers of the third and following centuries; and it was then a common thing to see persons of your sex to follow in those deserts the strictest discipline.   About the year 1734 the town of

Ephrata was founded as a rendezvous for all solitary persons which have dedicated themselves to perpetual virginity, and have hitherto lived scattered in the wilderness; in which town one corner was allotted to the Sisters, and accordingly two deputies were sent to the Hon. Thomas Penn, your worthy consort, to Philadelphia, to ask permission to lay out said town on a barren piece of land. (For they have been there scrupulous to take out patent), which he not only granted, but also promised his protection, although they were afterwards compelled by necessity to take a patent.

This is the origin of a small republic, which sprung up in the heart of North America, and whose fame in a short time penetrated not only through the British provinces, but also through all Protestant kingdoms of Europe. It arose from the dust with incredible celerity, and such strict discipline, that never a potentate had soldiers which understood their corporal maneuvers better than those members understood their spiritual one; for besides their hard labor, they maintained fasting and watching in such a degree that they justly might be put in the scale with the said fathers in the wilderness; for which cause not only all the governors of this and sundry of the adjacent provices, but also many other gentlemen, had the curiosity to see the new Commonwealth.

It is remarkable that after it came to its meridian it began to decline, which was occasioned by deaths and desertion, partly by intestine broils; a proof that no church whatever can here be of perpetual lustre. Should I enumerate to your Ladyship all the battles, skirmishes and temptations we had during that long course, it would swell up this letter to a large volume, for we had against us not only the powers and principles of darkness, but also all carnal men, with whom did sympathize our own flesh. Six years ago departed this life our worthy President, who had founded the order, and then the generality did conceive new

hope, that our fatal period was nigh at hand; but the hand
of God did strengthen us that we closed our ranks anew, and
by his gracious interposition the expectation of our
adversaries is again frustrated. The number of Sisters at
present is twenty-six.

I am persuaded that many of the British dominions have
favored our institution, being well adapted to raise the
spirit of ancient Christianity, and I humbly think that your
Ladyship is among that number. I have the assurance that
none of them shall fall short of their expectation; since
for the sake of the honor of God, and the common
edification, this institution is erected. Not by any man's
selfwill, but immediately by the hand of God, although he
employed proper means to do it.

Perhaps I have ventured too much upon your Ladyship's
patience, and I will therefore conclude with the humble
supplications to the throne of Grace, that God would take
the whole Honorable family, and particularly your worthy
consort and your Ladyship's person, under his peculiar
protection, and save them from all evil, in which I
subscribe myself your Ladyship's obedient servant,

                                        P M

P.S.--When I did communicate this letter to the
Sisters, their two matrons, together with the whole society,
desires [sic] me to send their humble respects to their
patrons.

Esteemed Friend,

Thine Letter have I received, and on perusing the same
found, that it was something more weighty than curiosity,
which governed thine pen. Seven and fifty years are now
most elapsed, when a serious reflection for my salvation
moved me, to enter into a contract with the Supreme Being,
which was confirmed by the holy baptism after the mode of
the first Christians. This was followed by a penitential

life, which was very rigid, as it then was customary in our Society. I kept a regular course in my life, and was very strict in my addresses to the throne of grace, also that mine outward life willingly submitted to the dictates of the spirit then being at the helm in the Society. These successes had so animated me and my fellow-travellers of both sexes, that we all became rank Enthusiasts. But to return to my own Person. I cannot say, that I have thoroughly lost this my primitive zeal; but in process of time I met with many great obstructions. For when our heremetical Life was changed into a monastic one, I had the mortification to see that the convents and all their corners were filled with Magistrates, in order to prohibit false Altars to be erected for the selfishness. And now was between the poor devotees of Ephrata and the wool-headed African Scalves [sic] no other difference, than that they were white and free sclaves. Further, when I had distinguished myself by meritorious works, it proved the Justice of God, also that I suffered for it as a criminal: this contest did grow in proportion so as my zeal did increase. All this did open to me a door to many reflections, for it seemed to me, that our God, hath an exclusive right to be called good, in which I was confirmed by our Master himself, who would not be called good. It is a debate in the church yet undecided, in what light good works should be considered whether necessary or noxious, as it said, that we come to salvation by grace. In my opinion all such good works, which stood their trial, are declared genuine and meritorious. The greatest honor which our Master received in this world, was this, that He was ranked among malefactors. From these circumstances it appears that the great contest between God and men did derive for things, which are called good and are not, which is hypocrisy. To serve God is the heaviest work in this world: a criminal under sentence of death may receive pardon, under condition;

but what shall he do, who had served God to the best of his knowledge, and yet is under sentence of death, this is hard to determine.

The sufferings which were in Christ, made great progress in our days, and prognosticate a great revolution in the church, and as they have reached almost their highest pitch, perhaps they will next come to their period. The Spirit, under whose influence we are, at present takes strongly hold of the bodies, and will no longer be deceived by a hypocritical worship, where a pretence is made to serve God in spirit, when the body is sold away to vanity and luxury.

If some expressions are defective, I ask pardon, it comes from age and weakness, and what is here wanting, the Spirit, thine heavenly conductor, will fill up, to whose manuduction I sincerely recommend thy person. For thine care to maintain my character I thank thee, and hope, thou shall herein not be deceived by me.--Finally, do I recommend thee to divine protection, and am thine unworthy Friend.

Ephrata, the 16th of Jan. 1772.

                                                    P.M.

Respected Friend,

The account given by a British officer of Ephrata in the Museo, is scurrilous and sordid, and considering the kind reception, he met with here, as he confesseth himself, unjust and ungreatfull in the highest degree. What was his intention thereby, is hard to tell. If he sought to hurt my credit, he deceiveth himself, unjust and ungratefull in the highest degree; for what is the loss of the character, if we have the answer of a good conscience within. It is thine obliging visit, which had constrained me, to meddle with this business, which is without the line of my conduct.

Had the officer, when he was here, unmasked himself, the marks of a Deist might have appeared on him, if not an Atheist, for from Deism to Atheism is an easy descent. As they are noxious to the Christian cause, the Apostles have strictly charged their followers, to have nothing to do with them: for they are always accustomed to a swim at the top, like cord-wood. Thee has desired me to mark out in said account, what was true or not; in answer to this, I tell thee, it is no truth in it at all, and how could truth come from a malicious heart? the Officer must have been very inimical against our Society, and when he did compose his account, it is probably, that he was in liquor, which opened the recesses of his heart. There is a sort of men, which hate us mortally because of our principles, and as it may be, that the officer is a great advocate for the prolification-law, he might have taken an offence at seeing the same disregarded in Ephrata. However must I do justice to him in that, that he was so honest as not to blow in the whoremonger's trumpet, as others have done, when he saw here the free conversation of both sexes, of which among the adherents there is no precedence.--For in Egypt, where monastic life was first hatched out, was the river Nile the division line between convents of both sexes, and when there a young monk accidently saw a female being, he did run off, as if he had seen a dragon. Considering this, and the encomium he gave me, (altho' it is not true,) when put together in the other scale, maintain the balance. Truth must bear a contradiction. I am not an advocate of my own cause, but am greatly indebted to my friend Esquire Barton, that he has done it.

The case of Caspipina differs much from this, his account of Mount Zion is wrong, it is only a small eminence and is situated within our village. What he farther doth allege of our merits in saving other, which might lessen the merits of Christ, for which he was pleased to call us a

deluded people, these things were spoken in common discourse, we have no creeds, our standard is the New
Testament. I have always carefully avoided all polemics,
and study to live in peace with all denominations.

Excuse my brevity and undigested matter. If I can do
thee any farther service, I shall be to thine disposal. God
preserve thee from the vices of this age, and conduct thee
by his Holy Ghost, through many temptations to the land of
promise. This is the wish of thine Friend,

Peter Miller.

Ephrata, the 5th of Sept. 1790.

P.S. The officer's whole account of our life is wholly
superficial: the motives, we had in following this life,
are to him a mystery, he says: that an aversion of social
life, (he means marrying) brought us together. The gentleman thinks, perhaps, that we were a race of Pre-Adamits,
which had no connection with Adam: for as he is a
naturalist, he will not admit, that we have been brought
together by the immediate hand of God, but that our living
here was only an accidental thing.--But he deceived himself,
for when we settled here our number was 40 brethren, and
about so many sisters, all in the vigour and prime of their
ages, never before wearied of social life, but were
compelled by the hand of God, with reluctance of our nature,
to select this life, and that under a penalty of forfeiting
our Salvation in case of refusal. I once more beg pardon
for the inaccuracy in writing--vale.

Esteemed Friend,

In obedience to the invitation, given in thine last
letter, which came to hand the first of this instant
December, I do send this answer: If the contents do not
merit thine applause, I hope thine censure will be
moderate--our knowledge is but partial. That the kingdom of

Christ in its approach is so long retarded, comes partly from our own unbelief and ignorance. It is now generally allowed, that the first man was created after the image of God: (which image was the Son of God,) into a most perfect independence, without which he could not represent the independent being of the Deity, for the copy must answer to the original in every respect. And if he had been created into any degree of subordination, his fall might have been prevented, he being destituted of a free will.

Yet no sooner had he by his fall forfeited the great dignity of this independence, the law of nature did bring him and all his posterity into subjection and servitude. But as by this fall the connection between God and his weakened image was not dissolved, he proposed to maintain an exact parallelism between himself and his weakened image, also that the copy could represent the original, in which the love to his image moved Him to proceed so far that he suffered Himself to be incarnated, and lay in Bethlehem as an innocent babe. We are under a necessity to assert this, that we might give reason why God in His proceedings with men regulates them Himself after their capacity, and condescended so much as to give them laws which were against His holy nature. No wonder is it therefore, that even in our days war is declared consistent with the will of God, viz: they take the condescending, the permissive will of God for His most perfect will, which is a great error. To give thee here of an instance: At Mount Sinai God promised the children of Israel a Sacerdotal Kingdom, or as St. Peter says, a royal priesthood, after the order of Melchisedeck, where the priest or king offereth himself for the sins of the people. In this sense Moses received the Ten commandments, of which one was: Thou shalt not kill: not alone no men, but no creature whatsoever, for a law spoken in so general terms might be extended so far, as the sense will permit. But Moses in a Godly zeal broke the two tables: and although God made two other tables, yet were they laid by in the ark of the covenant, for the use of the millenian church or of the peaceful kingdom of Christ, meanwhile were both the Jews and Christians in their respective dispensations, governed by the laws of the broken tables. And now God, having found by experience, that the Jews had no capacity to receive a superior light, altered his scheme, and gave them laws, which were not good, and statutes, in which they could not be saved, as Ezechrel (Ezekiel) [sic] says.

As concerning our transactions during that long term of our residence at Ephrata, I wish I could satisfy thine curiosity: I have published a Chronicon Ephratense of which I could make thee a present, if thou art master of the German language. However I will do something to satisfy thee. In August 1730, I arrived in Philadelphia, and was there at the end of said year, upon order of the Scotch Synod, ordained in the old Presbyterian meeting house, by three eminent ministers, Tenant, Andrew and Boyd. Having officiated among the Germans several years, I quitted the ministry, and returned to a private life. About that time our small State was in its infancy: I never had an inclination to join with it, because of the contempt and reproach which lay on the same; but my inward conductor, brought me to that critical dilemma, either to be a member of this new institution, or to consent to my own damnation, when also I was forced to choose the first. In my company had been the School master, three Elderlings (Conrad Weyser one) five families and some single persons which has raised such a fermentation in that church, that a persecution might have followed had the magistrates consented with the generality. We have been incorporated with said congregation in May, 1735 by holy Baptism: when we were conducted to the water, I did not much differ from a poor criminal under sentence of death. However the Lord our God did strengthen me, when I came into the water, and then I in solemn manner renounced my life with all its prerogatives without reservation, and I found by experience in subsequent times, that all this was put into the divine records; for God never failed in his promise to assist me in time of need. At that time the solitary brethren and sisters lived dispersed in the wilderness of Conestoga, each for himself, as Hermits, and I following that same way, did set up my Hermitage in Kulpehakin at the foot of a mountain, on a limpid spring, the house is still extant there with an old orchard. There did I lay the foundation to solitary life, but the melancholy temptations, which did trouble me every day, did prognosticate to me misery and afflictions: However I had not lived there half a year, when a great change happened: for a camp was laid out for all solitary persons at the very spot, where now Ephrata stands, and where at that time the president lived with some hermits. And now, when all hermits were called in, I also quitted my solitude, and exchanged the same for a monastic life: which was judged to be more inservient to Sanctification than the life of a hermit, where many under a pretense of holiness did nothing but nourish their own selfishness. For the brethren now received their prior, and the sisters their matron, and we were now by necessity compelled to learn obedience and to be refractory was judged a crime little inferior to high treason.

At that time works of charity hath been our chief occupation; Conestoga was then a great wilderness, and began to be settled by poor Germans, which desired our assistance in building houses for them; which not only kept us employed several summers in hard carpenters-work, but also increased our poverty so much that we wanted even things necessary for life. At that time entered the constable the camp, and demanded the single man's tax; the brethren differed among themselves in opinion, some paid the same, but some refused, and claimed personal immunity, for in the eastern country the monks and hermits collected every harvest by their labour so much grain, that they supply'd yearly all the prisons in Alexandria with bread, wherefore Theogosius magnus and other emperors declared them free from all taxes, and that we were not inferior to them. However the constable according to order summoned some wicked neighbors, and delivered six brethren into the prison at Lancaster, where they lay ten days: but the magistrates set them again at liberty, a venerable old justice of peace offering himself for a bail for their appearance at courts, his name was Tobias Hendriks. The court came on and when the brethren appeared before the board of assessment, the fear of God came upon the Gentlemen, who were their Judges, when they saw six men before them, which in the prime of their ages by penitential works hath been reduced to Skeletons, that they used great moderation, and granted them their personal freedom, under condition, that they should be taxed as one family for their real Estate, which is still in force, altho' these things happened fifty years ago.

But when we had formed ourselves at Ephrata into a regular society; our Prior, taking advantage of our blind obedience, we were insensibly arrested by him to meddle with worldly things farther than our obligations did permit, altho' he kept the brethren under a severe discipline: we erected a grist-mill with three pair of stones, a saw-mill, paper-mill, oil-mill, fulling-mill, had besides three wagons with proper teams, printing-office with sundry other trades, and as money came in every day, it was laid out again upon interest contrary to our principles. Our president never meddled with temporal things, yet as long as our prior stood to him in subordination, we were not permitted to stop him in his proceedings. But at last did he conceive a notion, to make himself independent: and this was the proper time for us to renounce to him obedience, and also did we strip

him of all his dignities, and this was the greatest con-
vulsion, which our State suffered since his existence. The
prior now quitted the camp, and established a new settlement
for hermits on the banks of the new river, which he called
Nahanaim; but after many vicissitudes, which he experienced
there, at last he and his natural brother were taken
prisoners by seven Mohawks, and sold to Quebec, from whence
they were transported to old France, where, after our Prior
had received the tonsure and became a friar of their church,
they both died. I believe I gave thee an account hereof in
my former letter. Remember: we have lost our first Prior,
and the Sisters their first Mother by offices, because they
stood in self-elevation, and did govern despotically: no
wunder, [sic] when the civil State must experience the same
symptoms, the desire to govern is the last thing, which dies
within a man.

The President died July the 6th, 1768, which was a
great Stroke for me, as I was obliged to succeed him. I
besides many other stood under his manudirection, which was
so severe as any related in the Roman church, above 30
years. He was a most extraordinary product of this century.
The Dissertation on Man's Fall mentioned in the Edinburgh
Magazine is his work. I have printed thereof 1000, but have
no more to present to thee. When in the late war a Marquis
from Milan in Italy lodged a night in our convent, I
presented to him the said dissertation, and desired him, to
publish the same at home, and dedicate it to His Holiness,
and all their devotees, it would be considered as the
greatest rarity which ever came from America. The fall of
man is not sufficiently known in their church. I asked once
my friend Pater Geisler, an honest Jesuit, now deceased:
what reason he had, to remain single? he said: nothing but
the Edict of His Holiness: but this did not satisfy me.

The question is now much agitated, whether our order
will be propagated to posterity? In my opinion he will,

according to the Substance, but in what form he will appear in after-times, is to me a mystery. Our president did once declare to his Intimates, that he hath received assurance from God, that seed of his work shall remain until the second coming of Christ.

And here I shall conclude, leaving these matters to thine consideration. Age, infirmity and defect in sight are causes, that the letter wants more perspicuity, for which I beg pardon. Meanwhile, I remain

Thine sincere Friend

Peter Miller.

Ephrata, the 5th of Dec. 1790.

THE ROSE OF SHARON

The Rose

or

The Spiritual Betrothal of the Pleasing Flower
of Sharon to Her Heavenly Bridegroom
to Whom as Her Leader, King, Spouse, Lord
and Bridegroom She Promised Herself
Eternally.
To which is added [a description of] her
Full Support of and Obedience to Her Spiritual
Leader, Mother and Director and [of]
the Faithfulness and Duty expressed between her
Members and toward themselves
Given by their Spiritual Father and Founder,
Through Whose energy this whole Spiritual
Community was Established as was the no less
Worthy Community in Zion.
Ephrata, the 13th day, the 5th Month, 1745

Although our mind is not fully fitted for the task, to describe in many words this our worthy community at Sharon called the Rose, yet we cannot pass by the opportunity of giving some information of her virtues, interiority, nothingness, temperance and rejection of all visible things which be outside Christian and Church discipline.

It pleased the wisdom of our God to allow a light to shine in the darkness of this sad, fallen and very dark period of the Church. Those who do not have clear eyes are yet further blinded by this light's appearance so that many falter, stumble and fall at bright mid-day. Because of this many reasons arose to call this beautiful light a black darkness. Because this beautiful light of the world shone so firmly and sharply in the eyes of all that their lights went out and their false appearance fell to the earth, such great wrath arose along with this evil cry that the whole work was almost set at nought. But, because the work was established and begotten under great long-suffering, patience and endurance, everything was able to maintain its health for the most part in such difficult times by a holy sinking-below-itself until the bad weather passed. All of this was forseen from the very beginning .... The Founder and spiritual Leader of the whole work studied and learned all his subjects in the school of suffering ...

[A discussion of the leader's suffering and endurance before the eventual success of his project.]

In the meantime it came to pass that two lovely sisters (one Anna, the other Maria) received a heavenly call and together agreed to go into exile away from their father's house for the hope of eternal life.

They both took their bundles and started on their sad journey. On their way they sought out the well-known and spiritual leader named C[onrad] B[eissel] now Father Friedsam honoured by God. He received them with great joy, and immediately looked for means to build for them a small house. He even worked with his own hands and spared no pains until it was finished.

Who would have thought that in the exalted wisdom of God, so weighty a proof of his wonders, was placed in these two humble lowly vessels, for they were both very young. The eldest named Anna soon fell into a high passion and caused the younger named Maria much sorrow and trouble because she was much too deeply enamoured in God, and sought to subjugate her whole life by the bitterest penance, such as fasting, vigils and mortification of the flesh. This the other sister for certain reasons could not endure, and became so embittered that she, without any thought or consideration, in a completely disturbed state of mind, beat Maria. This is not surprising when [we consider] how in later times she so miserably crossed the spiritual leader whom she herself honoured. She [Anna] also fell into the most dreadful brutality that it would not have taken much to cause a blood-bath. She brought so much disgrace and shame upon the work of God that it is not to be described here. In the meantime the innocent lamb [Maria], the younger sister, endured her tyranny with great patience, and swerved not a hair's breadth from her duty, earnest fasting or the mortification of the flesh, until her body became so emaciated that her spiritual leader and father confessor admonished her about it, and with a loving reproach told her that she was overdoing the matter. Then, like a dutiful child she gradually yielded, but with no other thought than that, by holy obedience, she would please God the more. Once it happened that her spiritual zeal constantly increased so that she went to her spiritual leader, and

addressed him with these words: 'Brother (for he was then
called), I have a strong desire within me to have a nun's
habit made for myself.' Then the small herd of sheep was
still scattered here and there, and not yet gathered into
one fold. The spiritual father soon noticed that there was
more in this little movement than what appeared upon the
surface, so without much delay he helped to bring the work
to completion. Although the contrary minded sister appeared
to consent and entered into it, her perverse spirit increased, so that to all appearances the outlook was that it
would end in a complete failure, as was shown later. But
let this suffice about the two sisters. We will now leave
the one, and confine ourselves to the other, and relate how
she afterwards erected our dearly beloved society of spiritual virgins and gathered them together as brides of the
Lamb. Under the leadership of this person, it was never a
question who was most competent in the society to bear the
honorable title of Spiritual Mother, for as soon as she
entered upon that office all was changed. There came a
demand for a life under rule and discipline. As a result
the above-mentioned lover spent the time of her hard service
among her sisters. Soon the longing came for a well ordered
and circumscribed rule of table discipline. Then they
sought to distinguish the time for sleeping and waking, and
as everything was viewed with moderate discreetness, it was
sought to arrange the matter that nature as a spiritual
vessel and instrument was not blunted nor made uncomfor-
table, but rather willing and eager for the service of God.
Thus the hours for sleep amount to six hours. When the meal
is finished in the evening from the second to the fourth
hour [7 to 9 P.M.] the time is occupied in school practice,
be it writing, reading or singing, after which the three
hours, fourth [9 P.M.] until the seventh [12] are given to
sleep. The seventh hour [12 to 1 A.M.] is devoted to the
mass and Christian and divine psalms and hymns are sung and

holy prayer attended until the ninth hour [2 A.M.] after
which three hours, namely from the ninth until the twelfth
hour [2 A.M. to 5 A.M.] are given to sleep. Thus the time
is passed from night until morning, and everything is done
within holy bounds and in regular order. The awakening
takes place at the twelfth hour [5 A.M.] and [is done] in
the greatest order. The time is given to holy contemplation, until the first hour [6 A.M.]. Then each person goes
to her regular employment given them by the overseer until
the fourth hour [9 A.M.] which hour is also devoted to a
little spiritual and bodily refreshment. Little can now
intervene to prevent one from one's bodily employment until
the twelfth hour [5 P.M.]. Then an hour is given to holy
and divine contemplation until the first hour [6 P.M.], when
the meal is prepared with great care and takes place, at
which more attention is again given to obedience and
moderation than to the kind of food prepared.

On account of many and various inner and outer troubles
of the body and spirit, we have not been able thus far to
advance in our worship of God and public devotions as we
ought to have. As in the sixth hour of the night our sleep
is broken by two hours of worship, even so it would seem
proper that the time of labor be interrupted by one or two
hours. Although we are used in all things to advance with
quiet and gentle steps, we are not completely guiltless in
this matter. God, however, will give us our heart's desire,
although the present time may not allow us to make a complete plan how the time is to be kept. Thus far the
Tabernacle of the Covenant with its gate to the Court,
beyond which is the Holy and Holy of Holies, where God can
be served without intermission, has not yet been erected.
Therefore we will attempt at least a prophetic account, how
it might in time come to pass or should be. As the whole
matter is now in fairly good order from evening until
morning nothing more will be said, but we will speak only

of the time from morning til night; and as the worthy Society has thus far handled the time fairly well until the fourth hour, we will not mention the routine but make a beginning with the twelfth hour in the morning [5 A.M.] and show how the whole day is to be kept.

In the usual manner all are to be awakened at the twelfth stroke [of the hour] after which, all, after being awakened, are without delay to assemble at their devotions, which are to continue for an hour or longer if so desired. When this is over, all are to go to their regular occupation until the fourth hour [9 A.M.] and as nothing of interest takes place then except a little lunch, it is well to say that if any are so far advanced in meditation as to leave this hour pass by, it ought to be given over to an hour of short private meditation. The fifth and sixth hours [10 A.M. to 12] are to be devoted to work, but the seventh [12 to 1 P.M.] is to be devoted with special diligence to prayer as a midday mass of 1 hour, and in the twelfth hour in the evening [5 P.M.] before going to the dinner they are to assemble and hold another devotional meeting of 3/4 hour which will prove a glorious preparation to our meal. Firstly, before we pore over the whole matter, and give our final testimony and blessing over the entire inheritance of the Lord, we will first share the special benison and solemn invocation of each one, and make our beginning with the afore-named founder and director and then divide the society into seven classes.

May the lovely words of the Lord in the Lord's inheritance and the odour of roses and lilies spread out in the house of our God. May Maria, a mother for the troubled and joy for the downcast be and remain exhalted and in the sight of God. She will be given [the power] to speak wisely and to act intelligently. May God bring it about that her work gives good counsel and her activity brings forth piety. May the fruit of her labour be blessed; may her growth always be flourishing and lovely; may her boughs and branches spread out as an oak tree. May God bless her potential and make her a rich mother so that her children go up as lilies by the brook . . . [Similar eulogies over the Subprioress, overseers and each of the sisters who are divided into seven classes]

Now, before we continue in this whole matter, we will take our refuge under the wings of divine mercy and pray for grace, assistance, and help that He guide us so as to act wisely and have holy thoughts. Thus, we plead unto you with one voice: 'O thou mother of all things, protect thy servants from all deceitful snares of this world, and make them worthy to be received up and into the choir of everlasting virginity. We also commend unto you, our spiritual leader and director, together with all who are concerned for us, so that we may gain the jewels of the celestial bride. May it be granted unto them to speak wisely and act prudently, so that we, under their guidance may be brought under your fetters, bonds and subjection, and thus be and remain your true servants and pupils in all time and eternity. Amen.

Upon this our unanimous sacrifice and willing subjection to the rules of our order and the divine wisdom, we wish to make the beginning and write down the names of all those virgins who have taken vows, are betrothed and stand bound in love and faithfulness.

[A list of the names of the sisters]

We rejoice in the favour of our God; we rejoice in His goodness; we rejoice in his grace and mercy which gives us drink at the breasts of his consolation.

Sister Thecla has conquered. She has conquered and has come to honour among the virgins of the Lamb for the bows of the strong are broken and those, who are weak, clothed with honour and glory . . .

[Similar eulogies for all the sisters]

Now we wish to give an orderly account and to tell of
the circumstances and opportunities which gave birth to our
well known spiritual clothing and of various rules of the
order which arose in the orderly practice of all. Included
as well are other useful teachings.

As it came to pass that the society of persons appeared
to increase, and the souls were attracted and called together by the only-begotten loving Spirit of Jesus Christ
(one came from here and the other from there), all kinds of
fashions and manner of dresses were gathered together. This
did not accord with the only-begotten Spirit of Love who was
the cause for the souls to resort to our spiritual-household
or family, that they might again obtain from God their support of the Spirit. As this did not seem to coincide, but
appeared at variance, it happened that once upon a time, our
Father or spiritual leader elevated by God, explained the
sources of the many diversities of the clothing as a matter
entirely defective, and which could not exist according to
the close rules of the Spirit. He came to consult about
this with several of us Sisters, and said that the matter
was not to be continued, nor could it be in accordance with
a cloistered or communal life according to Christian or
divine conduct with and among each other.

Because our comport in clothing appeared to be entirely
in contrast to the internal Spirit of Love, these speeches
were well received by us. And we soon accommodated ourselves after this conference to change the various colours
of our clothing, inasmuch as we were still blended in a
multitude of colours. Thus we were first assisted to take
into hand the unity of colour. Therefore we accordingly
selected what we thought was the most diverse; we chose the
black colour for our clothing. Thus the multitude of colour
was changed into a certain unity, but to an actual unanimity
of the clothing itself, we were not helped; as such was a
weighty matter, to find something between both [extremes],

which the secular spirit had not previously applied in some
other way. The matter could not be reached quickly, but the
instruction had to be obtained from God himself. Finally
after a long embarrassment, and painful desire of the
spirits intimately enamoured in God it was given unto our
Father or spiritual leader blessed by God how to act in this
matter. So it happened that there was found among the most
venerated brethren one by the name of Martin Brämer, who now
has passed from time into eternity. The Lord reward him on
the day of Eternity for his pains and faithfulness which he
demonstrated in this sorrowful struggle. This brother whom
we have mentioned, at that time had the sewing for the
brothers and sisters in his hands. With this brother our
spiritual leader consulted about the circumstances of the
whole matter and how and what had happened. Then some of us
Sisters were found who specially urged that the habit of the
order should now be taken up and adopted. So with the
consent of our spiritual superintendent this brother was
chosen and at the same time was instructed by our superintendent, how and in what manner he was to make the clothes.
Consequently it was concluded to first fabricate the habits
for the sisters who agreed [in the matter]. At first it was
held that white woolen cloth should be taken, and that the
clothing should be arranged as follows: a long frock plain
and straight, narrow sleeves without facing, so that consequently the whole frock was to be narrow and close, so that
it is more like unto a penitential robe than one for inciting worldly pomp. What further concerns the veiling or
covering of the countenance and the body, is this: over the
frock follows a loose veil without hood, which is back and
front almost as long as the frock, only that there is a
little contrast in one from the other. After the veil follows a cover or hood which back and front reaches a little
below the girdle, so that the shoulders and the countenance
may by it be hidden and covered, and further, there is still

a wrap or mantle which is closed all around, wherein the whole body can be muffled from top to bottom, and be covered. This is not usually worn, except in wintertime, to the midnight masses, during the devotional hours as it is designed as a cover or protection against the cold of winter, and all of these clothes were made from white woolen cloth. Therefore it was customary to wear them only in winter. In the summer we wear even similar clothing as is commanded, only that they are arranged to the summer season, as the former are for winter. Therefore we usually use cotton cloth, or else take a light flaxen cloth. To this habit belong shoes of uncoloured leather, with low heels, rounded front, plain and straight. This now is the habit of our Order, which is worn for our bodily [comfort] and separate uses. Further we are in earnest intent, that in all our actions both outward and inward the unity of the Spirit be felt and perceived. Therefore it is especially seen, too, that this order of habit be assumed; wherefore it is ordered and directed, some for the holy mass, the other for sacred duties [such as] going out to houses to break the Bread, to proclaim the death of the Lord Jesus or otherwise when visiting in a communal manner. For wintertime it is unanimously agreed that the wraps or mantles be usually worn to devotions, the masses, and general meetings. For going out, visiting or performing sacred offices it is ordered that the loose veil and clothing be worn, and it is not allowed generally, that one robes herself in one way and another in a diverse manner.

Further, this is now to be our rule: when summer time approaches, that owing to the heat we can no longer wear our winter clothing, the winter habits are to be discarded by all at the same time, and the regular and well ordered summer habits assumed, which as before stated are to be of light linen or cotton cloth, all to be supplied with hoods and veils. It is understood that none is to act as she

pleases. It is also ordered that as soon as the summer
season is over, the winter robes be assumed by the whole
society as the rule demands, so that all look alike, no
matter how many there may be.

Novices shall abide by the same rule, so that no dis-
sention arises in the Society. Although we have not mentioned any specified time for said changes, let this be the
rule: at the end of the second month [April] the winter
habits are to be discarded and the summer habits assumed,
which shall be worn in general use until the end of the
seventh month [September] when the winter habits shall again
unanimously be assumed, so that in the outward appearance of
the clothing, the unanimity of the spirit be not contradicted.

Now we will describe the rule and use of our every day
clothing, and in what manner it is to be worn. First, we
have a knit gown of grey fabric, just as nature supplies it.
To this gown belongs a hood of the same fabric, only it may
be of coarse flaxen cloth. It is arranged as follows: it
is to be deep over the face, so that the head may be covered
and enveloped. From this a veil is to hand from the front
and back, long enough to be caught by the waist girdle. In
front under the chin there are to be two small lapels to
further hide the body. For daily use knit socks are to be
worn in place of shoes, they are to be made like shoes,
reinforced with a coarse woolen cloth or thin leather sole,
so that our walk may be quiet and silent. Our every day
clothing is to be the same summer and winter. Mention was
made of black dyed clothing, but as these gradually faded
until they again were of normal colour, it is henceforth to
be the rule, that no colour is to be considered in our
spiritual society or family except such as is the result of
nature. Much more could be said upon this subject, which
might appear trivial, but unto us are sacred mediums and
motives of spiritual life, as we well understand the meaning

of the spirit, where all goes and aims toward a spiritual and divine union of the souls.

What shall we say more of the quiet souls justly enamoured in God, how they arrange their lives and conduct, so as to please only and alone their King of Heaven, whose kingdom is not of this world. Therefore our life and conduct cannot agree or conform to the world, whether it be in eating and drinking, sleeping or waking, in clothing or other requisite things pertaining to the natural life. Therefore we have taken it into the hand to deny and refute such engagements, and have schooled ourselves to be moderate in our eating and drinking, and subsist upon little, that with scant preparation, not according to the usual desire of nature but merely reflecting upon the necessity of human frailty, the spirit may the more readily accomplish its divine task. Our sleep we have also arranged so that we can without great difficulty keep the time of our midnight vigil. Thus we make no further preparation when retiring to rest, than to lie down in the clothing or habits we wear during the day. Our couch is a bare bench, the pillow, a small block of wood, or small straw pillow, more frequently neither. In this matter every one has her option. O! blessed souls, who are thus enriched by the King of Heaven, that they be worthy to go out with Him before the city and help carry His ignominy until death. Souls which the Lord at the proper time will exalt and set in honour in the house of our God.

[God is a God of order. We thank our spiritual leader for guiding us to this order. The Lord Himself must be the reward on the Day of Judgement for those who attend to this order of worship, who prayed in His holy temple without ceasing and who walked the paths which denied the ways of this world. We await new heavens and a new earth in which peace and righteousness will dwell. We now describe other rules of order.]

First follows our daily school practice and labours before God done so that we can bring our bodies under earnest subjection. So that the spirit may not be pained or hindered in its daily routine, we regulate all our work so as to mortify the body under the spirit and bring it under bit and bridle, so that we can control it and guide it to the proper uses of the spirit.

As we have first renounced all vanities of the world, our future conduct will be guided according to the discipline of the body. We will begin by limiting to the utmost our eating and drink, sleep and waking, so that our whole life and conduct show forth that of a suffering and dying pilgrim upon earth. For this reason we have divorced ourselves from the ways and customs of this world, and daily and hourly learn the manner and laws of our crucified Jesus, who instructs us in all things and taught us to deny self, and to take up the cross and follow Him.

Then again is to be mentioned what is requisite to keep duly and properly within bounds. Firstly, it is meet that we keep proper with our eating. As it is set inevitably that there is to be but one meal a day, it will be held in the evening, and great stress is laid that the entire Society assemble at it. It may happen during the day that one takes perhaps a bite of bread, owing to weakness. This is not prohibited to such as feel the necessity for it. Let them partake of the same as a special gift, and acknowledge themselves debtors before God, and pray to Him to grant the strength yet wanting. What further concerns our virginal discipline: before the meal, all shall be served, and none shall have the right to exercise their own will, but show due respect. Whatever else takes place is an exception and not within the rule of discipline.

Concerning our sleeping and waking, which is also within divine and regular bounds, six hours are designated for spiritual and bodily rest; the remaining hours of the night we spend in dutiful spiritual and bodily exercises, for these six hours are kept with great strictness. For this purpose, one sister is ordered to see to the awaking of the whole Society. When the time for sleep has expired, she is to light the candles and lamps in every room to awaken the sisters from their sleep. This order is changed weekly from one class to another. One can not do it any less frequently than appointed in the rule but if one wishes to do it more often, one may. The six hours of rest can be passed by each soul as she pleases. They can either sleep or stay awake, for they are given over to her welfare. The remaining time, however, which we have already said is to be passed in dutiful exercises, comes under our virginal rule of discipline.

What then further concerns our relations with and toward one another, is this: it is to be held in all seriousness and diligence, so that our life be modest, quiet, tranquil and retired, so that each becomes an example for the other, and exemplifies the secret course of life and communion with God. All levity and needless gossip with one another or light laughter are not to be thought of, nor shall occur in this spiritual society. Therefore it is un-necessary to make much of this rule, as it is not considered and much less likely to occur. It is further to be noted of the mood of the hearts and souls who have sacrificed their whole life unto God, and live for him in the silent contem-plation of their heart, and walk in his ways: should it happen in our spiritual society that we have to go out among mankind, be it as a visit or to follow the natural inclina-tion of our mind to call on friends or relatives, it is known to God how it all causes pain to both heart and spirit. There is no greater pain than this as it is all so contrary to our virginal discipline and can never agree with, when it is done by reason of the weakness of the spirit, and not according to our rule. Therefore we count it a disgrace when it occurs and we note it. We are then bowed down in our hearts because we have no right to do such a thing and [when we do] our calling is not properly followed. Therefore we know that we are guilty before God in that we yet lack the most perfect [way of life].

According to our virginal discipline no visits can be permitted except such as are called for by an urgent necessity and if it were possible to be relieved entirely, it would be to our pleasure; then we could live entirely to the duties of our calling. But so long as circumstances demand that such is to be in our Society, which for spiritual and corporeal reasons cannot be obviated, it is necessary that we bring them under order and within bounds, so that the desire lead not our perverse nature into temptation under the pretext of performing necessary spiritual duties. So that such things cannot occur so easily an examination should be made [in each case to determine] whether it arises out of a need, of a natural desire, or out of the duties of the inner walk with God. [If it is the latter] it can easily be noted in the movements of the mind ....

Further it is ordered that the sister selected as the overseer of her class is to be the absolute ruler and guide, governing herself so that the souls who stand before God and have been placed under her charge by the superior of the whole society are equally treated; that to none is given too much or too little; and when anything happens, no matter in which class, if one or another has any desire to go out, the sister overseer, as the supervisor, is to well interrogate the souls of their desire for the proposed visit and learn whether their desire be a dutiful one of the mind or one of our perverted nature, which generally emanates from the uncontrolled will, not yet brought into subjection under the holy will of God and our discipline.

[There is much to do in our spiritual calling which ought not to be set aside for light reasons, or because of our deformed nature which we must daily and hourly mortify]

O holy death, thou life of immortality too little known among those souls called in a general call. Therefore we have committed ourselves especially to walk upon the secret and hidden path of the cross of Jesus Christ and to follow it and not to leave it until death cuts us off and casts us over into eternal life. O how unpleasant and difficult is it until the true Nazarean life is once again born in us, until we can all freely enter the Lord Jesus' will and deny things allowed and not allowed so as to be and remain alone devoted to and members of the Lord in time and eternity.

We then experience how painful and narrow is [our] walk until we again are brought completely under the free grace and love of God where no external law is any longer necessary, where Jesus Christ is in and through all the end of the law in us. O how many heavy works and difficult tasks must we not pass by until we are once again able to gain or be brought to the contemplation of God. Therefore it is our duty to take every means and law upon ourselves against human faults and original sin which cause us much pain, misery and need on the way to God ... before we think to achieve the heights of perfection where we as the purchased and chosen of the pure lamb are able to live and walk unpunished before God's seat of grace.

Moreover, it is yet to be noted that it is very necessary and good that we properly and correctly distinguish and search the movements in and out of our mind [to determine] what are the movements of our actions . . . if they are finally the working of the will or if they are ruled and directed by the most perfect will of God. In a resigned will more external virtues can be brought forth than in the most perfect will, for in the resigned will there is yet much life support to hand. God oversees us and gives much to us and does not hold our soul so closely to account as he does when it has gone over into following the perfect will of God. Then it is much different than before. Then we do not only have to order everything here alone in the outward virtues of external piety. Then we have to give over the good we thought we had received in God and was ours to be completely cast out and rejected with pain and bitter suffering. Then the soul is naked and emptied of all external self-chosen virtues; it must go into the wilderness completely alone and bereft of all protection and consolation of creatures. Then it is much different than earlier when our understanding and reason were able to grasp and understand matters. Then the love of God keeps a completely different house with our acts, life and walk than earlier when we thought it was good to act in external services and images . . . [This was] before we achieved the ability to practice the perfect will of God. When we receive the loving embrace of our heavenly bridegroom he lovingly and consolingly calls to us and says: Come my beloved and chosen bride. I will lead you into my garden of love and joy and will offer you the lovely odour of many beautiful kinds of flowers which are the virtues of God-loving souls. I will lead you and guide you to the fountain of life so that your thirsty and dejected spirit can rejoice and refresh itself and I will rule, order, direct and reign in it until I take you completely up and into my secret and faithful loving communion and I will remain and dwell with you without change of time. Before we can be brought into the perfect, open, free will of God we must be practiced in working and labouring the lowest rungs of the resigned will . . . .

Concerning the sisters who find themselves chosen as overseers, they are to instruct well the souls and daily and hourly remind them of their hidden walk in faith with God, and to steadily maintain that relationship until our labor and trouble have reached a blessed end, and seek to discourage all unnecessary goings out to visit natural friends or acquaintances; further, to instruct and remind them that the tongue of truth hath taught and said that whosoever doth not give up father, mother, brother and sister, yea even his own life, cannot be my student nor follower.

Further, it is to be noted that when one or another sister in a class finds that she wants to go out, be it either by duty or permission, she is to know that such is not to be according to her desire, but only after a previous application to the overseer of her class, who can investigate whether to grant or refuse and act as she thinks best the matter stands before God, assuming that the monitors will so shape their lives that they prove a bright example to their subordinates, who shall have confidence in their director.

First of all, in every class of sisters who live together a certain one shall be appointed, she shall have supervision over all matters, opportunities and conditions as they present themselves. What her duties are to be will be briefly stated: Be it known that such a sister is to strive in all earnestness that her life and walk be without fault or blemish in the society, and she must be in unity and full accord with the spiritual and personal poverty and deprivation whereby our laudable community is blessed by God . . . . To such a sister all power may be given, and she is to use her best endeavor for the souls and take heed of the outside trifles, such as the carrying of wood, kindling of the fires, drawing water, lighting the lights. The time of awakening is to be well noted, and the rule for locking and securing the door is to be well seen to, so that all unseeming going and coming may be stopped. Then the society can all the more easily walk within the confined discipline of the rule of the spirit.

Concerning the locking of the door, it is ordered that when the time comes for awakening, the appointed overseer, of whichever class she may be, shall designate a sister whom she considers most trustworthy to unlock the door as the clock strikes twelve in the morning [5 A.M.] and they shall remain open until the second hour [7 A.M.] then be closed until the seventh hour [noon] and they shall remain wholly or half open until the time for sleep, when the fourth hour [9 P.M.] strikes, from which time the doors shall remain securely locked during the whole night, as the rule of the night naturally calls for locked doors. This attention and order is chiefly vested in the first and third classes, and they will govern.

[We wish to make a few comments on the duties and work of the sisters who find themselves as obedient children in the society in which they are to endeavour to learn to receive the virtue of God in the highest grade. It can be seen in our actions how near we are to this; if we continually speak about others we have not come to it. Therefore learn to deny yourself and be the smallest in the flock of Christ.

By such activity, beginning with ourselves we can once again lift up our empty and dejected hearts. How far are you from the right path if you judge someone else. God is always working for our salvation even if we do not understand it. He often brings suffering to us.

There is nothing more beautiful and glorious than for our whole lives to come under the Holy Spirit.

We can praise and thank God much for his love given so richly to us.

Therefore rejoice, O chosen of the race of the Lord for you will flourish and blossom, and your growth will spread in the new world.

Not everything can be said that the spirit experiences and enjoys in the hiddenness.

Our whole life consists in continued mortification.

O fullness of divine grace, flow out upon me.

Here follows a short statement or additional register

of names which is set against the first register and rules
for living in case there are souls in the society, from
those who have taken vows who do not live according to the
rules and do not wish to come under any sisterly rule of
life and discipline.

Therefore in each of the classes there shall be a
certain sister, who stands in the name of the whole society,
to have the oversight in a peculiar, circumspect and con-
scientious way (in accordance with the above rules of
discipline) in no less a manner than falls in the course of
duty.   In punishing an oversight such a sister shall be
earnest and quick, as if walking before God.   If, then, a
sister does not live in accordance with the Christian rules,
and refuses to accept her punishment, she shall be reported
to the overseer or to the mother superior, who will then
rule according to the counsel and will of the higher mother
of celestial wisdom.   Here the mother heart will argue in
patience and love for a betterment.   If, however, after such
admonition the evil is not abated it is a proof that such a
soul is perverse and incorrigible; so her name is to be
stricken off, for a time, from the upper register, and be
posted here in shame and disgrace.

With such souls one ought to deal fairly sparingly for
a time in trust, openness and love, because by their own
will they have turned away and have not directed themselves
to penitence of heart and change of mind. Spiritual trust
and openness can only with difficulty be given to such impure souls without great loss until one can sense true penitence and change of mind, and that they have denied their
own self will and nailed it to the cross and have given
their hearts as students to Jesus Christ and have submitted
to all the rules of God which hung over them and draw themselves to God and their neighbours as penitent souls for
their full healing.   Then they can once again be taken into
full association in the heart of the faithful society of

love and their names are to be taken out of this second register and written into the first with those who have taken
vows and bound themselves to remain faithful until death
under the blood-flag of Jesus Christ, and have signed their
name as a testimony of this. This second register must
remain as it is, set against the first so that if souls who
have signed the first register have not kept the rules
according to their promise or signature, their names are to
be stroked out of the first register and written into the
second so that they know that they are responsible to keep
what they have promised [to keep].

- End of this Procedure -

[A short description of the procedure for dealing with
those who are not faithful to their vows. One year of penitence is required after they request that their names be
once again entered into the first register]

[The third register on novices. The novitiate is to
last for a year and a day. If they are not decided after
this time they are to leave. No one may enter younger than
eighteen and a half years.

Meditations by various sisters of the community among
which the following by Sister Hannah is an example:]

O dearest love, we praise the great goodness and faithfulness which you have eternally placed over us. Your blessing must remain with us so that we flourish and blossom so
that we grow from class to class and bring forth our fruitfulness into the new world.

O how beautiful will be the sight of it, how glorious
it will appear when the whole divine race which has hoped in
so much pain for so long under the cross will grow into a
perfect community where the sweetest harmony, the angelic
and heavenly Choir will be heard ...

Conclusion

[God has graciously visited us. We are no longer as we

once were. In the fullness of time the heart of God revealed itself to the fallen human race. A virgin conceived and opened Paradise or a way into the new world for the fallen children of man] How must the kingdoms of this earth tremble before this miraculous birth. O, what great excellence will be revealed when the whole fullness of this race, the wonders of time, the mystery of eternity will be revealed and shown forth, when all the children of this heavenly founder, mother and queen of heaven out of whom they are born are together like the dew at dawn. For this reason they will be called the race of virgins and children of Paradise, and will be possessors of the new world.

[Out of this high miraculous birth of the Son of God and the Virgin Mary this society arose, born as a miracle, in mystery without human action. We must see to it that we do not shame our race and come to the new world where the holy man Jesus, the first born of this race, keeps his house. We participate in his glory.]

God Himself is our reward and shield on whom we trust. We wait upon the goodness which he will show to us and cling to the heart of his love. There Christ Jesus is in us, He who was given as our Sanctifier and Redeemer from the Father. Out of His fullness we have all received grace for grace and have been richly given drink at the breasts of his consolation and love. To Him be honour into eternity. Amen.

We close now with these words:

O fountain of salvation! O abyss of eternal love! O eye of eternal wisdom who has looked upon and made itself known to us. Truly, you are the uncreated sea of God and His love. You, You are the Source and the fountain of living water which flows into eternal life. Therefore to you belongs all dominion and power into the infinite eternity of eternities. Amen.

May the Lamb clothe us, and be and remain the only

cause of this whole Society. May His eye guide us and His step mark our path until we have reached the full end and completion of our work.

-The End-

THE EPHRATA CHRONICLE

by

Lamech and Agrippa

How Ephrata was Founded, and Ordained
for the Settlement of the Solitary

Ephrata is situated in Lancaster County, thirteen miles from Lancaster, eighteen from Reading, and sixty-five from Philadelphia, in an angle where two great highways intersect each other, the one from Philadelphia to Paxton, the other from Reading to Lancaster. The Delaware Indians, who inhabited this region, named it and the stream that flows past Ephrata, *Koch-Halekung*, that is Serpents' Den, on account of the many snakes found there. The Europeans kept the word, but pronounced it Cocalico, which is also the name of the township. The inhabitants did not value the land, as being unfruitful. A Solitary Brother, Elimalech [Emanuel Eckerling] by name, was the first one to build on this barren spot; and he gave his little house to the Superintendent [Conrad Beissel] when the latter fled thither. Thus it appears that the founding of Ephrata sprang entirely from a providential occurrence, and not from the premeditated will of man. After the foundation of this wonderful household, which made fools of so many both in and outside of its limits, had been thus laid, the further building up of the place was not permitted otherwise than with the severest self-denial on the part of the builders; wherefore also so many strange events happened. This is the reason, too, why the tempter prevailed against it in nothing, although the enterprise was often delivered up to him by God that he might sift it; for he could find in it nothing of man's will, even as the Superintendent frankly said to one who asked him whether he had built up the work: No, for the whole thing was against his conscience. In a certain place he speaks further on the subject thus: "So then Ephrata is now built up out of this soul of suffering, endured in the conscience for the sake of God's kingdom."

Here in this wilderness he fixed himself as though he intended to live apart from men to the end of his days. He cleared himself a tract of land, and cultivated it with the hoe, and in general made such arrangements that, in case men should again deliver him up, it would not be any loss to him. It is easy of belief that in the short period of his seclusion, during which men left him in peace for awhile, his addresses to the virgin Sophia were redoubled, for it was then he composed the beautiful hymn, "O blessed life of loneliness when all creation silence keeps." He often told what pains it cost him in the beginning to free this region from the evil spirits which hold dominion over the whole earth. If this seems strange to anyone, let him read Otto Clusing's Life of the Fathers in the Desert; there he will find more about such things.

The congregation now, after having been robbed of its teacher, held its meetings with a housefather named Seal-thiel [Simon Landes]. But so many legal quarrels took place that they were called the "court meetings." Meanwhile the Superintendent found an opportunity, and summoned the heads of the congregation to his new dwelling place, where they took counsel with reference to the general matter, and finally opened another meeting, after the Superintendent had been withdrawn for seven months. It was held for the first time on September 4th 1732. About this same time the Solitary Brethren also made up their minds, and moved after their spiritual leader, and built, in the winter of 1732, the second house in the Settlement. Their names were Jethro [Jacob Gast], Jephune [Samuel Eckerling], and Martin Bremer, the last of whom was the firstling of those who fell asleep in Ephrata. This was not the end of it, however. Soon after two of the Sisters who had earliest been devoted to virginity, A[nna] and M[aria] E[icher], also came and asked to be taken in. The Brethren, who went according to the Fathers in the Desert, of whom it was known that they did not tolerate such a thing among themselves, protested against it to the Superintendent as being improper and perhaps a cause of offense. But he was not of their mind. It seems that he foresaw in the spirit what would be the outcome of the matter. The result was that a house was built for them on the other side of the stream, into which they moved in May, 1733, and where they lived until the Sisters' Convent was founded. In the following year another house was built, for two brothers, Onesimus and Jotham [Jorael and Gabriel Eckerling] otherwise called Eckerlin. This was followed by the common bake-house, and a magazine for the supply of the poor; with these building stopped for a while.

These matters created a terrible stir in the land, especially among the neighbors, who were partly degenerate Mennonites and partly spoiled church-people. They did all against these newcomers that one could expect from that kind of people devoid of all fear of God. Once they, without warning, set fire to the forest, in the hope of burning down the Settlement; but the fire turned, and laid in ashes the barn of a householder with all its contents. Then they began everywhere to warn one another against seduction, parents warned their children, and husbands their wives. This was among the common people; but the great ones of the land harbored the suspicion that the Jesuits had something to do with it, so that the Brethren were often asked, when they were seen to have gold, whether they had brought it from Mexico. Such were the sorrowful times wherein the foundations of Ephrata were laid; they were specially like unto the times of Nehemiah and Ezra.

About the same time, in the year 1734, the awakened in Falckner's Swamp, it being the seventh year of their awakening, began to break up and move towards the Settlement, which increased the alarm in the country. They bought up from the spirit of this world the regions around Ephrata, so that in a few years the country for from three to four miles around the Settlement was occupied by this kind of people. Wherever there was a spring of water, no matter how infertile the soil might be, there lived some household that was waiting for the Lord's salvation. Afterwards these regions were divided up, and each one received its own particular name; one was called Massa, another Zoar, the third Hebron, and the fourth Kadesh. After these, the awakened from the Schuylkill also came and settled down around the Settlement. From them the Sisters' Convent gained a number of members; but only two, natural sisters, endured to the end. These have finished their course, under the names of Drusiana and Basilla. The rest were gathered in again by the spirit of the world. How the Superintendent must have felt through all this, can well be imagined. He knew well that it all would be reckoned to his account and to that of the good that had been entrusted to him. He was so little proud of it that, on the contrary, he used to say that God had sent all these people to him to humble him; wherein many of them spared no pains. He was to each that which each one sought in him -- to this one a saviour of life unto life, to that one a saviour of death unto death.

Before I close this chapter what happened in the country with a Frenchman named John Reignier must yet be reported. He was a native of Vivres in Switzerland, and professed to have been awakened in his seventh year; but he was not completely rid of the upspringing flames of masculinity within him. He came into the Settlement just at a time when the Solitary Brethren were in deepest earnest; but they had not the gift of discerning the spirits, so that he could insinuate himself among them through false powers of light. The Superintendent, to whom this person's true condition was manifest, warned them against his seduction. But they were already so taken up with the man by reason of his semblance of holiness, that these warnings did not impress them. As in everything he avoided the middle path, he at length led them into strange extravagances, so that they bound themselves with him not to eat any more bread. Accordingly they gathered a great store of acorns. But judgment followed them, so that their store of provisions was devoured by worms. He even went further, and taught them that it belonged to holiness, after the example of Elijah and other saints, not to dwell in any house. The Superintendent finally determined to bring the affair to an end, and prevailed upon the Brethren to build a hut for the man, hard by the Settlement, where he was maintained at the general expense. At last, however, he lost his reason, whereupon the Brethren rid themselves of him. Afterwards he joined himself to one Gemaehle by name, by whom he had himself baptized. The two then went through the country as Apostles. As such they aroused much attention everywhere, especially in New York in the Jew-school. Such is the power of perversion. At length he made a journey of 600 miles, with bare head and feet, through the great wilderness to Georgia, where he joined himself to the Moravian Brethren, who took him to Herrenhaag, where the *Ordinarius Fratrum* [Count Zinzendorf] wedded him to a wife, with the following wedding discourse: "See, dear Brethren, here is a proud saint from America, whom God hath cast down so that he must now celebrate a marriage with a public harlot." This would have been a good opportunity for him to humble himself; but instead he repaid these kind offices with evil, which was published to his shame in Frankfurt. Nevertheless for a while all went according to his wishes; for they sent him as a laborer to St. Thomas. But when from there he came to Bethlehem, and they were going to bring him under the strict regulations of the congregation, he left their communion again. Thereupon he came to the Superintendent a second time, who took his Delilah from him and put her into the Sister's Convent, at which he rejoiced and had himself received into the Brothers' Convent. But his wife became regretful and demanded her husband again, to which he was forced to yield against his will; this gave him such a shock that, for the second time in the Settlement, he lost his reason. When he came to himself once more, the old brother-hatred towards the Superintendent again became alive in him, so that he uttered many slanders against him and his about whoremongering. But, as the name of Brother was therefore taken from him, he and his wife moved away, and at length he ended his restless life at Savannah in Georgia. God be merciful to him on the day of judgment!

To this time it yet belongs that the Superintendent with several Solitary Brethren made a visit to Oley, where the powers of eternity were remarkably manifested. They came into a house where the daughter was a bride, who at first sight let herself be so overpowered with these forces that her earthly bridal love fell dead before them. Without the bridegroom's knowledge she followed the visitors, and in the Settlement took her vows of eternal virginity among the original Sisters. Whereupon her parents followed her; but she continued to shine among her sex by her virtuous walk, until at last, under the name of Berenice, she finished her course, which is recorded in heaven, because for her future glory's sake she denied herself her carnal bridal-couch here below.

Ephrata is Occupied by the Solitary of Both Sexes;

Divine Worship is Instituted; and the Communal Life is Introduced

After the Superintendent through an awakening in Tulpehocken had received valuable re-inforcements for his divine work, and thereby was made aware that God was with him, he took advantage thereof, and instituted measures for building a meeting-house to God's glory; for hitherto the meetings had been held in private houses. For its erection both the Solitary and householders willingly contributed their share. The structure contained, besides the hall for meetings, also large halls fully furnished for holding the *Agapae,* or love-feasts, besides which there were also cells built for the Solitary, after the manner of the old Greek church. At that time it happened that a housefather handed over his daughter, a young lass, to the Superintendent, with the request that he should bring her up to the glory of God. Anyone else would probably have declined such a present; but he regarded the matter as a providential leading, received her, and had her serve him for a purpose, namely, to found the Order of Spiritual Virgins. She with two others were given a residence in the second story of the church-building just mentioned; which latter was named Kedar. These four Sisters were the first who bound themselves by a pledge to a communal life; but the one who gave the first occasion to it, at last forsook again the narrow way of the cross, and joined herself to a man, after having lived in their convent many years, under the name of Abigail. Soon after this the Superintendent quartered four Solitary Brethren in the lower story of this house; which increased the suspicion against them, for no one would believe that matters could go on properly thus. The Superintendent, however, cared more to have an essential separateness, than that there should be an outward appearance thereof which might not be real. Consequently there finally came to be as unrestrained a life in the Settlement as though all were of the same sex. It must be granted the Superintndent that in this respect he went further than some before him in the conventual or celibate life; for where others went out of the way of danger, he plunged his followers into the midst of it.

When the house Kedar was finished, a general love-feast was held in it, contributed by the households to the glory of God who had made known his wonders in these heathen lands. Messengers were sent out into the country to invite to it all friends and well-wishers. How greatly this displeased the Prince of Darkness may be judged from the fact that, at this very time, at midnight, the Superintendent was so severely belabored with blows from an invisible power that he was forced to take refuge with the nearest Brethren; upon whose authority it is here mentioned. After this, although the love-feast was held, only a few of the invited guests came; and these were more offended than edified thereby, because they saw how a Brother during the feetwashing kissed the Superintendent's feet, and said: "These feet have made many a step for our welfare." Soon after this the Superintendent instituted a visitation through the country as far as New Jersey. It consisted of twelve fathers of the congregation, and everywhere occasioned great wonder, partly because so many respectable men permitted themselves to be governed by so humble and despised an instrument, and also because they saw among them a man so famous in the land as C.W. For the latter was so far brought down by works of penance, and had let his beard grow, that hardly anybody recognized him; besides which he had voluntarily offerd up, for the glory of God, a part of his possessions towards the upbuilding of this new economy.

Even before Kedar was quite completed, the nightly divine services among the Solitary in the Settlement had been commenced. They were called Night Watches, and were held at midnight, because at that hour the advent of the Judge was expected. At first they lasted four hours, so that from this severe spiritual exercise one had to go at once to one's physical work, which was a sore crucifixion of the flesh; afterwards, however, the time was fixed at two hours. At first the Superintendent himself presided at them, particularly when both sexes met together; and he did so with such power of the Spirit that he never let them come to the bending of the knee so long as he noticed that a ban was on them and there had been quarrels, when he had to have recourse to scolding until finally their eyes became wet with tears. Moreover he taught them on both sides, as a priestly generation, to lift up hands unto God on behalf of the domestic household, which was so sorely bound under the yoke of the world; and that this was the continual service of God. In succeeding times he withdrew from this service, out of consideration for the work, lest it might become constrained on his account, and waited upon God in his own house of watching. Then each meeting had to help itself as well as it could; though whenever quarrels arose at the service, and he was asked for help, he never failed to give it.

This record would be imperfect if here were not inserted also an account of the zeal of the congregation. For after it had taken the Superintendent as its priest, the worship of the congregation lay nearest his heart. The confidence which every household at that time yet felt towards him (for as yet there was no one who doubted his divine mission) was such that all their real and personal possessions were in his hands, and they would not have refused, at a mere wink from him, to give up all for the glory of God. At that time every house in the congregation stood open to the poor. Accordingly when such persons applied to the Superintendent, as was common, he would ask one housefather after the other, during meeting, whether he had any money; and he was seldom disappointed in his confidence in them. Was there any charitable work to be done, then an investigation was made after meeting, and his work for the following week appointed for each member who was able, when often many a one devoted his own share to the use of the poor. This method continued for many years, but has now been abrogated by death.

In autumn of the year 1735 all the Solitary, of both sexes, who had dwelt as settlers scattered through the country, moved to the Settlement. Thus this holy mode of life, over which God had poured out the powers of the new world, was brought to its end in Pennsylvania, and will hardly be revived again; for other schools afterwards arose, and when God wants to transfer any one to a higher duty, he makes his former estate to be sinful for him, otherwise would no one be brought to renounce it. In this same movement the afore-mentioned teacher of Tulpehocken in a letter to the Superintendent asked to be taken up in the Settlement. The Brethren did not think that such a one would be able to endure the severe mode of life, and advised against his reception. But the Superintendent had greater faith, and through his mediation he moved into the Settlement that autumn yet, and several of his household followed him. The rest fell away again from their testimony.

After the meetings had been held for a short time in Kedar, the following changes took place: A widower of property in the congregation, Sigmund Landert by name, felt himself obligated in his conscience to offer up his possessions to the glory of God; wherefore he asked the Superintendent's advice, who counseled him not to do it. But he soon came again, full of sorrow, and made this proposition, namely: that if he and his two daughters would be received into the Settle‐ent, he would build out of his means another house of prayer adjoining Kedar, besides a dwelling-house for the Superintendent; then Kedar might be changed into a Sisters' Convent. This, the Superintendent saw, was from God, and accordingly agreed to his request. Here one can see how in those days the Spirit reigned and manfully urged them on, with the power of apostolic times, to a communal life. More such cases occurred in those times. Among the rest, a housefather sold his property, and, in apostolic wise, laid the price thereof at the Superintendent's feet; who used it for God's glory, and incorporated him and his family in the household at Ephrata, where, after much faithfulness in God's work, he ended his course under the name of Macarius. The erection of the church now went forward without hindrance; for the housefather before referred to brought all his possessions into the Settlement, besides his two daughters, who entered the Sisters' Convent. The younger of them had recourse to the world again; but the older entered into her rest, at this same Convent, in November of the year 1773. Their father, however, who was a skillful mechanic, rendered good service in building up the Settlement; and after a holy poverty and abnegation of all things had become his portion, he went home to his eternal fatherland under the name of Sealthiel; he had proved by his example that a domestic household may be dissolved through the heavenly call.

This house was a sightly structure, furnished with a hall for love-feasts, and one for meetings, which had two "portkirchen" for the use of the Solitary, besides a gallery occupied by gray-haired fathers; here and there, moreover, texts in black-letter were hung. This beautiful building, after having stood about four years, was razed to the ground again, the cause of which can scarcely be com-

prehended by human reason; the standard is too limited. The
Superintendent's followers were confounded in him, and knew
not whether the erection or the destruction of this house,
or both were from God. Other persons held him to be a
sorcerer, and said he had made fools of his people. It is
probable that a hidden Hand made use of him, in this wise
symbolically to represent the wonders of eternity, after
which the veil was again drawn over the affair; for there is
a likeness in its history to that of the temple at
Jerusalem, which, after it was scarcely finished, was
plundered by the king of Egypt. Since a dwelling had been
erected for him adjoining this building, he was now for the
second time obliged to abandon his seclusion and therefore
removed into the confines of the Sisterhood. Here God made
use of him to found their Order; whereupon he devoted himself wholly unto them. For it is to be known that at his
first awakening at Heidelberg he came unto the Virgin above,
through whom the whole creation is restored again to God,
and who was enamored of his *limbum* beyond measure, which was
one cause of his many sufferings, for she wished to have him
feminine and quite subject unto herself, whereas he was
still possessed of the ardor of rising manhood. Now however
the graft of the upper virginhood was through him to be
implanted in others for the spread of God's kingdom.
Wherefore his spiritual daughters were sent unto him in the
bloom of youth; all of whom, without distinction, he received. Whoever came to him at that time saw with astonish-
ment his whole house filled with his spiritual daughters;
and as he then had reached his fortieth year, it is easy to
imagine what temptations he had to endure in his natural
body, in reference to which he once declared that he had
really first learned to know his Father in his fortieth
year. Before his death also, he placed among the many
blessings God had shown him this, that he had preserved him
from the allurements of the female sex.

At this same time when the female part was incorporated in his household, and while the Brothers' Convent was being built, the Superintendent was impelled to lay the foundations of the communal life. Accordingly all provisions were delivered to the Sisters in their kitchen, who daily prepared a supper for the entire Settlement in a large dining-hall, they being separated from them by a dividing screen. Everything, withal, was done in order and reverently according to the leading of the Holy Ghost, and under the supervision of the Superintendent, so that the powers of the new world were markedly manifested. After this had continued for half a year, and the common household of the Sisters had been dedicated, the Brethren were again dismissed in peace, and the Superintendent restored to them their prescribed rations.

At this time the *Lectiones* were first instituted in the Settlement; namely, the Superintendent ordered that weekly, on the evening of the sixth day, every one should examine his heart before God, in his own cell, and then hand in to the Superintendent a written statement of his spiritual condition, which he read at the meeting of the congregation on the following Sabbath. These confessional papers were called *Lectiones*, and several hundred of them were afterwards published in printed form. It is remarkable that the most unlearned and simple-minded stated their condition so artlessly, unreservedly, and simply that one cannot but be astonished at their simplicity.

Concerning the Spiritual Course of the Church in the Settlement;

and the Various Prophetic Gifts

As introductory to this chapter it is to be remarked that all the mysteries of eternity, in order to be manifested in time, must clothe themselves in a body, otherwise they cannot impart themselves to man; and everything divine that does not become human, remains unfruitful, for fruitfulness lies in the body; and therein is contained the mystery of the incarnation of Christ. As has been remarked, there was intrusted to the Superintendent, at his conversion, a good thing, which he in general calls the fundamental good. Note well, reader, it is the goodness of God, which ruled before the fall, whereby the fallen angel became the devil, and over which Adam stumbled too, which therefore will also become a cause of restoration. Now, the fall might perhaps have been prevented if the cherub had sooner been placed as guardian over man, as was afterwards done. But the pure simplicity of God did not permit him to know this, otherwise he would have become impure. Now, Adam was created to repair the evil, and he should have taken the Virgin into his domicile. It happened with him, however, as with the fallen angel, he wanted to have the good in his own peculiar possession, and therefore God was obliged to construct a helpmate for him out of his own body, so that he might by all means have something over which to rule.

With this good the Superintendent was loaded at his
first awakening at Heidelberg; for in conversion everything
depends upon the first impregnation. Hence his portion, and
that of all who came nigh him, was such a bitter one. When
he was obliged to enter the world of men with this good, he
foresaw the danger of losing it, and that if he would
maintain his post, he would call down upon his head the
hatred of all the children of Adam; and this was also the
case. For many of his followers, who seemed to have much
love for him, when they noticed that they could not possess
themselves of his good, but rather that it sought to possess
them, exchanged their love for a deadly hatred. It was
noticed that his first followers, who entered the work with
him before the schools of the solitary life had been opened,
either suffered shipwreck, or had to pass through seasons of
sore trial, because they pocketed too much of the good into
their natural life. Among the first belong John Landes and
A[nna] E[icher] who have been mentioned before, and of whom
the first became a thistle on the road, and the other, one
of his spiritual daughters, became offended, and ended her
life in that state. At this dangerous post all the
Eckerlins were wrecked, especially that one of them who was
Brethren's Prior; for in spite of the fact that he was an
ardent wooer of the Virgin, his efforts only resulted in
bringing her under his man-power. The Superintendent once
warned him not to presume too much upon the good, when he
wrote to him, in the 66th of his printed Letters: "If you
should find that the body seems heavier than the feet and
ankles can bear, remember that this may be because of the
superfluous breast-milk which you drank so abundantly on the
mother's lap, and that the difficulty will be helped of
itself by your merely weaning yourself from the mother's lap
and breast."

After the Solitary in the Settlement, however, were
lodged in their convents, the schools of the solitary life

began, where such lessons had to be learned that one often almost lost sight and hearing, and to which the oldest Solitary ones had become as little used in their hermit-life as the novice who had been received only the day before. And now the cause became known why the hermit-life came to be changed into the communal; and that the holy fathers in the desert had erred when they maintained that the foundations of the Solitary life were to be laid in the convent, but that its perfection would be reached only in the desert. The Superintendent now so managed with the good, that while everyone might partake of it, yet no one could gain selfish possession of it. He was on his feet day and night, and whoso wanted to be rid of him had to lock his door at night; for he was in the service of the four living creatures which have no rest by day or night, so that he was often accused by his calumniators of being under the spur of his natural spirit. There was accordingly a constant stir in the Settlement, so that, if anyone were absent but for three days, he became a stranger, and had much trouble afterwards again to work his way into the order of affairs. No one would have been able, even though he had lived in the Settlement for many years, to give a correct description of the course of events there; it was inconceivable, and at the same time highly offensive to the mere reason. Falling and rising alternated continually; he who to-day was exalted on spiritual heights, to-morrow was laid low; and this was un-avoidable. He whom the Superintendent took into his confi-dence, was elevated on high; he from whom he withdrew it, sank down again, sometimes even into the darkest depths; where then he was nailed to the cross; which things happened frequently. Here was the post of danger, where many of his followers were offended in him, and afterwards closed them-selves against him, some of whom, through God's grace, were loosed again upon their death-beds, as the Brother Peter Gehr mentioned above; others bore the offence with them into eternity, in spite of the fact that he offered them the peace of God in Christ Jesus; wherefore it may well be said: Blessed are they who are not offended in me. Others combined themselves against him, and though they accomplished nothing, they yet often drew deep furrows across his back. In the bestowal and withdrawal of his confidence he was immoderate. When he imposed himself upon one, the sharpness of his spirit pierced such an one through bone and marrow, so that he soon was too much for him. But if he withdrew himself, he did not show himself for a long time, for he had no need of men since he had his power from above. In his intercourse he was not natural, and they who were nigh to him had to adapt themselves accordingly; wherefore no one could lay hold on him with his personality. Divine worship he appointed for the most inconvenient time, at midnight, and took special delight in the spirit if he could carry it on until daylight. If anyone offered him refreshment, he often said, "It gives me none," for his emaciated body was nourished by the Word that proceeded out of the mouth of God, otherwise he could not have endured such severity. When, constrained by love, he was often seen to eat during the day, it nevertheless made no change either in his body or his spirit, for he was a living skeleton until his death. Whenever he went into the Sisters' convent the whole house was moved; and when out of every corner they called to him, he was pleased with this open-heartedness, and said: "The young birds have the same simplicity when their provider comes to feed them." He was most careful to maintain the equilibrium of the Settlement, for God had placed the balances in his hand; and although, during the revolt of Korah, he was for a time deposed from the government, still finally it all fell into his hands again. His house was an asylum and city of refuge for all widows, orphans, and destitute ones; and whoso could reach its borders was safe against the avenger of blood.

As such discipline, so unpleasant to the flesh, was imposed upon the good Brethren of the Settlement, the passion of the body of Christ increased among them; whoever beheld them was amazed at their lean and pale appearance. This was indeed made known to the world by writings, but no one entered into the secret of it, because they were reticent and silent about it.

Now we again come to the Brethren in Zion. After Brother Onesimus had been made Prior of the convent of Zion by the Superintendent, the latter gave him his intimate confidence and fellowship, by reason of which the Prior ruled the Brethren with such severity that, if anyone lifted but a hand against him, it was an understood thing that such an one sinned against God, and jeopardized his eternal salvation; and though they often intended to rebel against him, yet they feared the Superintendent, whom they held to be an ambassador of God. Thus the Prior brought the Brotherhood into such thralldom that the only difference between a Brother of Zion and a negro was that the latter was a black and involuntary slave, while the former was a white and voluntary one. Yet one must bear witness of the Prior that he never ordered another one to do anything that he would not himself have been willing to do; for he was the first to go to work, and the last to leave it. It was, however, soon evident that it would cost the Prior dearly to maintain this intimacy; for the Superintendent was exceedingly watchful lest his fellowship should be misappropriated, and if any did do so, he was excluded by him. Now the Prior had three brothers after the flesh, who indeed were continually striving with him for the priesthood, but who nevertheless always stood up for him when he was attacked by others. It was also correctly supposed that the Mother of the Sisters was another cause of his fall and of his later tearing himself away from his spiritual Father, in that she brought to him much sympathy from the Sisters'

House; for she sought to further her own profit by stirring up differences between the Superintendent and the Prior. In spite of all this, however, everything went on all right for awhile. The Prior showed all conceivable honor to his spiritual Father. He wrote several books in praise of him; and in his letters to him he always called him a Holy Father, and although such eulogies did not blind the Superintendent's eyes, it yet kept the Prior in his good graces, which also was very needful, for there were already various ones in the Settlement who would have liked to have him overthrown. The Superintendent, moreover, had a superhuman fidelity to him, and gave him every protection, even though the entire Brotherhood was against him. Once it was proposed to elect a new Prior, which the Superintendent granted. The votes were gathered, and it was found that the Prior lacked two votes of being elected. Then the Superintendent, who, by virtue of his office, was entitled to two votes, cast these for the Prior, and so again secured the office for him. The greatest difficulties at that time were caused by the Night-Watches of the Brethren in Zion; for despite the fact that at that time several of the Brethren had already for ten years lived a Solitary life, there yet was no comingling of spirits among them, still less anything priestly, that might have filled in the breach and closed up the fissures. The Prior, however, was seized by the spirit of office, so that he considered himself bound to bring the Brethren under; if he had not done so, his conscience would have smitten him. This occasioned much quarrelling at the divine worship, which at times was kept up for several hours. But whenever they called in the Superintendent, he soon had everything adjusted to everyone's satisfaction. In those days many an one may have cried unto God for release from this spiritual tyranny, but the answer to their prayers was postponed for yet greater trials. Meanwhile Prior was diligent in his office. He employed two Brethren who

had to transcribe his writings; and if he was tired of
preaching at the matins, he had his Lectors who had to read
from his writings the rest of the time, wherefore many an
one in his vexation exclaimed: "He preached us to death
again!"

Unedifying as these things may seem, it must yet be
confessed that there was no lack of that essential of true
service of God, the crucifying of the flesh; hence we make
remembrance of those blessed times when, beside these
sorrows, the spirit of prophecy also manifested itself so
strongly. The Superintendent in those days was lifted above
the world of sense, and had surmounted time with its
changes. His hymns composed then are full of prophecy, and
belong to the evening of the sixth time-period, that is, to
the holy Ante-Sabbath. They represent the mysteries of the
last times so impressively, that it seems as though the
kingdom were already dawning. It appears that it was the
intention to set upon a candlestick the wonders of the last
times through the revelation of the heavenly Virgin-estate
and of the Melchizedekian priesthood in America; for that
these hymns were given unto him in visions he at times
betrays, when he adds, "This did we see in the spirit,"
while ordinarily under similar circumstances he is very
self-reliant. All these hymns are to be found in a new collection under the title *"Paradiesisches Wunderspiel."* Soon
after he undertook an important work in the spirit, namely,
he investigated what must have moved God to have so many
animals slaughtered in his service for the redemption of
man, which his righteousness would not have permitted if
animals had not guilt resting upon them because of the fall
of man. About this he became spiritually exercised, and produced a singular writing which he called *"Wunder Schrift."*
Because he thereby disregarded nature too much, he con-
tracted a severe illness. On account of its excellence it
was printed in English with the title: "Dissertation on

Man's Fall." Unless, however, the reader is versed in the
spirit of the Virgin-estate, it is somewhat unclear in its
expressions. In it, however, he has opened up a far outlook
into eternity, and has gone further than even the holy
Apostles in their revelations, bringing glorious things to
light concerning the Mother Church, and how the Father
finally shall deliver his office to the Mother; similarly
concerning the Sabbatic Church in the time of the bound
dragon; what God's purposes are with this Church; and why he
permitted her to be so severely tried by Gog and Magog.

His followers had their part also in all this. Through
their heavenly calling they were instructed thoroughly to
plow up their human nature as being the soil into which are
to be sown the seeds of the new manhood; and because thus
their humanity was under the sword of the Cherub, God opened
unto them again an entrance unto the tree of life, so that
they again ate of the *Verbo Domini*, and so satisfied themselves with unceasing prayer as though they had been at some
sumptuous banquet; all which Adam forfeited when he descended to earthly things. How otherwise would it have been
possible for them, amidst their severe labors, to live in
such abstemiousness? The attractions of the angelic life
had overcome all mercy towards the body, so that the Superintendent was obliged to restrain many an one in his too
great zeal. It was now no secret among them any more how
Adam before the fall had eaten; also how it was still possible to live without animal food and without evacuation of
the bowels. Clement of Alexandria, [miscellaneous], Lib.
III, left a glorious witness of this, where he says: "Jesus
ate and drank in ordinary fashion, and did not expel the
food from him;" so great power of abstinence had he, that
the food within him was not consumed, because there was no
corruptibility in him.

It was remarked that afterwards the spirit of prophecy
descended upon the offices, and therefore hit also the Prior

of the Brethren and the Mother of the Sisters; even as among
the Jews, when the spirit of prophecy entered into the room,
the high-priest began to prophecy.   The Prior wrote so much
at this time, that he employed two Brethren in copying; but
as he was then himself but only rising, his witness also was
confused and unclear.   His writings were kept hidden by his
admirers long after his death; but now no one knows anything
of them.   After the prophetic spirit had withdrawn again
into his chamber, an echo of it yet remained from the time
of the bound dragon or the Sabbatic Church, with which the
meeting was entertained for years.   Herewith we will close
this chapter.

A New Convent for the Sisters is Built, Called Sharon:

The Singing-Schools come into Vogue at the Settlement

Above we mentioned that the Superintendent informed the congregation at a meeting that it would be necessary now to build a chapel for them in order that the domestic household need not be dependent on the Brotherhood in Zion, as this had been a cause of offence to several families who left the Community. Hereby you can see again that the Superintendent stood under a high hand, since two chapels had already been built in the Settlement, and one might well have asked, who gave him the right thus to put a load upon a whole Community, and had God not secretly urged him on to this work, the people would certainly soon have been done with him. But he had learnt so much by experience, that nearly all the awakened, having expressed displeasure for a time, will soon again prepare for themselves a resting place in the ease of their natural life, and he, therefore, always took care not to relapse again into comfort after so tedious a journey. He consequently frequently used to say that he had renounced himself to such a degree that not even a melting-pan was left him.

The building of this new church was commenced in spite of all opposition, and finished in September, Anno 1741, after the Community, together with the Brotherhood, had worked at it for ten months. In December following, the house was consecrated by a meeting and love-feast, and called Peniel. A brother, Elimelech by name, who has been made mention of before, was put over the house as Superintendent, and divine service was held therein for one Community until 1746; but how it happened that Peniel with all its belongings got into the hands of the Sisterhood, will be mentioned in its proper place.

Soon after these events, the house-fathers and mothers were induced to attempt to bring their state to a higher condition, for they were convinced that it was founded on sin, and they knew that Rudolph Nägele and Sigmund Landert, who still lived at that time, had succeeded. The Superintendent gave his moral support to the matter, although it was conjectured that the affair was instigated by the Eckerlins, for it was known that they intended to turn the farms of the household into convent-land. Meanwhile the households courageously furthered the work. They built a great convent adjoining their chapel. The same was divided into two parts, of which one was arranged for the fathers, the other for the mothers. Besides this the house was provided with rooms, chambers and a hall for love-feasts, just as it had been done in that of the Solitary. And in order that the house might be thoroughly incorporated into the Community of the Solitary, some Brethren of Zion moved into it, and administered their divine service, because at the time a particular harmony existed between the two Orders, since both held the unmarried state high. After the household was thus arranged, a venerable house-father, John Senseman by name, was installed as steward, who had the management of the household. But, when the house was to be inhabited, the house-mothers objected, and said: They had first again to be on a free footing, and this must be done by divorce; for, although they had thus far lived a life of continence, they still stood under the will of their husbands, and lived at their mercy. The Superintendent granted their request, to which the care for their eternal salvation

had actuated them. Consequently one of the Brethren had to
write the letters of separation, which afterwards, being
sealed, one part handed to the other.

    This new institution was for some time richly blessed
by God, for these good people were not only very simple
minded, but bore a great love towards God; they also were
very benevolent and harbored many poor widows whom they
maintained out of their own means, so that their household
resembled a hospital more than a convent. But the tempter
pressed so hard upon this work, that it was sifted to the
utmost, and at last broke up. The beginning was made by the
house-mothers, every one of whom, being excluded from
creature-comfort, took hold again of her husband; and this
was not to be wondered at, for their children, who they had
vainly hoped would follow them, remained on the farms in a
neglected state, and drew the hearts of the mothers towards
them. Another cause was added, for about this time the
Eckerlins, who had been a great defence against the natural
life, left the Settlement. When the Superintendent observed
that the means of the household were not sufficient to
continue in these limits, he again gave these dear people
their liberty, and advised every house-father to again
receive his helpmate, which they did, and then all the
letters of separation were burnt on one pile. And thus,
according to human insight, we often work in vain when we
think to have done our best; as happened to these dear
people, all of whom have by this time entered eternity,
where they perhaps received through grace what they strove
after with great labor here below. For although God cannot
allow man to believe that success rests with himself, (how
else could he be humbled?) yet he will not allow anyone to
be deceived in him. Oh, that such a zeal might awake again
within the household! Then salvation would obtain in all
the boundaries of Israel. The people of the household,
therefore, moved upon the farms again, and left the widows

and all the rest of the poor to the Settlement, who were maintained in Zion by the diligent labor of some of the Brethren, until at last they died. The expenses which the household had incurred were partly refunded, as much as possible. For instance, one house-father was paid with 100 acres of land; besides, the Zion's Church was handed over to them. In return, they renounced all claim on the newly erected house, which later on was given to the Sisters as their convent, and called Sharon; they have possession of it at the present day. Thus God secretly carried out his counsel, and helped them to a house, and the households unknowingly had to assist him in it, which God at the day of judgment may remember to their benefit. Although the Superintendent has been falsely accused of having outwitted the households, this is only another proof that Ephrata was not built after a previously conceived plan.

Now we will again return to the Solitary. Thus far they had sought self-sacrifice in hard labor; but now the Superintendent was urged by his Guide to establish higher schools, of which the singing-school was the beginning. This science belongs more to the angelic world than to ours. The principles of it are not only the same all over the world, but the angels themselves, when they sang at the birth of Christ, had to make use of our rules. The whole art consists of seven notes, which form two thirds and one octave, which are always sung in such a way that you do not hear the tone which stands between two notes, thus occasioning a sweet dissonance, which renders the art a great wonder. It is also remarkable, that, although so great confusion of languages arose, the singing remained untouched. But as everything necessary in the Settlement had to be stolen from the world-spirit, so also in respect to singing. The Superintendent did not know anything about it, except some notes which he had learned on the violin. But a certain house-father, by the name of Ludwig Blum, was a

master-singer, and was also versed in composition; he once
brought some artistic pieces to the Superintendent, which
induced him to make use of the Brother in his church
building.

Now those of the Solitary, of whom about seventy of
both sexes were in the Settlement, were selected who had
talent for singing, and the above mentioned Ludwig Blum,
together with the Superintendent, arranged a singing-school
in the Settlement, and everything prospered for a time. But
the Sisters at last complained to the Superintendent that
they were sold to one man, and petitioned him to manage the
school himself, saying that they would steal the whole secret of the schoolmaster and hand it over to him. The Superintendent soon perceived that this advice came from God, for
as the event proved, quite different things were hidden
under it, for which the good school-master's hands were not
made. And now the Sisters told the Superintendent everything
they had learnt in the school, and as soon as they saw that
he had mastered the art, they dismissed their school-master,
at which he took such offence, that he left the Settlement,
and did not walk with them any more, and when asked, why he
had left the Settlement he said: "The singing broke my
neck." Before he left he made the following declaration to
the Superintendent: "A king's daughter took a poor
peasant's daughter into her company, because she was gifted
with various arts and abilities; however, after she had
learnt all her arts, she thrust her off and banished her
into misery. I, therefore, ask the Superintendent, whether
the king's daughter treated the peasant's daughter justly?"
The Superintendent thereat showed him all kindness, and
promised him, since there was not anything more for him to
do in the Community, he would go with him in spirit, and
remember him in his prayers before God. He afterwards
showed him much favor, and thus the Superintendent was
against his will inveigled into this important school.

Before the commencement was made, he entered upon a strict examination of those things which are either injurious or beneficial to the human voice, in consequence of which he declared all fruit, milk, meat, to be viands injurious to the voice. One might have thought that he borrowed this from the teaching of Pythagoras, in order to break his scholars of the animal habit of eating meat, of which habit he was never in favor. When bringing all this before the Brethren for examination, they observed that he crossed some words with his pen, by which he had declared the love of women as also injurious to the voice. When asked why he did this, he answered that some might take offence at it. But the sentence was retained with full consent of the Brethren, and the writing was added as preface to the hymn-book. This was but fair, for who does not know that carnal intercourse stains not only the soul, but also weakens the body, and renders the voice coarse and rough; so that the senses of him must be very blunt who cannot distinguish a virgin from a married woman by her voice. Much concerning the fall of man can be explained from the voice. It is a well-known fact that the voices of nearly all people are too low, and this occasions the sinking of the voice in church-songs. On the contrary, it cannot be explained how the voices of friars who keep their vows change for the better; he who in his youth was a skillful bass singer, may become an excellent tenor singer in his old age.

But he also added to the things necessary to be observed in united song, that godly virtue must be at the source of our whole walk, because by it you obtain favor with the spirit of singing, which is the Holy Spirit. It has been observed that the least dissension of spirit in a choir of singers has brought confusion into the whole concert. The singing-schools began with the Sisters, lasted four hours, and ended at midnight. Both master and scholars appeared in white habits, which made a singular procession,

on which account people of quality frequently visited the
school. The Superintendent, animated by the spirit of
eternity, kept the school in great strictness and every
fault was sharply censured. The whole neighborhood,
however, was touched by the sound of this heavenly music, a
prelude of a new world and a wonder to the neighbors. But
it soon appeared what God intended with this school.
Afflictions were aimed at, and these were plentifully
imposed upon both sexes, in so far that a lesson seldom
ended without tears; although within the Brethren the
essence of wrath was stirred. And though strange scenes
occurred, no one ventured to check the Superintendent, for
so far everyone believed that he acted as God's commis-
sioner, until at last Samuel Eckerlin, one of his principal
adherents, when required to submit to the rules, left the
school, whereby he fell under the hatred of the Brethren,
and his spiritual growth faded in consequence of it.

The Superintendent conducted the school with great
sternness, so that whoever did not know him, might have
thought him to be a man of unchecked passions. At times he
scolded for one or two hours in succession, especially when
he saw that they were under a ban, and at such times he
looked really majestic, so that even his countenance
glistened. When the Sisters saw that a continual quarreling
was going on in their school, they took counsel among
themselves to find out the cause of this quarreling, and
came at last to the conclusion that it must be in the
difference of sex, and, therefore, determined to give up the
school. But they were greatly mistaken in the cause. It
was the very opposite. For God assigned to him a dangerous
post, where many a saint had already lost his crown; besides
some had even tried to cut off his locks, and who knows
whether some such people were not among his choir. Meanwhile
they sent a Sister, Tabea by name, who was bold enough for
such a mission, to inform the Superintendent that they

would break off all connection with the school entirely. Thereupon the Superintendent asked them, whether they would free him of all responsibility before God, to which they answered "Yes." Thus was the spiritual union between the Superintendent and the Sisters sundered by this imprudent counsel, and he entirely withdrew his favor from their house.

About this time a young man, named Daniel Scheibly, was bought from a ship by the Brethren, and because he was of good manners, they extended to him the right hand of Brotherhood. Because the above mentioned Sister Tabea had thrown off the yoke of Christ and was become a freed woman, she incautiously engaged in a secret correspondence with this young man, and at last promised to marry him. Such an uncommon thing in the Settlement soon became rumored abroad. A conference was held about it, and she was asked by the Brethren why she had seduced their servant, and they demanded back the money they had expended for him; but at last they came to an amicable settlement for conscience sake, and relieved her of the debt. Finally the time of their marriage arrived. One of the house-fathers was to officiate; then, while she stood before him in the dress of a matron, having laid aside the habit of the Order, and the moment had arrived for them to be united, the Superintendent called her apart, and took her again under his protection; whereupon she dismissd her bridegroom and again entered the Sisters' House. To atone for the scandal she had caused she shed many tears of fervent repentance, by which she washed off the stain from her habit, wherefore also her name Tabea was changed to Anastasia, which means "One risen from the dead." Her bridegroom, however, left the Order, and fell back into the world.

The example of this Sister influenced the others again to submit to the guardianship of the Superintendent, so that the school was re-commenced. Soon after a choir of Sisters appeared in the meeting, and sang the hymn, "God, we come to meet Thee," with five voices, which was so well received in the Settlement, that everyone had his name entered for the choir, so that one did not know who should perform the outside work. But this heavenly art also soon found its enviers, for one of the house-fathers publicly testified and wrote against it, but the Brethren reprimanded him and said: The wisdom of God had ordered this school to their sanctification, they had sweated in it and endured school discipline, therefore they would not permit a stranger to interfere. After the Superintendent had with much trouble broken the ice, and taught the first principles of singing to the scholars, he divided them into five choirs with five persons to each choir, namely, one air, one tenor, one alto, and two bass singers. The Sisters were divided into three choirs, the upper, middle and lower; and in the choruses a sign was made for each choir, when to be silent and when to join in the singing. These three choirs had their separate seats at the table of the Sisters during love-feasts, the upper choir at the upper end, the middle at the middle, and the lower at the lower end; in singing antiphonally, therefore, the singing went alternately up and down the table. Not only had each choir to observe its time when to join in, but, because there were solos in each chorale, every voice knew when to keep silent, all of which was most attentively observed. And now the reason appeared which induced him to establish such choirs of virgins. It was with him as with Solomon, he was zealous to make manifest the wonderful harmony of eternity, in a country which but lately wild savages had inhabited; for God owed this to North America as an initiation into the Christian church, therefore these choirs belong to the firstlings of America. The contents of these songs were entirely prophetic, and treated of the restoration of the image of Adam before his division, of the heavenly virginity, the priesthood of

Melchizedek, etc. The gift of prophecy overflowed the Settlement like a river at that time; and close observation showed that the beautiful sun of Paradise had then already reached its meridian, but afterwards inclined towards it setting, and was at last followed by a sorrowful night, as will be shown in its place. This wonderful harmony resounded over the country; whoever heard of it, wished to see it, and whoever saw it, acknowledged that God truly lived among these people.

And now let us tell for the information of those who are versed in this art, how he explained the first principles of singing so simply that even a child could understand them; therefore he did not care for the artificial terms of the masters, which rather obscure than enlighten the art. Accordingly, whenever he took a hymn in hand, in order to compose a tune to it, he was careful to represent the spirit of the hymn by the tune; then after he had composed a choral-song, he fixed the metre, not according to custom, but as the nature of the thing required it. He, however, soon found out that some of the melodies were very strained, and that notes occurred which did not belong there. Thus he discovered the key, for every key has its own peculiarity, and adopts only such notes as are natural to it, and this is the reason why the melodies of Lobwasser have a stained sound, because the key to them was not understood, and notes were thus used which were not suitable. In order that he might not make mistakes in composing, he had for each key certain dominant notes, commonly four to the octave, which he called rulers, but the three other notes, servants. Thus in the f tunes, f, a, c, f, are the rulers, but g, b, d, the servants, and although it sounds ill if a servant is made ruler, the composer, nevertheless, must know when it is proper to swerve into another key. This gives a very charming variation to the song, provided it resolves itself again into the original key before the end. The Superinten-

dent was a master in this, but his scholars suspected that
he had done it in order to find a cause for fault-finding
with them; for as soon as they changed to another key their
voices fell into disorder.

When he attempted to compose the bass and middle-voices
he encountered new difficulties, for you must know that vo-
cal music, as well as *mathesis*, have their unalterable first
principles, which angels even observe in their song. These
he did not know, neither was he able, like masters in
music, to find the concordance by means of instruments; at
last he invented certain schedules, a special one for each
key, in which he laid down the proportion between the
soprano and the other voices, whereby composition was
greatly facilitated. For instance, in the key of *f*, the *f*
in the soprano corresponds to *a* in the tenor, and *c* in the
alto; the bass, however, has the octave of the middle
voices. All his tunes have two basses; but he also composed
some for six voices, and even for seven, namely, two soprano, one alto, two tenor, and two bass; for that purpose,
however, he after all had to use two octaves. His last work,
by many masters declared the most important, were the
choral-songs. They were brought to light, partly printed,
partly written, Anno 1754, under the title: " Paradisisches
Wunderspiel, Paradisiacal Wonder Music," which in these
latter times and days became prominent in the occidental
parts of the world as a prevision of the New World, consisting of an entirely new and uncommon manner of singing, arranged in accord with the angelic and heavenly choirs. Herein the song of Moses and the Lamb, also the Song of Solomon,
and other witnesses out of the Bible and from other saints,
are brought into sweet harmony. Everything is arranged with
much labor and great trouble, after the manner of singing of
the angelic choirs, by a Peaceful one [Friedsam, i.e.
Beissel] who desires no other name or title in this world."

It is reported that the angels singing antiphonally

appeared in a vision to St. Ignatius, and thus their methods found their way into the church. It is possible that in former ages they were more in use in the convents; now but little is known of them. Yet one of these tune-books came over the ocean, and we are informed that, being engraved on copper, it was printed at Augsburg; but we cannot answer for it. When already half the Settlement was burdened with this work, the house-fathers, too, came to engage in the wonderful music, for the powers of eternity, which were embodied in it, had such an effect that whoever heard the song was forcibly attracted by the goodness of God. Some time during the night was fixed for the school-hour, and two Brethren were appointed teachers; but they showed such diligence in the school during winter that they neglected their domestic duties, which rendered it necessary to close the school. But the Superintendent, in consideration of the fact that such gray heads had paid so much honor to the work of God, in so far that they suffered themselves to be children again, had a music book for four voices written for them, which he presented to their Community. Their veneration for this music was so great that everyone wished to possess the book, and whoever had it accordingly fell under judgment, as happened yonder with the ark of the covenant. The book thus wandered from house to house, till at last nobody wished to have anything to do with it.

After the Superintendent had accomplished such an important work for the benefit of the spiritual Order in Ephrata, it was resolved, at a general council, that both convents present him with a worthy reward as a testimonial of filial esteem. This was to consist of two complete music books, furnished for all voices, one of which was to be made by the society of the Brethren, the other by that of the Sisters. Both parties put their most skillful members to the task. On the part of the Brethren three of them worked at it for three-quarters of a year. It contained about 500

tunes for five voices; everything was artistically
ornamented with the pen, and every leaf had its own
head-piece. The Superintendent's name stood in front,
skillfully designed in Gothic text; around it was a text of
blessing added by each Brother. The work of the Sisters was
not less remarkable. It was artless and simple, but
something wonderful shone forth from it, for which no name
can be found.

These two books were reverently presented to him, and
the Brother deputed thereto thanked him in the name of the
whole Brotherhood for his faithfulness and care. He
accepted their present graciously, and promised to remember
them in his prayers. There were some instances when the
Superintendent showed himself to be a great man, and this
was one of them. Many might object that he was ambitious,
but those who know him more intimately, know how far he was
from it. But the fact is, he was to make manifest the
manners of the New World among his followers, and how
everyone must esteem his neighbor higher than himself; and
herein did his disciples faithfully follow him, according to
the simplicity of those times

Before we conclude this chapter, let us mention the
writing-school, where the writing in ornamental Gothic text
was done, and which was chiefly instituted for the benefit
of those who had no musical talents. The outlines of the
letters he himself designed, but the shading of them was
left to the scholar, in order to exercise himself in it.
But none was permitted to borrow a design anywhere, for he
said: "We dare not borrow from each other, because the
power to produce rests within everybody." Many Solitary
spent days and years in these schools, which also served
them as a means of sanctification to crucify their flesh.
The writings were hung up in the chapels as ornaments, or
distributed to admirers.

The Community at Ephrata is Extended by an Awakening,

for Which Two Brethren of the Baptist Congregation,

George Adam Martin and John Horn, Prepared the Way

This awakening took place during the above-mentioned war, and may have commenced about the year 1757. The members of this awakening, as well as their teacher, George Adam Martin, before this belonged to the Baptists, but left that congregation, induced by circumstances which had their first start with the said George Adam Martin. The causes of this separation are too outrageous to call for a special investigation here, and besides it is not permitted to trouble the reader with the like of it at this place. But because the said George Adam Martin handed in a writing, in which he minutely described how he was awakened, and how he had lived for a time with the Baptists, but at last united himself with the Community at Ephrata, we will give an extract from it, and then leave it to the consideration of the reader. This document is the answer to the question of a friend, why he had separated from the Baptists and gone over to the Seventh Day Saints. He speaks thus of his conversion: In the year 1733 I was strongly moved to repentance and a change of life, and all without any man's intervention, which confused me so that I did not know what to do. For my heart was troubled. Wherever I went or was my conscience was so disturbed that I avoided all company and felt grieved at any vanity I met with. I was constantly

frightened and alarmed, for my conscience smote me everywhere; besides I was young, bashful and timid. I therefore
went about like a lost sheep, and thought all people better
than myself, which opinion indeed I still have. I never
looked for much from men, and if I occasionally listened to
some one preaching, I was not frightened by it, because I
felt myself more damned than any preacher could damn me;
nevertheless some little hope remained, and I thought
perchance I might yet be saved. Being in such a condition I
was baptized on my faith in the year 1735. This I did to
honor God in Christ Jesus and intended to follow him; but
had no further thought about the piety of a Community,
because my inner troubled state did not permit me to think
about other things. All my thinking and striving were only
as to how I might enter the kingdom of God.

      After my baptism, when alone in the woods, I knelt down
behind a tree and prayed. After I had finished it came into
my mind to open the New Testament, and whatever I found
under my right thumb that should be my precept during life.
Then I turned up: "Study to show thyself approved unto God,
a workman that needeth not to be ashamed, rightly dividing
the word of truth" (II TIMOTHY, II, 15). This troubled my
mind excessively; sometimes I took it to be a temptation;
then, again, as if I had tempted God; and again that the
Spirit had mocked me. Taking all together I did not know
what to make of it. To become a workman in the church of
God, that I dared not harbor in my mind. Soon after I was
led into such temptation for about sixteen weeks that I
incessantly heard nothing but: "You are damned! you are
damned!" This frightened me so that I enjoyed neither
sleep, nor eating or drinking. My father asked me what was
the matter with me, but I dared not tell him, for I thought
that never before had a person lived on earth in such a
damnable state. At last I was delivered out of this
bondage, received pardon, and became a recipient of the

gracious visitation of my God in Christ Jesus, and of the power of regeneration, of which before I had known nothing. Thus by grace and compassion alone I became one of the redeemed of the Lord. After this I became cheerful and joyous in my Saviour, Jesus Christ, diligently read the Bible, exercised myself in prayer, took pleasure in divine things, and meddled with nothing but what concerned my salvation; besides I held the Brethren in high esteem and had a sacred regard for everything good.

It happened in the year 1737 that my Superintendent was called upon to go to the great Swamp, in order to baptize several persons. When he announced this at the meeting and asked who was willing to go with him, I was willing to go. After our arrival, when the meeting was over, the persons to be baptized were introduced, and a passage from Luke XIV was read to them, about the building of towers and waging war, which also was customary among them even in Germany; for when I was baptized this surprised me, and I did not know what to think of it. It was done as often as persons were to be baptized; so that you did not know whether you were to build or not, to go to war or not, or whether God had 10,000 and the devil 20,000 men. As soon as you came to the water the hymn was usually sung: "Count the cost says Jesus Christ when the foundation Thou wouldst lay," etc. which A[lexander] M[ack] had composed already in Germany. When these confused transactions were now also enacted here, as was customary, it suddenly seized me so that my limbs trembled, and it flashed like a flame through my whole being, and before I knew it I heard myself speaking in an overloud voice. I was frightened at myself, for I thought of nothing less than of speaking. I said that it was not the Lord Jesus' intention to bring such things before candidates for baptism, for their purpose was to enter into their covenant with God by baptism, and to build upon the rock Jesus Christ; those who wished to build a tower besides

the temple of God might have such things brought before
them. This speech frightened everybody, and all were silent
and dumb. At last our Superintendent, M[artin] U[rner] of
blessed memory, said, "What shall we do then, for something
must be said to the people." Without taking thought I answered: "The 18th Chapter of Matthew, about exhortation and
punishment, might be read;" which proposal was adopted from
that hour, and is still customary with them to this day.

This was the first stumbling block I found in their
doctrine. But because they adopted my suggestion throughout
the whole country, and no person moved against me, but all
were surprised and thought that this movement on the part of
a young man which they saw and heard was the work of the
Spirit of God, I greatly honored them, since they in so
childlike a way gave all the honor to God. Moreover they
now noticed me more, especially did my Superintendent love
me until he died, and he was much grieved when he had to
lose me. But I did not respect the household of the
Congregation, and nothing of the kind touched me; but I was
earnest in my calling to gain favor before God by my life
and behavior. I took no offence at any person, nor did I
seek their esteem; I only endeavored to follow the dictates
of my conscience. But it happened by and by that they,
contrary to my wish, chose me as their Superintendent, after
I had already obediently moved across the waters of the
Susquehanna. Before this occurred it happened that Count
Zinzendorf and many of his Brethren came into the country
and occasioned a great stir, especially by his conferences.
And because all denominations were invited to them, I too
was deputed by my Superintendent to attend them. When I
arrived at the conference, which was held at Oley, I found
there some of our Baptists, Seventh Day men, Mennonites and
Separatists. The Count himself was president, and for three
days I heard queer and wonderful things there. After my
return home I went to my Superintendent and said that I

looked upon the Count's conferences as snares, for the purpose of bringing simple-minded and inexperienced converts back to infant baptism and church-going, and of erecting the old Babel again. We consulted with each other what to do, and agreed to get ahead of the danger, as some Baptists had already been smitten with this vain doctrine, and to hold a yearly conference, or as we called it, a Great Assembly, and fixed at once the time and place. This is the beginning and foundation of the Great Assemblies of the Baptists.

After this general meeting had been established, the opportunity was offered to speak of various matters whenever we met, and since most of the Baptists who had laid the foundation of their Congregation in Schwarzenau, were uneducated arch-idiots and ignoramuses, their followers, of course, brought their absurd notions also to this meeting, always appealing to their predecessors, saying the old Brethren in Germany did so, and we must not depart from their ways.

When I heard this I contradicted them, which occasionally gave rise to disputes, in which I always had P[eter] B[ecker] and M[artin] U[rner] and most of the common people on my side. But among other things something once occurred which appeared to me to be heretical, for when A[braham] D[ubois], who still was one of the first, once said that our old Brother A.M. had believed the same, I was at once aflame and boldly contradicted it. But another Brother, M[ichael] Frantz took the affair out of my hands and said: "If it had not been for this I should not have joined the Brethren." To this I answered: "Then you have a poor reason for your change of religion." Meanwhile ears were pricked up and the matter was talked about, and I said I did not know how Christ Jesus could call himself a son of man if he had not taken upon himself something from the Virgin consecrated for this purpose, for it was evident that she never had known a man. Then M.F. answered that he had not received more from the Virgin than a wanderer who passes through a town receives from the town; or than a ball which passes through a gun, or the water which runs through a pipe. I was frightened at such an expression. M.U. sat alongside of me and said: "May God protect us against this!" But he whispered into my ear: "Speak out against this, it is heretical; do not spare it." I then said that if it were as they said it would have been all the same whether the Virgin was holy or not; a wanton might then as well have given birth to him since he received nothing from her, which is blasphemous to think and far more to say. This frightened them so that they left off defending this thing; the dispute, nevertheless, lasted two days before this Mohammedan Goliath was slain. It may be thought that I have deviated too far from my reasons why I left the Baptists; but no, these are the very reasons, for I took offense at the foundation and origin, because the originators deviated from their aim and basis, which in my opinion is the love of God towards all men, and formed a sect, like the Inspired, out of the great awakening which had taken hold of them in Germany, and aroused strife and hatred by their disputes. This George Gräben told them to their faces, and especially to A.M., at a public meeting in Holland, being inspired to it, saying: "You and all of you are dead, and have died to the life of God;" all which was listened to by W[illiam] K[ebinger] who had just been liberated out of the prison in Gülch, where he had been incarcerated for the sake of the truth; he told me all this. At the very commencement they adopted needless restrictions, in that they did not allow any one who was not baptized to partake with them of the Holy Sacrament. Had they not been so sectarian in this matter, and been more given to impartial love, they would have found entrance to more souls in their great awakening and largely promoted the glory of God. But, instead, sectarianism, quarrelsomeness and discord spread through their whole awakening in Germany as far as to Switzerland. Therefore, also, the incomparable teacher, J[ohn] N[aas] separated from them, and stood alone, until he went to America and arrived in Philadelphia, to which place A.M. went to meet him, and entreated him for God's sake to forget and forgive what had happened in Europe; to which the same agreed. A.M. by his diligence also prevented the above mentioned J.N. from coming to Ephrata at the time of the awakening, otherwise he would have been a victim of it too, for his testimony concerning the renunciation of the world was as similar to the testimony in Ephrata as one drop of water is to another. He afterwards moved to Amwell, in New Jersey, and superintended the Community there. I visited him there several times, and was much edified by his conversation, and pleased and surprised at his great and sound mind and the gifts which God had bestowed on him. I might here mention many things which he made known to me. He told me that A.M. had been an honest and faithful man, but that he lacked enlightenment. Perhaps this was because they had fallen out with each other about the incarnation of Jesus Christ. He said to my face, "You will not agree with these people," meaning the Baptists; "either they will reject you, or you them, for a truly converted man cannot live with them; and I," he added, "should I live another year, shall again withdraw from them." But he died within that very year, and is buried in Amwell, among the twenty children, all of whom lie buried around him.

With Christian Libe, who also was a preacher among them, strange things likewise happened. He was taken prisoner in Basle, where he was engaged in divine afairs, and was sold into the galleys, but ransomed after two years. At last he settled in Creyfeld, where he and the above-mentioned J.N. superintended the Community, until they at last had a fall-out, because J.N. called him a pill-monger publicly before the whole Congregation, and then left.

But Christian Libe tried to continue the Congregation, although everything wasted under their hands; the Brethren who had been prisoners withdrew, the whole Cogregation was given up, and everything went to ruin. He himself became a merchant, and even at last a wine merchant, and married out of the Congregation, against their own rules, and not a branch is left of their Baptist business in all Europe. Such matters, and many others not mentioned, prove to me that their fundamental principles cannot endure before God and the world; for they neither know, nor are they able to conduct the office of the new covenant, because they have no true knowledge of salvation, nor of the righteousness which avails before God, and is reckoned to us as faith; but they want to force and perfect everything through righteousness, by punishing, condemning and avoiding, which is not according to the new covenant, but the letter of the law, consisting of commandments and laws.

If God had not spared a branch of the root of Hochmann from Hochenau, the whole brood would have died at birth, like the Baptists of Munster. This innocent branch was P.B., who was a spiritual son of Hochmann, but was baptized, and came to live at Creyfeld, where he energetically exercised the gifts he had received from God, in singing and fervent praying, to the benefit of the Congregation; although he was otherwise no orator, but led a quiet life. Soon after he had to experience what he had not expected, for his spiritual Father had taught him peace and love; but here he heard much quarreling and strife, which soon deeply grieved him. It happened that a young Brother, Häcker by name, who had studied, and who was full of love and an intimate friend of the said P.B., wanted to marry the daughter of a merchant, who also had been baptized into the Congregation, but still served the Mennonites as preacher, because they did not wish to lose him, and gave him a yearly salary of 800 Gulden. This man was glad for such a son-in-law, and married them with great pleasure, not thinking that it would produce such a great excitement in the Congregation. But when the affair became known the tumult in the Congregation became so great that Christian Libe, the second teacher, and with him four single Brethren, rose up against it and excommunicated said Häcker, though J.N. and the Congregation wished only to suspend him from bread-breaking. This godless excommunication ruined the whole Congregation in the town of Creyfeld. I heard the blessed teacher, J.N. say that more than 100 persons in Creyfeld had been convinced in favor of the new baptism, but on account of this ban everything was ruined and killed. And since no Moses was there, who might have sent Aaron with the censer, the fire of the ban burned on and consumed the whole Congregation, which still pains my heart whenever I think of it. But it touched poor Häcker most, who took all the blame on himself. The spirits took possession of him so that he fell sick and died of consumption; as they were converted people they were able to accomplish something. His good friend P.B., however, was with him in his utmost need, up to his death.

After this P.B. concluded to move to Pennsylvania, and when this became known several others moved with him; but the spirit of discord and ban also moved with them, and so wounded and corrupted them on the other side of the ocean, that they could hardly be cured in America. But God, nevertheless, took care of this branch, that it should bear fruit from the root, and brought it about that the German ban-branches were broken off, in order that this branch might have room to grow, and at last it blossomed and bore fruit in America, as in a garden of God. But the dear soul, P.B., could not attain his object, for the wild Baptist ban-branches always tried to paint a European shadow before his eyes; so that he died having fellowship with hardly anyone, for none of them understood his nature. Now I return to our yearly meeting, at which the European ban-branch continually became a topic of conversation, so that you always had to contend with these quarrels, until A.D. and M.F. at last died. Then other and thinner branches came forth, with which it was still more difficult to deal, until at last they put me out. Then I thought the affair would end, but it only commenced in earnest; for as quiet as ever I kept they let me have no peace. I was heartily tired of their affairs. Some, however, still adhered to me and could not leave me. They also were suspected and were avoided on my account, for whoever would not ban me himself had to be banned.

Now I became puzzled, for the wild European ban-branches threw such a shade, mist, darkness and gloom over the eyes of my mind that I could not see the light of the sun in the Gospel. I still lay buried under the hellish ban-doctrine, and my conflict was very great, for I was even afraid to doubt the ban-doctrine. In Germany I should willingly have entered the highest classes of the high schools, but here I had to attend high school against my will, had to learn the language of Canaan, and to begin with A. This, indeed, appeared very strange to me, because nearly everybody who knew me considered me a great doctor of Holy Writ. There I lay under a heavy rod, severely beaten both by God and men, for the treacherous dealt treacherously with me and I was so lean. (Is. 24:16.) For the justice of God pursued me and all the good in me was turned into evil, because I had taken it as my own. Here my earnestness was turned into hypocrisy, my singing and praying into boast-fulness, my preaching into vanity, my journeying and visiting into an outrunning of God before He had sent me. My friendliness was dissimulation, my weeping and my tears a sectarian longing, my conversation with men on religious subjects a fraud, my piety a mere show, my reading and my studies a prying art, my desire to convert men a rebellion against God. For the cursers cursed me (namely, the old Baptists), and those who are ready to awaken the Leviathan (Job 3:8); for whoso banneth he curseth. Here I had to learn the language of Canaan, willing or not willing, like Balaam, who, whether he wished or not, was compelled to bless and could not help it, however much he wished to curse. (Num. 23:20.) Here, then, God severed all fellowship of my conscience with the European ban-teachers and showed me how their foundation was laid in cursing and blessing. For, if a person does not wish to be blessed by them, they curse him like those who curse and who awaken the Leviathan, and they rejoice in the ruin of such people and say that that is the judgment of God (see A.M.'s little book, pages 107, 108, 109; also the answer to Gruber's twenty-second question), at which talk any one instructed by God should verily grieve in his heart. May God preserve mine and everybody's heart from such a doctrine, because it is so far removed from the doctrine of Christ, which teaches: "Love your enemies; bless them that curse you!" May God, the Almighty, have mercy.

Therefore I believe that the European Baptists have no business in America, but that they escaped hither as fugitives from the Spirit of God, which would not allow them to build their nest in Germany, because they were corrupt in their principles; for without knowing it they had been cheated by the spirit of Balaam, who rode and struck the she-ass before he was sent. (Num. 22.) I further believe that it would have been better for the American awakenings if they had never come to America; but flight is permitted in the Old and New Testaments. However, had they fought out their fight in Europe, since they were there awakened, it would have been more to their honor. For although I disagree with their fundamental principles in time and eternity (except baptism, the Lord's supper and the rite of feetwashing), I nevertheless respect them before God, but especially A.M., a man who suffered much for God, in spite of the great and grave errors which he had, like many of the saints; for a man who with his congregation leaves his inherited religion, leaves Babel and Egypt, experiences what one who is no leader cannot experience, as did Moses, John Huss, Martin Luther, Ulric Zwingli, Menno Simon, Count Zinzendorf, Conrad Beissel, etc.

There never was a false prophet, who had not also some truth.

There never was a godless person, who had not before been converted.

There never has been an accuser of his brother, or a despiser of his mother's son, who has not had the covenant of God on his lips and proclaimed the laws of God.

There never was one who cursed, who had not before known how to bless.

There never went a person astray, who had not before been on the right way.

There never was a liar, who did not before fall from the truth.

There never was an enemy, who was not a friend before.

There never was one who recognized the truth, before he recognized the lies in himself.

Now I will briefly answer a second question: How and why I might have joined the Seventh Day Baptists? Although you might as well have asked: How and why I might have joined the children of God? For my Congregation is the largest of all, since I am at one with all who belong to the kindom of God. (Matt. 12:50). But I must begin my narrative at the beginning. On my account nearly sixty souls were banished (a likeness to John 9:22), because they would not believe in lies, nor follow the envy of their preachers; therefore we formed a Congregation. However I continued to preach as before, and there was great commotion throughout almost the whole land, so that I was in demand at

Conestoga, Philadelphia, Germantown, Conewago, Monocacy, as far as Virginia. And although I kept up fellowship with all unsectarian souls, I, nevertheless, was most intimate with my own trusty Brethren and Sisters. About this time Brother Frederick Fuhrman held a love-feast, to which all this little flock gathered and some were baptized; this was the first love-feast. But the Congregation increased in membership by baptism, so that during a journey of four weeks twenty-six were baptized and twelve love-feasts held. But as the affair progressed it happened that I was expected at Conestoga. I, therefore, got ready, and three Brethren with me. I long before had intended to see the Brethren at Ephrata. When we arrived at Lititz I sent two of my Brethren by another way to those who expected me, to announce to them that I was there, and if they wished to have a meeting held the said Brethren should come to Ephrata before the meeting and notify us. I and my Brother, John Horn, however, with staff in hand, went direct towards Ephrata. Following the road we first arrived at the Sisters' household, though we did not know who lived there. We went to a worthy matron and asked where Friedsam lived. She showed us the way. We went straight to it and knocked, when old Nägele came out and asked where these men came from. I answered that we came from far, for I did not wish them at once to know who we were, for they know my name but not my person. Then he said: "Come in then," and opened the door. The old Father reverently rose and received us with a kiss, and the others did the same, for he had visitors at the time. Then he made us sit behind the table, he sitting before it, and said: "Where do these dear men come from?" I answered: "We come from far" (for I restrained myself). He asked: "But from where?" I said: "From Canecots-chicken." He said: "Then you know George Adam?" I answered: "Yes, we know him well." He spoke: "Ah, how is he?" I said: "As you see," for I could no longer hold back

"Ah," he said to this, "are you George Adam? here lies the letter which you wrote; we were just speaking about you when you knocked." We continued the conversation, and nothing was said on either side to which we both did not agree.

While conversing thus animatedly, a Sister entered, brought a tub of water and an apron, put them down and silently left; who she was, and who had ordered her to do so, I do not know even to this very hour. The old Father rose and said: "Come Brethren, sit down here, I will wash your feet." So he washed our feet, and Brother Nägele dried them for us. Then I said: "You have washed our feet, now let us also wash yours," to which they consented; so I washed their feet, and Brother Horn dried them. When this was done, he said, "Let us go into the Sisters' house." I said I should like also to visit my old pastor M. and Brother Obed. He said that could also be done, but desired that we first should go to the Sisters' house. We went there, and they prepared a splendid meal for us, during which we all the time continued our conversation; but nothing was said on which we did not agree. After this we ascended the hill where Brother Obed lived. On the way up he said to me, "God has done this, that you had to come to us, for with us everything lies prostrate, and we have for years been unable to hold any meetings; I hope you have come to raise up again the fallen down hut." I was surprised at this candor, and thought perhaps there was some trick behind it. But I afterwards learned that it was sincerity, and through all my life until his death, I never heard of un-faithfulness in him.

When we arrived there, and had welcomed each other, he said, "How do you do, Brother Obed? How about heaven?" Such speech continued and all was harmony, which pleased my Brother Horn so much that he afterwards remarked: "You will not bring me away from these people again, do what you please;" which I heard with pleasure. At the close of the visit the old Father asked whether we would not like to visit the Sisters? I said we had no time now, we expected two other Brethren who had left us at Lititz, who were to inform us where and when the meeting was to be held. "Why, do you know what," he said, "I will make them assemble in their prayer-hall, so that you can see them all; it is also desired that you should make an address to them;" and this it was resolved to do. After this we visited our old pastor Miller, who reverently received us, and met us with all the modesty becoming an honorable man. In the course of conversation I asked him whether he did not still owe something to the R. He said, "I no longer have a drop of blood in me that is R----d." I said, "That is not what I ask." "Oh!" he said, "I understand; not only to the R----d but to all men, whatever I have and can;" which pleased me.

Meanwhile it was some time before our two Brethren arrived, and reported how it was to be. At the same time news arrived that the old Father and the Sisters had assembled in their prayer-hall, and were waiting for us. Since our number of visitors was now again complete, we were all conducted thither by the old Brother Eleazar, and were shown to our seats. An inward emotion here seized me; my spirit felt the presence of a divine majesty; the veil was removed, in which all the nations are enveloped. I saw the pathway of the saints into the holy of holies; the spirits kissed each other in stillness, and a divine, holy, mutual, and profound unity was entered into without a word, voice, utterance, or speech, for there reigned silence for a long time as if no person were there. Smell, taste, feeling, even seeing and hearing, all were one, just as I have seen two small flocks of sheep unite in which there were no rams.

At last my spirit was called back again. My eyes were full of tears when the Sisters began to sing a hymn, as well as I remember: "The streets of Zion are desolate;" which brought tears to many eyes. After this was finished, I spoke: "You sang a hymn for us, let us now also sing one for you." Then we sang the "Song of the Lilies," but as it had escaped my memory, I asked Brother Horn for the words, and he told them to me; then we sang it to the end, which simplicity astonished the Sisters. After quiet was restored, I made a short address, although I felt no particular inclination to speak. I had various impressions from the spirit of prophecy, but since our time was limited we had to accommodate ourselves to it. Thus everything passed most pleasantly. A fellowship was formed, and the unity of spirits concluded without a word, without conditions, without questioning as to how or when, without care, without labor, without fear, without distrust, without consideration; in love, with love, through love, out of love, and for eternal love; and neither world nor time, neither flesh nor blood, neither friend nor foe, neither the present nor the future, neither fear nor death, neither devil nor hell can break it, for Two became One, and were One before they knew it. And thus it is with all who are truly born again; for they are children, sons and daughters of God Almighty. So far the record.

Such are the particulars of this important union, related by the Brother himself. It must be known, however, that in spite of his banishment he still had a strong following among the Baptists, who were honest people, and began to think that he had been unjustly treated; and who, therefore, were disposed to stake their lives on his innocence. The most prominent of these were John Steiner, John Horn, Peter and Abraham Knipper, Frederick Fuhrman, George Scheitler, Peter Zug, Finck, etc. But the reception of these two Brethren brought about great changes; for, in the first place, these two visiting Brethren were seized with holy wonder when they saw that the union was made in the spirit without any words, as they had thought that articles of agreement would be laid before them. Afterwards the old hatred between the two Communities was again revived on this account, for the reception of Brother G.A., nullified the ban which the former Brethren had laid on him; all of which happened in the prayer-hall of the Sisters, as above mentioned; for there the holy Mother came down from above with the oil of anointing, and healed his wounds; wherefore he was often heard to say: "Rejoice with me, for I have found the piece which I had lost." It appears that the Superintendent had received, as a trust from God, a blessing for the B---- Community, of which they would have become partakers had they humbled themselves; for he was the greatest stumbling-stone which their Community ever encountered. But because they failed to endure the test, the choice fell upon another. For we must concede to this Brother the honor that he was the first among them, who arrived at a holy harmony and yet remained a Baptist. For all of this people who had joined the Community before him, sent their letters of withdrawal to their people, but Brother G.A., above spoken of, was faithful to their statutes, and neither a second baptism, nor the Sabbath, nor any of the various other ordinances of the Community, were urged upon him. Therefore it was ordained by God that Brother G.A. was to earn the blessing, which their whole Community might have had; and the Superintendent once addressed the following impressive words to him: "You shall be blessed, and also remain blessed." When, shortly before his death, he once more visited the Superintendent, the latter said to him: "My salvation rests in your hands." All this created an extraordinary esteem for the Superintendent in this good Brother, and all the letters he wrote to him were full of special expressions of love, while the superscription sometimes contained the title: Pontifex Maximus.

Some of the Baptists who saw a little further, expected that the Superintendent's bearing towards this man would subdue him sooner than all their bans; but in the Community

in and around Ephrata he occasioned great excitement, especially in the households. For up to this time the priestly
office had been in the hands of one of the Solitary, but now
the domestic household also wished to have part in it, which
brought with it such temptations, that one housefather,
J[ohn] S[enseman] declared on his death-bed that this
Brother would be the cause of the Community's destruction.
But because the Superintendent was the first to condescend
to him, there was no help, everybody had to follow suit; and
if any one had not done so, judgment would have come upon
him, so that he would not have dared to lift up his hands
towards God. All this was not unknown to the said Brother,
therefore he once declared that all the good in Ephrata
rested in his hands. After the visit was now concluded with
blessing, the Superintendent dismissed them with letters of
recommendation to the Brethren at the Bermudian. Soon
after, moreover, he sent two of the oldest Brethren,
Jehoiada and Lamech, to the Brethren at the Bermudian, and
expressed himself in the following manner, namely, that they
should receive Brother G.A. as if it were himself. This
was saying as much as that they should take him as their
priest, which greatly troubled them, so that they protested
that their priests lived in Ephrata. A venerable
house-sister was even seized with a fatal sickness on that
account, of which she died; it happened to her like to the
wife of the son of the priest Eli, who, when in labor, was
more concerned for the glory of God, than for her own child,
and said: "The glory of Israel is taken captive," (I Sam.
4:19.) But after they had learned to submit to God's
wonderful guidance they became one Community, for before
this they lay under suspicion, because most of those who had
moved away from the Community at Ephrata had done so for
improper reasons. If you wish to build churches you must
lay the foundation on the lowliness of Christ, else you
build in the air.

Through this movement a door was opened for a new church-period, during which much important spiritual work was transacted. The Superintendent called the awakening at Antitum from this period on, the Eagle church, after the fourth beast in the Apocalypse; although these good people considered themselves too lowly and unworthy of such a high title; but there was another secret connected with it. The Superintendent, who, during his whole awakened condition, stood in the service of the four beasts, about this time came under the dominion of the Eagle, wherefore the renewal of the Eagle's youth showed itself so much in him that he was entirely pervaded by it during his old age. During his first journey from the Settlement to Antitum he carried all his ecclesiastical vestments with him, because not only the oldest Brethren from Bethany, and the house-fathers, but also the oldest Sisters of Sharon, with their Mother, were his companions. They who beheld the glory of these two flocks of lambs when they united into one at Antitum (and many who saw it must still be alive), will well remember that then their mountains leaped for joy like sheep, and their hills like lambs, at the generation of the celestial Mother, which shall at last take possession of the Kingdom, when the adulterous seed is destroyed from the earth. The Superintendent made this whole journey on foot, except when they forced him to make use of a horse, and then he said: "In this way I cannot be edifying to anyone." In this lively spirit he was seen to travel over mountains and valleys, and no hut was too poor for him to enter with his company. And now the fire of the awakening spread over the whole region of Antitum. Many secretly stole away from their houses and ran after this wonder, for the former Brethren of Brother G.A., in order to put a stop to this awakening, sent two of their Brethren, John Mack and Staub, to all their houses to warn them against being seduced.

During the whole journey the Superintendent gave

strange evidences of his humility and obedience. He never
sat down in a house until the father of the house showed him
a seat, which some observed and remarked: "He is more
strictly led than we." But the circumstances forced him to
this, for he was hired in a vineyard which already had its
husbandmen with whom he might easily have interfered; on
which point also a law was made in the *Jure Canonico*: *Quod
unius ecclesiae unus debeat esse Sacerdos*: that each church
should have but one priest. When it was resolved to hold a
bread-breaking, and a priest was required for it, his
humility taught him to make room for Brother G.A., who, in
consequence presided, though their love-feasts were at the
time still held in Corinthian fashion, and not in the manner
in which they were held at Ephrata. Soon after another
breaking of bread was held, the administration of which they
conferred on the Superintendent, which he promised to undertake on condition that they would permit him to break in the
manner in which he had been taught. To this they would not
agree. They said: "It is strange that you make such a
difference in such small matters;" to which he answered:
"It is also strange that you, to whom I yield in all points,
cannot yield to me in this one point, which my conscience
demands." Then they gave him the permission, and from that
time they celebrated all their love-feasts in the same way
that is customary with the Brethren at Ephrata. The reason
why the Superintendent took offence at their way of breaking
bread was because they were of opinion that all must be
equals; and, therefore, they did not wish to allow any
prerogative or privilege to any one person among them. On
this account some of them were not pleased when the
Superintendent, at a large meeting, held in the house of a
Brother named Joseph Greybühl, while the whole congregation
were on their knees, consecrated this Brother by laying on
of hands, and thus confirmed him in his office. After the
Brethren of Antitum had dismissed the Superintendent and the

other visitors in peace, they went on their homeward journey. The spirit of awakening about this same time caused so much work between Ephrata, Bermudian and Antitum that visitors were continually on the march to and fro, which nourished the mutual love. For the Superintendent had scarcely settled down in his seclusion again when a new visit to Antitum was prepared for, which started six weeks after the first. The Superintendent charged another Brother with it, and ordered some Brethren and Sisters of the Settlement and some of the oldest house-fathers to accompany him. The Superintendent himself was at Antitum three times, and this in his old age, when his task was fast approaching its end. But those at Antitum reciprocated by many a fatiguing journey to Ephrata. For at that time the fire burnt in the Philadelphian church, which each and everyone at Antitum tried to keep up, even at the risk of his earthly possessions. At this time the before-mentioned Brethren, G.A. and H., paid a new visit to the Settlement, in order to see the Superintendent once more, for they expected that he would soon leave his earthly tabernacle. The Superintendent received them with open arms and held a love-feast in their honor. After this the said Brother G.A., accompanied by some of the Fathers and some Sisters from Sharon, paid a visit to Philadelphia, but his companion meanwhile remained quietly in the Settlement; and after their visit was ended in blessing they gave the last kiss of peace to the Superintendent, for they did not see him again after this. Thus they returned in peace to their home. And with this we will conclude the chapter.

Concerning Various Strange Affairs Which Occurred in the Country

About the Same Time, and in Which the Superintendent was Interested

At that time an old Separatist who had been the Superintendent's travelling companion across the ocean, Simon König by name, joined the Community, and thus another opportunity was given the Superintendent by spiritual alms to help an unfortunate, who had failed in his calling, to rise again. The way in which the said König was brought to the Community was quite extraordinary; for he had lived seventy days without any natural food, which produced such a change in his nature that he afterwards could not live in society any more. He published in print his own account of his reception, in which he calls the Ephrata community the most noble in the world, at which his Separatist Brethren took great offence; but it happened to him like the new wine which bursts the new barrels, for the Pentacostal wine had intoxicated him. It is however to be deplored that such a paradisiacal foretaste was followed by such sad consequences; for not long after this he fell under displeasure, and left the community again, which he had extolled to the skies; and although several attempts were made to snatch him out of the fire, everything was in vain, and he passed into eternity during his alienation.

Now we come to the history of the spirits, which took their beginning in Virginia during January, 1761, and were

laid at Ephrata in the following spring; but to understand
it several other circumstances have to be mentioned also.
There were two young married persons in the Community of
Ephrata who were anxious about their eternal welfare; but
because, according to the usage of those times, the wife
entered upon the practice of continence without consent of
her husband, he fell into great temptation, and at last
sinned with a neighboring widow whom he had served in many
ways. Because on this account he lost his fellowship with
the community, he took his children and the said widow with
him to Virginia, and left his first wife in the Community.
After he had three children by the widow, she died, and he
married a person of noble birth, who had just arrived in the
country, and who called herself Henrietta Wilhelmina von
Höning, but who did not bring the best character with her
into the country.

It happened in January, 1761, that as this third wife
of the man mentioned (his name was C.B.), was slumbering, an
old woman appeared to her, who, according to the description
given by her, must have been the above mentioned widow. She
took hold of the arm of said third wife, and placed her on a
chair, and that part of the arm which she had taken hold of
was blue for several days. Then she said to her: "Don't go
away, but remain here with my husband, I am an old woman and
do not mind it; I shall go away again; you are the third and
legitimate wife. And because you are good to my children, I
shall reveal everything to you, for you will not be here
much longer. Go into the kitchen about the twelfth hour;
there behind the tin closet you will find money." Afterwards
she and her husband searched the kitchen and found it there
hidden, in paper money. After this the spirit played a
strange comedy with this person for four weeks, so that she
thought it would cost her her life, as she suddenly spat
half a pint of blood. Every night the spirit revealed some
of the money which the woman had during her lifetime

purloined from her husband, and which was found in the places where she had hidden it. But it appears that the spirit must have been greatly under the influence of a fierce temper, for whenever it was not obeyed, it would tear the clothes from the body of the wife; and that was a common thing. If she rode behind her husband her shoes and stockings were taken off her feet while sitting on the horse. Did she go to a neighbor, it always cost her part of her dress, which was torn; but if she remained at home, there was a continual racket all around the woman. Sometimes all the books were thrown down from the shelf, and hardly was this done when the tea-service followed and was broken to pieces. At length the report of these strange matters spread over the whole country, and a messenger, B. by name, was sent from Winchester to inform himself accurately about the thing. He spent the night there; but during the night the spirit rioted in throwing, knocking and pounding so that the afore-named B. commenced to curse on his couch, which so exasperated the spirit that it dragged the couch on which three persons were lying around the room, though B. resisted with much force. Then the spirit took hold of his arm and tried to twist it, whereupon he cried out in fear: "Lord Jesus, what is this?" Now the spirit fell down upon its knees before him, pushed him back with both its hands, and disappeared.

They several times heard the spirit utter the word Conestoga, at which place they had formerly lived; and because the wife was always seized by the arm by the spirit they interpreted it to be the spirit's meaning that they should go to Conestoga. In this they were not deceived, for as soon as they had resolved on this move two spirits appeared; the last stood behind the first and was quite tall and lean, which made them think it was C.B.'s first wife. Whenever the first said to his wife, "Come!" the second would stand behind and beckon with its hand that they should

come, and behaved very devoutly. After the wish of the
spirit in regard to the journey was divined it plainly told
them the whole affair, namely, that they were to go from
Ephrata to Conestoga; about the twelfth hour of the night
they should enter the great hall over the church, and to
this place Conrad (this was the Superintendent whom the deceased during her lifetime had highly esteemed), Nägele, her
husband, and a Sister who had long ago died (most likely
Anna Eicher), should also come; it and Catharine (the first
wife of said C.B.) would also appear, for they had died
unreconciled with each other. Then the following two hymns
were to be sung: "Oh God and Lord," and "Dearest Father, I
Thy child." After this they should clasp each other's
hands, but she should put her hand on them and say: "Christ
is the reconciliation of us all; may he help you and forgive
you your sins, and wash you with his blood." On this journey to Ephrata it was observed that as often as she tarried
longer than necessary the spirit became uneasy and threw her
shoes towards the door; and in Lancaster it also tore her
clothes in sight of all the people in the tavern.

When they arrived at Ephrata the Superintendent was
away from home on official duties, and of those present none
was inclined to meddle with these things. A Brother, therefore, was sent to him to tell him that his presence was
required in the Settlement. At first he refused and said
there would be a meeting next day, at which he had to be
present. But the night following he received other instruc-
tions and travelled home with the Brethren. He considered
that these people and their important experiences had been
sent to him by God, and as such accepted them. The meeting
was held February 3d; it began at the eleventh hour of the
night and lasted two hours. Besides those three persons
from Virginia, eighteen from Ephrata were present, and among
them those whom the deceased had especially named; but the
chief person with whom the spirit had had to do refused to

be present until she was persuaded to it after much trouble. The meeting was commenced by reading the last chapter of JAMES, and after the first hymn had been sung, all knelt down; but when the spirit was mentioned in the prayer, strange emotion took possession of her, and she was seized by great fear, so that her husband and step-son had to support her. It was noticed at the time that her necker-chief became sprinkled with blood while they were on their knees; there were thirty drops, but where the blood came from did not become evident. This was the only extra-ordinary circumstance that happened at this meeting, for the spirit did not appear according to promise. But when the reconciliation was about to take place, the above mentioned person refused to do anything in the matter, and tried to put the management on others; but she was told that it was her duty, and that none else could do it. At last it was thought advisable that the two daughters of said C.B. (the one by his first wife, who was a member of the Sisterhood, the other by his second wife), should perform the act of reconciliation instead of their mothers. They clasped their hands, and the third wife spoke the above-mentioned words over them; then the exercises closed with prayer.

After this act the spirit did not trouble this person any more. The opinions which were now and then passed on these occurrences we will leave untouched; but as the Superintendent clearly expressed his opinion on them, we will lay it before the friendly reader for further consi-deration; it was as follows:

I cannot help but say a little something about what happened to me last night during my spiritual labor, espe-cially since I expressed myself pretty plainly yesterday. In the first place, yesterday I had a very strange revela-tion to my spirit before the mercy seat, and in my usual manner, in the spirit of the prayer. I went to lie down to sleep at the proper time and woke up again at midnight, as, indeed, is commonly the case. I looked at once for the mercy seat and put my incense on the altar, and it filled my house. After a while I again lay down to rest on my bench, but soon I had to get up again in order to offer incense, so I took my golden censer and made the fire burn high; but myself remained bent low to the earth in prayer and intercession for the oppressed and innocent, and that God might vindicate his great mercy, goodness and compassion towards the innocent, just as he had sought to vindicate his honor on the unrighteous through his righteousness.

After this sacrifice I lay down again to rest, slept for a while, and when I awoke looked around and waited in spirit for my watch-word; when it was told me that we labored in vain about this spirit; that we would be rid of it if the stolen goods were returned to their proper place; not indeed as the spirit had ordered, for then we would become partakers of its sins. For no part of them can be laid on the altar of God; it would not bring honor even to use them as alms, for it is written: "I hate robbery for burnt offering;" and again: Who restoreth to the debtor his pledge and payeth back what he hath robbed. Without this neither sacrifice nor prayer can be pleasing. It was further told me that if it were right, nobody could for conscience sake take away any of the money from the children for whom it was intended, for this would deprive the father of his honor and parental right, and they, the children, would rob themselves of the father's blessing, for it is written: "The father's blessing builds houses for the children, but the mother's wrath plucketh them down."

Now I will speak: It came to my mind, after deep reflection, that N.N. is the first-born child, who in this affair is nearest related to the mother. If now this should be so, then she (of course, if the others agree to it), instead of the mother, should gather up all, and should lay the money away in an unclean place (he meant a secretary) until seven periods had passed, and should give up the mother and try to gain the heart of the father, where thus far she had been a stranger through the mother's fault, and therefore could not fully love the father, which brings upon us the mother's wrath which plucketh down houses. For by such work the kingdom of heaven is not gained; and so likewise, as I understand it, the spirit had not had a hair to give for the kingdom of heaven while it was in its body, and had nothing else to do but to torment innocent hearts, and so assist in the evil design, etc.

If the dear heart, N.N., cannot agree to this as above explained, to give up her mother with her evil doings and try instead to lay hold of the father's heart, which has as it is been sufficiently wronged by the mother, then it may happen that good fortune will not be with her in her future course, for the mother's curse destroys it. Should it, however, come to pass that the money could be disposed of as explained, and the spirit should continue to lay any claim to it, then we must do what we can. I also considered whether the spirit would not have lost its right if the money were only kept at those same places where the deceased had put it.   F., One who Possesses
                              Nothing on the this Earth.

The history and revelations of Catharine Hummer follow now in order of time, and although we may have no right to connect them with this chronicle, especially since they began outside of this Community, they, nevertheless, deserve to find a place here, partly because they are edifying and partly because the Superintendent esteemed the person worthy of his favor; the account however is taken from her own confessions and is as follows:

While sitting in the kitchen near the fire on the night of October 3d, 1762, between ten and eleven o'clock, somebody knocked at the door. I looked out, but nobody was there. It soon knocked again, and I again went out but found nobody. At last it knocked the third time, and going out and looking about I saw an angel standing at my right hand, who said: "Yes, my friend, it is midnight and late; the hour of midnight is approaching; alas, what shall I say? love has grown cool among the members. Oh, that this were not so among those who are Brethren in the faith!" Then he sang, that it echoed through the skies, and I thought it must be heard far and wide. When he had ceased, I said: "Shall I go in and tell my friends that they may rejoice with me?" He said: "No; they have lain down." I said: "They are not asleep." He said: "Yes, they sleep." Then I kept silence and thought, how well I feel, how well I feel! Thereupon the angel began to sing: "How well I feel, how well I feel, when our God doth show himself in spirit to my soul, so that within I leap and jump for joy, and bring all praise and honor to the Lord, although the tongue oft silence keeps." At the middle of the verse he told me to join in the singing; then he knelt down and I with him; he prayed fervently and beautifully for the salvation of believers. Now I wept for joy, and he dried my tears; but I dared not touch him. Then I said: "Shall I go and tell my friends?" He laid his hands upon my shoulders and answered, "My dear child, they are asleep." I said: "My dear friend, they just now lay down, they do not sleep." After this we again commenced to sing: "The children of God indeed sow in sorrow and in tears; but at last the year yieldeth that they long for; for the time of the harvest cometh, when they gather the sheaves, and all their grief and pain is turned to pure joy and laughter." Then I again said: "Shall I go in and tell my father that he may rejoice with me?" He said: "No, all your friends are asleep, and their hearts also want to sleep." Then I wept bitterly, and the angel asked: "Why do you weep?" I answered: "I have committed many sins and often grieved my Saviour." He said: "Do not weep, your Saviour forgave you your sins, for he knows that you have gladly listened to the good, and that you did not delight in the greatness of this world, that you have no pride in your heart, and that you have kept lowly company with the believers." Then the angel and I began to sing: "Who knows what shall come, what shall be our lot, when the Lord one day his own will take, his chaste bride so full of honor; he hath already kown her in his mind, she follows well his guiding hand and much augments his honor." Then we knelt and prayed again, and he prayed for the sinners. Then I asked for the fourth time: "Shall I go in and call my friends?" He said: "This is asked once too often; do you not know that the Saviour awakened his disciples three times?" I said: "This is too much;" and I wept. He said: "Weep not," and I kept silent. Then we began to sing: "O blessed he will be who shall enter in with me the realms of bliss; it surely is but right that we should here below us always well prepare." Then the angel began to speak and said: "My dear child, did you ever see such ungodly display? Did you notice the daughters of Jerusalem walking about in gay calico, of which things they have much on earth. They will be sent down to the wicked if they do not turn back, for they will not enter the kingdom of God; and there is still a great deal of this godless display upon earth; they will be shown down into hell. Then the Lord will say: Depart from me, ye sinners! I know you not! And then you will burn to all eternity and will be tormented from everlasting to everlasting."

Then he ceased to speak of these things, and we again began to sing: "They all will see at once with pleasure and joy the beauties of the heavenly realm; and the beautiful throng will walk two by two on Zion's meadows." Then, for the third time, we knelt down on the ground and he prayed about the sufferings and the death of the Saviour, and then we got up. Now he said to me: "Go in and lie down;" and said: "Hallelujah! hallelujah in Christ Jesus! Amen." Then he ascended towards heaven and spoke in a loud voice,

so that it reached to heaven: "Father, father, faithful
father!" and called out three times in a loud voice saying:
"I ascend into heaven." I looked after him until he disappeared from my sight; then I went in and lay down.

After this I lay in a trance for the greater part of
seven days and nights, so that my spirit was separated from
the body.   In this state I was led through strange conditions and dwelling places of spirits, and I saw such
wonderful things that I greatly hesitate to reveal them.
After this it became quite customary for me to talk with
good spirits and angels, and also to be transferred in
spirit out of my visible body into heavenly principalities,
just as if it had happened bodily.   The Almighty God in his
mercy also allowed me to translate myself in spirit into
eternity as often as I wished, either by day or night, and
there to see, hear and touch the divine wonders.   My body
was always as if asleep until my spirit returned.   I wandered through indescribable habitations of the blessed, and
saw innumerable hosts; and once I was told their number, but
I could not remember it.   Oh, what joy and happiness did I
there behold!   There you feel a bliss that is inexpressible
and cannot be described.   Now I will describe a few of the
divine wonders which Jesus Christ, who had joined me and was
my guide into eternity, revealed to me.

In the year 1762, on November 12th, my spirit was taken
from this visible creation, and out of my body, up into
invisible eternity.   There I saw all the prophets and
apostles, together with all the saints and patriarchs, and
heard one of them say these words to the pious: Hallelujah,
hallelujah, highly praised, highly honored; gather ye pious,
gather all ye pious to the great supper; rejoice ye all and
triumphantly declare how kindly the Lord leads you.   To the
godless the Lord will say: Depart ye wicked, I do not know
you, go with him whom ye have followed.   Then they will try
to excuse themselves and implore the Lord, but he will say

to them: Depart from me, ye evil-doers. And the Saviour
then will say: Come, all ye pious, to the great supper.
And they will hasten with gladness, and triumphantly shout
and say: Highly, highly be praised the Lord's precious
name! Then they will walk two and two on the meadows of
Zion; then they will walk even by fours. Oh, how will the
pious rejoice when the Saviour says: Come hither, ye pious!
Then they will hasten by fours, and the gross, godless sinners, by hundreds, and on the middle path by sixties; and
the unbelieving children, under seven years old, by twenties
on the middle path. Then they are again divided on the
middle path. What is here said about three paths is to be
understood as follows: We human beings know what is meant
by morning, noon, evening and midnight; in the same way this
is also to be understood in the other realm. When a man
dies and leaves this earthly realm he imagines himself alive
and does not know anything of his having died, and yet finds
himself a stranger on earth. Then he comes to a great road
that leads from Evening towards Morning; after he has travelled some distance on this road a broad road branches off
to the left, leading to damnation and hell. The road
ascends a little until it reaches a certain height, when it
suddenly descends, and there hundreds on hundreds are
travelling. But on the road which leads towards Morning
there sixties on sixties are travelling; this road leads to
the water mentioned, but the other one, almost directly
towards Noon, brings you to the water sooner. On this road
none but adults walk towards the temple of Mount Zion. Then
the angel said: "And then the Lord will say: Come ye pious
and baptized, who have persevered to the end, come over
here; come, you are baptized and have persevered to the
end." Again the angel spoke: "Behold the five chosen ones!
Oh, how glorious and how mighty! Behold the Father, and the
Son, and those three with him, God Abraham, God Isaac, and
God Jacob!" And one of the three went into the water and

baptized (what is not fulfilled here in this time must and inevitably will be fulfilled in the time to come). And the Saviour and the Father stood on the other side of the water, and the Saviour called the innocent by name, one after the other, to go in. Those who had here repented and believed in baptism he also called in. But those who had transgressed the Word of God, after having been baptized on earth, they must tarry at the water until they have repented anew. Those whom the world had bought, and who clung to it with their hearts, they must anew repent upon earth, for they must wait by the water and listen to what the Father preaches to them. These two, the Father and the Son, stood together on the other side. Then they also came to the water and preached, the Father to the godless, the Son to the pious. Now the pious also went into the water and were baptized, and the Saviour called to them to cross also; and they were glad and joined in the triumphant shout of the angels; and the angels stood in the water up to their hearts. I will yet add something important about baptism. I know a man, it is not necessary to mention his name, who when he died and came to the water was told that before he might cross he would have to be baptized. He answered that he had been baptized in his infancy, and had always thought that immersion was not so essential. Then he heard the words: Jesus too was circumcised on the eighth day, and nevertheless was also baptized in his thirtieth year; therefore he would have to follow, and so indeed he did. I saw him moreover until he had crossed.

After they had come out of the water they went away from it, the Father first, then the Saviour and the Three, and after them the angels. The further they went the more beautiful it was, bright and shining. These five sat down, then the baptized, then the angels singing most charmingly. The Saviour preached the Gospel; he did not preach as he had to the Jews in their synagogues. And after he had preached the Gospel, he also preached faith. Then they stood up and prayed mightily and gloriously, and Jesus told the pious to go their way, and they all departed; but the five chosen ones returned again to the water, and the angels accompanied them, and did as they had done before at the water. But the multitude of the pious, whom Jesus told to go their way, numbered one hundred; they departed and were prepared. Then one of the three went into the water, and also the angels up to their hearts. Then the Lord of innocence called out and said: "Come hither ye innocent, ye must be baptized." Then they will hurry into the water and be baptized; and when they come out, the Lord will call to them: "Come over here!" and they will go to the Five. But those who are baptized here, and fall away again, but repent again and are converted during their lifetime, to them the Father will say, when after death they come to the water: "Halt, halt!" and will preach to them and tell them what they have done; but the Saviour will preach to the pious. Then the Saviour will say: "Come also into the water, you must be baptized again;" then they will go into the water and be called over to the other side, shining and glorious in their beauty. Thereupon they all will rejoice with shouts and jubilation, because the Lord has led them so kindly. But to those who but half repented the Lord will say: "Depart, depart, depart from the middle road!" And when those come who here on earth stood by themselves, the Lord will say to them: "Depart from me, I know you not!" He will say: "No standing alone availeth here!" and they will be turned off with the godless.

Then the Saviour will say: "Come ye pious, rejoice and triumphantly shout, because the Lord leads you so kindly;" and he who baptized in the water said to me: "Behold Peter, and John, and James!" They were of the same degree; Peter and John had friendly countenances. Peter said to me: "Are you glad that your spirit will soon depart?! I said: "Yes, my friend, I am very glad." I sighed: "Come, Jesus, take me up." I was so happy, my heart was never quiet. Peter said: "Yes, my dear child, you shall soon join the five chosen ones." He continued: "They may keep your body, but not your spirit; I shall soon bring you up to me, as soon as your spirit departs from you; but your friends will sleep, and not see it." I spoke: "I am glad, my heart is never quiet; soon I shall rejoice and shout in triumph, because the Lord so kindly leads me." I was very glad that I had seen the believers in eternity; but my heart was very sad as they took leave of me; and yet I was glad, and hoped to see them again in eternity. It also gave me much joy that two of them returned with me to the water. Then one of them spoke: "The Lord will say to them that are exalted: Go down, you stood high in the world, you must now be made low; you were not satisfied with shelter and food. But to the humble he will say: Ye must be raised up, you were low upon the earth. But woe to them who purchase the world; they must go with the godless. Oh, how will the humble rejoice! for those who purchased the world and are citizens thereof, they will cry woe! over themselves; hallelujah, amen." When I came to this side of the water I began to sing: I shall love my Jesus until I am carried to the grave, and until he shall awaken me, and they shall write on my coffin: Jesus is my hope and my light; I my Jesus shall never leave.

Anno 1762, on December 6th, my spirit was again carried out of this visible creation and frame of flesh, up into the invisible eternity, again to hear something new. Then one spoke the following words, and spoke very loudly to those in heaven and on earth: "Rejoice and shout triumphantly, you will soon be led to your rest; rejoice with might, ye pious, you soon will find your rest. Hallelujah, rejoice with might! High, high, as high as you can extol, rejoice ye all and triumphantly shout, for the Lord so kindly leads you! Oh, how glorious and how mighty! Rejoice ye all and shout in triumph: come all ye pious, come to the great supper! Hio! hio! hallelujah! Oh, how glorious and how mighty; rejoice ye all and shout in triumph; soon all the pious and all the lowly will find their rest! Oh, what joy! oh, what delight! rejoice ye all and shout in triumph, hallelujah, hallelujah! Come ye pious, come ye all, come to the great supper!" The angel further spoke to me: "Behold the angels without number, behold how splendid and shining; behold how they protect the pious on earth! Oh, how glorious and how mighty! Who can number the angels who sit above and protect the pious on earth? Rejoice ye all and shout in triumph, the Saviour will come soon to take home all the pious, and with him his angels in white array; then heaven shall be barred. Hallelujah, hallelujah, rejoice with might ye pious, you soon will come to your rest! High, high, extol as high as you can! High, high as he can be extolled! Rejoice ye all and shout in triumph! Oh, how glad the pious will be! Oh, how blessed are they who believe that the Saviour died for the world and who are baptized in His name," etc.

On December 13th my immortal spirit was again carried up to eternity, and again heard the voice of a watchman resound aloud like a trumpet; the sound seemed to go through all the heavens and the earth. He again spoke: "Oh, how glorious and how mighty! Rejoice ye all and shout in triumph; behold how the Lord so kindly leads you! Rejoice with might, all ye pious, and ye pious all at once, come to the great supper!" etc., etc.

I find that these visions continued at least till April, 1765. The father of this person was a respected Baptist preacher. He, because he also had a great desire to build churches, made use of this circumstance and travelled through the country with his daughter, baptizing and preaching God's kingdom, whereby many were awakened from their spiritual sleep, some of whom he baptized in the stream

Codorus, at Yorktown. It is beyond description how quickly
this awakening spread through the country; people came from
a distance of more than sixty miles to the house of the
above-mentioned Hummer, so that the too numerous visitors
emptied these good people's house and barn of their provisions. Night services were then arranged, to which people
came every night; but if some tried to steal in from impure
motives, the Instrument [Hummer] was so keen to find it out
that they were exposed and excluded from the service. That
at the same time most charming hymns were sung by angels in
the air, I give on the authority of those who allege that
they heard them. Catharine Hummer, before mentioned, and
her sisters, showed from the very beginning of this awakening a particular esteem for the Solitary in the Settlement;
therefore it was hoped that this awakening would be of great
advantage to Ephrata; for as the Superintendent with a
considerable following of the Solitary was at this time
officiating at the altar in this region, these daughters
invited them to visit their house, and entertained them in
Christian love, even without their parents' knowledge, who
at the time were not particularly favorable to the visitors.
May God repay them for this faithfulness on the day of
judgment, because they without fear went to meet the
reproach of Christ and sheltered under their roof such
scourings of the world.

Thereupon it came to pass that two of them, namely, the
chief person, Catharine, and her sister, Maria, paid a visit
to the Solitary at a time when there was a service at the
altar, so that they were initiated into its mystery, which
produced great excitement in the whole Settlement as well as
in the Congregation, because the hope was entertained that
such respectable lasses would help to make up the church of
the 144,000 virgins of the Lamb, that so the new world might
the sooner become manifest. These matters at last induced
the Superintendent to write an edifying letter to the

Instrument, in which he, with his usual modesty, spoke in a very Christian way of this movement, and laid before this person certain signs by which to recognize whether the Spirit of Jesus Christ were its impelling force. He wrote as follows: "If our beloved and respected friend, or rather Sister, C.H., wishes to be fully assured of the spirit of her divine youth, or of what she has further to expect of the whole affair which happened to her, then let her preserve right relations with her virginity. If so be that the Princess on the throne is using her sceptre in this affair, then let her be of good cheer, the matter is all right, and no doubt concerning it need arise in all eternity; for the Virgin never deceives, because she is the mother of the eternal Wisdom, through which all things were created. If, however, the Virgin should have to lose her princely hat through the affair then it may be a result of the official or judging spirit of the fallen angel, administering his office for good and ill over the apostate life. But he does not get into the city of God or the New Jerusalem with his office, but has to live and lodge outside the boundaries of Israel; and at last will even be utterly expelled, when the mother-church or the church of the Holy Spirit shall wield the sceptre and the kingdom. Then, of course, all the offices created by the fallen prince of angels shall be abolished.

But it appears that after the above-mentioned person had changed her state and married, the spirit retired into its chamber again and the whole work stopped and fell into decay, which is usually the case with all angelic visions and revelations. May God grant that it may turn into a plentiful harvest in eternity.

Concerning the Last Circumstances Connected With the Life of the Superintendent, and How at Last he Laid Aside his Earthly Tabernacle

A father of old, when he was about to go home, and it went hard with him, raised his hands to God and said: "Lord, thou knowest I never let my prisoner escape." This can justly be conceded to the Superintendent also, namely, that he kept a sacred watch over his life from the first awakening unto his end. And as he was obliged to desist from his austere way of living, when compelled by God to mingle with the flood of humanity, so it was also observed that towards the end of his life, he again withdrew himself from close fellowship with any one, and led so secluded a life that even those nearest to him could not reach up to him in spirit. All his aim was not to stand in God's way in reaching the consciences of those who were intrusted to his care. For even as the good Master himself had to stand off, in order that the Spirit might be imparted to his disciples, so the Superintendent had to withdraw his fellowship even during his life-time, in order that his successors, weaned from him, might learn to walk on their own feet. The most important fact to be noted of his walk through life is, that all the strange situations into which he was brought during a pilgrimage of many years, could not turn him aside from the purpose once taken, to live a life disdainful of the world and serving God; of which he thus writes in a certain letter: "I know by this that I did not forsake my calling, because all carnal and worldly-minded people are still my enemies, just the same as at the time when I first entered upon this road." And to one of the Brethren who visited him shortly before his end, he said: "I am now again the same that I was when first exposed to the world-spirit, namely, an orphan." It surely is saying a good deal when a spiritual warrior can boast that during so long a time neither the flatteries nor the malice of men could lead him astray from his holy calling. But because he has been accused of having been addicted too much to strong drink for several years before his end, something would be wanting if this charge were not duly met. It appears that Providence ordered that he had to help his Master carry his shame even in this; for that God had lost sight of him so far as to permit him to again fall under the power of the things from which he had freed himself by his first repentance, is not easily to be believed, although one might, if it were necessary, make excuses on account of his old age and great bodily infirmities. This report he made excellent use of, and bore himself in appearance in such a manner that men were confirmed in their conjectures; for shame was his outer coat which he wore on his long life-journey so that his inner, pure white garment might be kept unspotted. But what great temptations this occasioned in the Settlement cannot be described; for if God intends to humble a people, he allows contempt to be heaped on its priests, and makes fools of its princes. And now all the Solitary revealed their real feelings towards him. His spiritual daughters who formerly would have gone through fire and water for him, now withdrew themselves from him; some of them who meddled too much with his frailties, had great cause to thank God that Noah's curse against Ham did not fall upon them. All of this, however, came from God, for had he died in the midst of the churchly honors which he had formerly enjoyed, his

loss would have touched the Sisterhood most of all, for next
to God, they esteemed their spiritual Father above everything. He once appeared to two of the Brethren in the form
of one who is drunk, when they put him under severe discipline; but he went straight home from them, and composed a
hymn about this occurrence, which soon after was printed and
distributed in the Settlement. This hymn shows that at the
time he had full possession of his senses. Two of the
verses are as follows:

> Once when I thought that I was from the illness freed,
>   In which for days and years I'd suffered grief, indeed;
> Some travellers came to me, all weary from the road,
> And gave me bitter gall, with blows a heavy load.

> Oh, God! I bring to Thee my woe and bitter pain.
>   Since Thou my Saviour art, to whom I ne'er in vain
> Did come, from early youth, for help to bear my cross,
> For heavenly bliss instead of pleasure's earthly dross.

Nevertheless some, especially of the domestic household, would have nothing to do with the matter, but kept
their senses in Christ Jesus, and said: "The Superintendent
stands directly under God's orders and is responsible only
to him." Herein he can be compared with David, whom the
Sanhedrin also wished to strangle; but David well knew with
whom he had to deal, and said: "Against Thee, Thee only
have I sinned;" and whoever of the Community reads this will
remember that all who laid hold of this presumed weakness of
the Superintendent fell under judgment. He once came to a
Brother in the likeness of one who is drunk, and took him
along to another Brother, where they prepared a love-feast.
After this was done, the Brother, as was customary, accompanied him to his house, where he had a very edifying conversation with him; so that the Brother perceived that his
drunkenness had been a holy pretence.

It was observed of him that towards the end of his life
he endeavored to remove all stones of stumbling out of the
way of the Solitary. His quarrel with the Prior, which had
lasted for years, he put entirely aside, and said: "I am

done now, and dare not go one step further." He also took a
Sister into his house, and went to the former Mother, Maria,
who also had stumbled over the rock of offense, and called
her his Sister, and offered her reconciliation in Christ;
but she in no wise accepted it.

He attended to his official business up to within eight
days before his death, when he officiated for the last time
at a love-feast, being already so weak that he said on the
way to it: "I am sick, I could just lie down and die." Three
days before his decease one of the oldest house-mothers,
Barbara Höfly by name, who thought very much of him, and was
also breathing her last, sent to him and asked for a visit,
even though he were not able to speak with her, if only she
might be permitted to see him. Although he was at the time
already wrestling with death he took a Brother along and
fulfilled her wish; she was buried yet before him. Another
Sister, who had only lately joined and came from a foreign
country, was also breathing her last at this time. She
prayed to God that he might let her die with this holy man,
and she also died yet before him. These are the travelling
companions who accompanied him to eternity. At last the 6th
day of July of the year 1768 came, when he laid aside his
mortal raiment. On the morning of that day he had yet been
in the Sisters' house, and nobody, therefore, thought that
his departure was so near; nor could the powers of darkness
prevail upon him to lie down on a sick bed. Meanwhile a
constant watch was kept, for strange happenings were expected, and that the powers of death would have a fierce
struggle with him, especially since he was an old soldier,
who was accustomed neither to call on men for mercy nor to
yield to the powers of darkess. But at last the news came
of his appoaching end, whereupon all the Solitary assembled
at his house. The Brethren stood nearest to him; behind
them the Sisters, and those who were of short stature got
upon benches to witness his sacrifice. In his last trouble

he clearly showed that he was anointed with the priestly spirit of Jesus Christ, for of all the adverse circumstances which had occurred during his administration in the Settlement, he declared himself to be the sole cause, and thus freed and acquitted all from every charge, and especially those who accused themselves of having misunderstood him. Then he desired the Brethren to bless him, and to receive him into their fellowship, which was done, for the Prior gave him his blessing with laying on of hands, and thereafter all the Brethren gave him the kiss of peace to take along on his journey. Then they persuaded him to lie down on the bench, and he was heard several times to repeat the following words: "Oh woe, oh woe! oh wonder, oh wonder!" But he did not explain himself about it, because his voice failed him, and soon after he fell asleep without a motion. Now the cry was, "My father, my father! The chariot of Israel and the horsemen thereof!" Yet nobody was seen to shed tears, but all thanked God most fervently that after so long a martyrdom he had delivered his servant from the body of this death.

These are the most important events in the life and blessed death of a man who was a great wonder in this century. The first impregnation for a spiritual life he received at Heidelberg in the Palatinate, when the great weight of the Spirit was laid upon him, which was one cause of his many succeeding passions. Many awoke to a spiritual life through his labors, and many strove earnestly to follow his footsteps; but they could not keep step with him, for he had so completely given himself to God, both body and soul, that he passed his life in wonderful strictness, even up to his death. The reason why most of the awakenings of our times come to such sad ends is, because people rely upon themselves, and do not renounce self more than their own interest demands, so that it may truly be said: All plans of self-interest bring death. It nevertheless remains a

great wonder that, after God called him from his blessed
life of seclusion to bathe in the flood of humanity, in
order to fish for people, he had so much faith that he could
risk his salvation on God; and it is a still greater wonder,
that surrounded by so many dangers in this human flood, he
did not forfeit his calling. And on account of this his
faithfulness did God crown him with praise and honors, and
ordain him to replace on the candlestick, at the sixth
period, both the priesthood of Melchizedek and the heavenly
virginity. Because this could not be done in Europe, on
account of the Beast's great power, God ordered it that he
came over the ocean into this country, where his doctrine of
the heavenly virginity and the priesthood, after some opposition, gained a firm footing, and where an altar was built
to the Lord in such wise that all awakenings not in harmony
with his testimony have no other effect than to bring forth
children into servitude.

Before him the wisdom of God attempted to reveal the
mystery of eternal virginity in the old countries, through
many precious instruments, of whom those dear men of God,
Godfried Arnold and George Gichtel and many others, may
especially be mentioned. The latter's success was great,
and I may well say that he had borne the light before the
Superintendent; but he remained a virgin, nor did he attain
to the secret nuptial couch of the Virgin Sophia, where
children are born; still less did he reach the covenant
household of Jesus Christ, but ended his life in a holy
separateness. It is known that he and his first co-warriors
were so severely sifted through the envy of the tempter,
that he, in order to prevent similar siftings, did not want
to allow two to live in one town. When we consider that the
Superintendent for about fifty years stood in a visible
organization in which under God's decree one rebellion after
the other broke forth against the testimony of God which was
entrusted to him, it must be confessed that he fought on

many more battlefields against the Prince of Wrath than did the venerable Brother Gichtel of blessed memory, and that he extended the borders of the generation of the divine Mother far more than he. It must also be conceded that the venerable John Kelpius, who had settled near Germantown with a company of spiritual wooers of the hand of the Virgin, as already mentioned, did much in spirit to assist the Superintendent in his church building. The same spirit inspired the sainted Kelpius that afterwards descended on the Superintendent; but when the good Kelpius departed this life, his work fell into the hands of the tempter to be sifted, and the spiritual ship broke up, so that Selig, Conrad Mathäi and some others, had to save themselves by swimming. The Superintendent's work, on the contrary, with better success passed to posterity, for eighteen years have passed since he was transferred to eternity, during which time the Order and the Community have been built up in the unity of the spirit, although with much opposition.

And if, as he maintains God promised him, a seed of his labors is to remain until the second advent of Jesus Christ, this does not mean that the Settlement of the Solitary shall stand so long; although they are just as well entitled to this as any congregation of Christ on earth. But we believe that it is to be understood more in a spiritual sense than literally: that wherever there is anyone in this country who has a matrix ready to conceive, there the Spirit, who in the beginning overshadowed the Superintendent, will also overshadow and impregnate him. All of which, however, must be taken figuratively and not literally. And because this country at last, after much opposition, received this ambassador, who had been driven out of his fatherland, and granted him and his whole family complete liberty of conscience, therefore it will always be blessed and be a nursery of God, which shall bear him much fruit, for the promise given to Abraham must be fulfilled: "In thy seed shall all generations of the earth be blessed." He was small in person, well formed and proportioned, had a high nose, high forehead and sharp eyes, so that everybody recognized in him an earnest and profound nature. He had excellent natural gifts, so that he might have become one of the most learned men if pains had been taken with his education. All secrets were opened to him, just as he wanted; and wherever he saw a piece of skillful work he was not satisfied until he had examined and understood it; he used to say it would be a shame for the human mind if it would be defeated in anything. He likewise was endowed with such a keen perception that he was enabled to discover with ease whatever might be hidden to others. But after he had dedicated himself wholly to the service of God these gifts were sanctified, and were used by him for the upbuilding of the temple of God in the Spirit. What he accomplished in the art of music, which he learned without any human instruction, has already been mentioned; he composed not less than one thousand tunes for four voices, of which none interfered with the other.

His printed hymns number 441. The reader will see his enlightened nature from them; many of them are prophetic, representing the near approach of the Sabbatic church, and the gathering together of the people of God. Of his printed discourses there are 66; besides which you will find many of his spiritual lectures printed. He also wrote many spiritual letters, of which 73 are printed; the rest are still in manuscript, but will also be communicated to the reader, though *sub conditione Jacobaea*. In conclusion we will here give the instription on his tombstone, from which the reader may learn both his natural and spiritual age:

"Here Rests an Offspring of the Love of God,

FRIEDSAM,

a Solitary, but later become a Leader, Guardian and Teacher of the Solitary and of the Congregation of Christ in and about Ephrata. Born at Eberbach in the Palatinate, called Conrad Beissel: Fell asleep July 6th, Anno 1768; aged according to his spiritual age 52 years, but according to his natural, 77 years and 4 months."

SOURCES OF
TRANSLATED TEXTS

1. "Preface" to Spiritual Letters translated from Geist-
    liche Briefe eines Friedsamen Pilgers, welche er von
    1721 bis an seine 1768 darauf erfolgte Entbindung
    geschrieben. gedruckt im Jahr 1794. Exemplar:
    Plainsfield N.J., Seventh Day Baptist Historical
    Society.

2. Mystical Proverbs and Poems translated from Mystische
    und sehr geheyme Sprueche, Welche in der Himlischen
    schule des heiligen geistes erlernet....Philadelphia:
    Gedruckt bey B. Franklin in Jahr 1730. [Exemplar:
    Plainfield, N.J.: Seventh Day Baptist Historical
    Society.] Translation of "Ninety-Nine Mystical
    Proverbs" based on English version published by B.
    Franklin (Philadelphia, 1730).

3. Maxims modernized from edition of Julius F. Sachse, "A
    Unique Ephrata Manuscript," Proceedings of Pennsyl-
    vania German Society 21 (1910), 34-44.

4. The Church of God translated from Die Kirche Gottes
    [Snowhill, Franklin Co., Pa.: Obed Snowberger, May
    1859]. Exemplar: Plainfield, N.J.: Seventh-Day
    Baptist Historical Society, Sachse Coll. 1872, No. 74,
    Case K.

5. "First Sermon" and Peter Miller notes from Deliciae
    Ephratenses translated by Klaus M. Lindner from
    Deliciae Ephratenses, Pars. I. oder des ehrwürdigen
    Vatters Friedsam Gottrecht, ... Geistliche Reden ...
    (Ephratae: Typis Societatis, Anno MDCCLXXIII) 1-35.

6. "Reflections" modernized and corrected from [Johann
    Conrad Beissel], A Dissertation on Man's Fall trans-
    lated from the High-German original. (Printed:
    Ephrata Anno MDCCLXV) [translated from ibid., 36-48.]

7. Spiritual Sermons translated by Elizabeth Sauer from
    Deliciae Ephratenses. Pars I, 104-108 (13), 115-118
    (15), 160-167 (25), 217-222 (36), 264-265 (49),
    277-280 (54), 314-317 (65).

8. Theosophical Epistles translated by Elizabeth Sauer
    from Deliciae Ephratenses Pars II. Oder des
    ehrwürdigen Vatters friedsam Gottrecht ....
    Theosophische Episteln ... (Ephratae: Typis
    Societatis, Anno MDCCXLV), 59-66 (1), 220-223 (43).

9. Mystic Church Document (authorship disputed--likely by
    Johannes Hillerbrand or Peter Miller) translated by
    Elizabeth Sauer from "Mystisches und Kirchliches
    Zeugness der Brüderschaft in Zion" printed by C.
    Sauer, Germantown, 1743 and reprinted in Johann P.
    Fresenius, Bewahrte Nachrichten von Herrnhutischen
    Sachen (Frankfurt am Mayn und Leipzig, 1747-51), III,
    410-417.

10. On the State of Adam translated by Elizabeth Sauer
    from ibid., 474-503.

11. The Naked Truth modernized from The Naked Truth,
    Standing against all Painted and Disguised Lies,

Deceit and Falsehood. Or the Seventh-Day Sabbath Standing as a Mountain immoveable for Ever, Proved by Three Witnesses which Cannot Lie. By M.W. [Philadelphia: Andrew Bradford] printed in the year 1729. Exemplar: Plainfield, N.J.: Seventh Day Baptist Historical Society.

12. The Rose of Sharon translated from Die Rose oder Der angenehmen Blumen zu Sharon geistliche Eheverlebnüs mit ihrem himmlischen Bräutigam, Welchen sie sich als ihrem König, Haupt, Mann, Herrn u: Brautigam, aufs ewig hin verlobt ... Ephrata den 13 des 5: Mon, 1745. (MS: Historical Society of Pennsylvania, Philadelphia, Pa., Ac 1924). Translation partially dependent on that of Julius F. Sachse, The German Sectarians of Pennsylvania 1708-1800 (Philadelphia: Pa., 1899-1900), I, 300-304; II, 181-201. Not translated are the Testament of Beissel, a note on Beissel's death and the obituary lists of the sisterhood appended at the end of the manuscript.

13. Selected Letters: The first letter of 1788 is a modernized version of a translation by Julius F. Sachse. [Exemplar: Plainfield, N.J.: Seventh Day Baptist Historical Society, Sachse Coll. 1872, No. 74, Case K.]: the translation is an extract and was corrected against the original in ibid., No. 15, Geistliche Schriften. The remaining letters are reprinted from Felix Reichmann and Eugene E. Doll (eds.), Ephrata as Seen by Contemporaries (Allentown, Pa.: Schlechter's, 1953), 111-112, 190-200.

14. The Ephrata Chronicle selected from Brother Lamech and Brother Agrippa, Chronicon Ephratense: A History of the Community of the Seventh Day Baptists at Ephrata, Lancaster Pennsylvania, trans. J. Max hark (Lancaster: S.H. Zahm & Co., 1889), Chapters 12, 14, 21, 24, 31, 32, 33.

BIBLIOGRAPHY

A. Major Works by Members of the Cloisters or Published by the Cloister Press

1729

Beissel John Conrad. Mysterion anomias. The Mystery of Law-
lessness: or, Lawless Antichrist Discover'd and
Disclos'd. Shewing That All Those Do Belong to That
Lawless Antichrist, Who Wilfully Reject the Command-
ments of God, amongst Which, Is His Holy, and by
Himself Blessed Seventh Day-Sabbath, or His Holy Rest,
of Which the Same Is a Type. For Thus Saith the Lord,
Exod. XX. ver. 10 The Seventh Day is the Sabbath of
the Lord thy God. Written to the Honour of the Great
God and His Holy Commands. By Cunrad Beysell
Translated out of the High-Dutch by M[ichael]
W[ohlfahrt] Presented in the year 1729.

Wohlfahrt, Michael. The Naked Truth, Standing against All
Painted and Disguised Lies. Deceit and Falshood. On
the Seventh-Day-Sabbath Standing as a Mountain immoveable for Ever. Proved by Three Witnesses Which Cannot
Lie. By M.W. [Philadelphia: Andrew Bradford] printed
in the year 1729.

1730

Gottliche Liebes und Lobes Gethöne welche in dem Hertzen
der Kinder der Weiszheit zusammen sein. Und von da
wieder auszgeflossen zum Lob Gottes, und nun denen
Schülern der Himlischen Weiszheit zur Erweckung und
Aufmunterung in ihrem Creutz und Leiden aus herzlicher
Liebe mitgetheilet. Dann mit Lieb erfüllet sein,
bring't Gott den besten Preiss und giebt zum Singen
uns, die allerschönste Weisz. Zu Philadelphia:
gedruckt bey Benjamin Franklin in der MarckStrass,
1730.

Beissel, Johann Conrad. Mystische und sehr geheyme
Sprueche, welche in der Himlischen Schule des Heiligen
Geistes erlernet. Und dan folgens, einige poetische
Gedichte. Auffgesetzt. Den liebhabern und Schuelern
der Goettlichen und Himmlischen Weiszheit zum Dienst.
Vor die Saeu dieser Welt aber, haben wir keine Speise,
werden ihnen auch wohl ein verschlossener Garten, und
versiegelter Brunnen bleiben. Zu Philadelphia:
gedruckt bey B. Franklin in Jahr 1730.

1732

Vorspiel der Neuen-Welt. Welches sich in der letzten
Abendroethe als ein Paradiesischer Lichtes-Glantz
unter den Kindern Gottes hervor gethan. In Liebes,
Lobes, Krafft und Erfahrungs Liedern abgebildet, die
gedrückte, gebückte und creutztragende Kirche auf
Erden. Und wie inzwischen sich die obere und

1732 - con't.

triumphierende Kirche als eine Paradiesische Vorkost
hervor thut und offenbahret. Und daneben, alt,
ernstliche und zuruffende Wächterstimmen an alle
annoch zerstreute Kinder Gottes, das sie sich sammeln
und bereit machen auf den baldigen; ja bald hinein
brechenden Hochzeit-Tag zu der Braut des Lamms.
Philadelphia: gedruckt bey Benjamin Francklin, in der
Marck-strass, 1732.

1735

Jacobs Kampff-und Ritter-Platz allwo der nach seinem
Ursprung sich Geist der in Sophiam verliebten Seele
mit Gott um den neuem Namen gerungen, und den Sieg
davon getragan. Entworffen in unterschidlichen
Glaubens- u. Leidens-Liedern. u. erfahrungsvollen
Austruckungen des Gemuths, darinnen sich darstellet,
so wol auff Seiten Gottes seine unermuedete Arbeit zur
Reinigung socher Seelen, die sich seiner Fuerung
anvertraut. Als auch auff Seiten des Menachen der
Ernst des Geistes im Aushalten unter dem Process der
Läuterung und Abschmeltzung des Menschen der Sünden
samt dem daraus ent-springenden Lobes-Gethön. Zur
gemüthlichen Erweckung derer die das Heil Jerusalems
lieb haben. Verleget von einem Liebhaber der Wahrheit
die im verborgenen wohnt. Zu Philadelphia: gedruckt
bey B[enjamin] F[ranklin], 1736.

1739

Zionitischer Weyrauchs-Hügel oder: Myrrhenberg worrinen
allerley liebliches und wohl riechendes nach
Apothekerkunst zubereitetes Rauch-Werck zu finden.
Restehend in allerley Liebes-Würckungen der in Gott
geheiligten Seelen, welche sich in vielen und
mancherley geistlichen und lieblichen Liedern aus
gebildet. Als darinnen der letzte Ruff zu dem
Abendmahl des grossen Gottes auf unterschiedliche
Weise trefflich aus gedrucket ist; zum Dienst der in
dem abend-ländischen Welt-Theil als bey dem
Untergang der Sonnen erweckten Kirche Gottes, und zu
ihrer Ermunterung auf die mitternächtige Zukunfft
des Bräutigams ans Licht gegeben. Germantown:
gedruckt bey Christoph Sauer, 1739.

1743

Hildebrand, Johannes. Schrifftmässiges Zeugnüss von dem
Himmlischen und Jungfräulichen Gebährungs-Werck,
wie es an dem ersten Adam ist mit Fleisch
zugeschlossen, aber an dem zweyten Adam bey seiner

1743 - con't.

Creutzigung durch einen Speer wiederum geoeffnet worden. Entgegen gesetzt dem gantz ungegründeten Vorgeben der Herrnuhuthischen Gemeine von einem heiligen Ehestand, daraus sie das Ebenbild Gottes auszugebähren vorgeben. Ans Licht gegeben durch Johannes Hildebrand, einem Mitglied der Gemeine Hesu [sic] Christi in Ephrata hausväterlicher Seite. [Germantown, Christpher Saur, 1743].

Hildebrand, Johanns. Wohlgegründetes Bedencken der Christlichen Gemeine in und bey Ephrata von dem Weg der Heiligung. Wie derselbe nicht allein in der Versöhnung Christi, sondern haupt-sächlich in seiner Nachfolge zu suchen ... durch Johannes Hildebrand. Bey Veranlassung eines von der so genannten Herrenhutischen Gemeine erhaltenen Briefs. Germantown: gedruckt bey Christoph Saur, 1743.

Mistisches und kirchliches Zeuchnüss der Brüderschaft in Zion. von den wichtigsten Puncten des Christenthums nebst einem Anhang darrinnen diesselbe ihr unparthey- isches Bedencken an Tag gibt von dem Bekehrungs-Werck der sogenanten herrenhutischen Gemeine in Pennsyl- vanien, und warum man ihnen keine Kirche zustehen könne. Germantown: gedruckt und zu finden by Christoph Saur, 1743.

[Eckerling, Israel]? Ein kurtzer Bericht von den Ursachen, warum die Gemeinschaft in Ephrata sich mit dem Grafen Zinzendorf und seinen Leuten eingelassen. Und wie sich eine so grosse Ungleichheit im Ausgang der Sachen auf beyden Seiten befunden. [Germantown: Christopher Saur, 1743?]

1745

[Beissel, Johann Conrad] 1690-1768. Urständliche und Erfahrungs-volle Hohe Zeungnüsze Wie man zum Geistlichen Leben Und dessen Vollkommenheit gelangen möge. Welche Ein Hoch-Erleuchteter und Gott- Ergebener Zeuge Jesu Christi. In Seinem Geistlichen Tage-Werck erlernet; Und dieselbe, bey unterschiedenen Umständen, an Seine Geistliche Kinder und Anver- wandte, eröffnet; Von denselben aber Um Ihrer Vortrefflichkeit willen, gesammlet und, zum Unterricht Anderer, ans Licht gegeben. Ephrata, in Pensylvanien, Drucks der Brüderschafft, 1745.

1745 - con't.

[BEISSEL, JOHANN CONRAD] 1690-1768. ZIONITISCHEN Stiffts I.
     Theil. Oder eine Wolriechende Narde, Die nach einer
     langen Nacht in der herrlichen Morgen-Röthe ist auf
     gegangen auf dem Gefielde Libanons, und hat unter den
     Kindern der Weisheit einen Balsemischen Geruch von
     sich gegeben. Des von Gott hoch begnadigten und be-
     adelten fürtrefflichen THEOLOGI der Mystischen
     GottesGelärtheit. Irenici Theedicëi. Aus welcher
     die Stimme des Brautigams die Gesandschaft des aller-
     reinsten Geistes der Himlischen SOPHIA empfangen zur
     Offenbarung der Paradisischen Jungfrauschaft: und ist
     gesalbet worden zum Priesterlichen AMt der Versöhnun
     in seiner Ihme von Gott anvertrauten Gemeine. Besteh-
     end in einer Sammlung geistlicher Gemüts-Bewegungen
     und Erfahrungs-voller Theosophischer Sendschreiben
     welche von Demselben An seine vertraute Freunde und
     geistliche Kinder sind gestellet, und nun um ihrer
     Vortrefflichkeit willen den Kindern der Weissheit zu
     einem geistlichen Unterricht gesammelt und ans Licht
     gegeben worden. Ephrata in Pennsylvanien Drucks und
     Verlags der Brüderschaft. 1745.

[Eckerling, Israel] b. 1705. Die Richtschnur und Regel
     eines Streiters Jesu Christi, welcher in die ewige
     Schätze der Weissheit verlibet ist. Als worinnen
     auf dem Weg der Göttlichen Reinheit die
     vortreffliche Tugenden der Keuschheit, Niedrigkeit und
     Demuth gefunden werden. Ephrata. Anno MDCCXLV.

[Eckerling, Israel] b. 1705. Ein sehr geistreicher Spiegel,
     als worinnen dass rechte Bild des einsamen Lebens
     erscheinet, und was eigentlich desselben Beschaf-
     fenheit seye, wann es seine rechtmässige Sache
     darstellet und ans Licht gibt. [Ephrata, 1745].

Die Ernsthaffte Christen-Pflicht Darinnen Schöne
     Geistreiche Gebetter. Gedruckt in Ephrata im Jahr
     1745.

Ernstliche ERWECKUNGS-STIMM In ein Lied verfasset Ueber den
     so lang gestandenen und grosen Cometen Welcher sich im
     X Monat des Jahrs 1743 das erste mal sehen liess, und
     10 Wochen lang gestanden. Von einem Freund zugesandt,
     Und, auf dessen Begehren, Zum Druck befördert. Zu
     Ephrata, MDCCXLV.

Gülbene [sic] Aepffel in Silbern Schalen oder: Schöne
     und nützliche Worte und Warheiten zur Gottseligkeit.
     Ephrata, Im Jahr des Heyls, 1745.

1747

Das Gesäng Der einsamen und verlassenen Turtel-Taube
    Nemlich der Christlichen Kirche. Oder geistliche u.
    Erfahrungs-volle Liedens u. Liebes-Gethöne, Als
    darinnen beydes die Vorkost der neuen Welt als auch
    die darzwischen vorkommende Creutzes- und Leidens-Wege
    nach ihrer Würde dargestellt, und in geistliche
    Reimen gebracht Von einem Friedsamen und nach der
    stillen Ewigkeit wallenden Pilger. Und nun zum
    Gebrauch der Einsamen und Verlassenen zu Zion gesam-
    melt und ans Licht gegeben. Ephrata, Drucks der
    Bruderschafft im Jahr 1747.

Hildebrand, Johannes. Eine ruffende Wächterstimme, an
    alle Seelen die nach Gott und seinem Reich hungernd
    sind. Oder eine Vorstellung, wie der arme Mensch im
    göttlichen Leben erstorben, und im 4 elementischen
    Leben aufgewacht nebst einer Anweisung wie man noch
    hier in der Zeit demselben Leben loss werden und bey
    Liebes-Leben die wahre Ruhe erlangen und der
    künfftigen ewigen Seeligkeit gewiss werden
    könne... Aus Erfahrung geschrieben ... von einem
    nach Gott und seinem Reich sehnlich sehnenden Hertzen:
    gedruckt zu Germantown bey Christoph Saur, 1747.

1748

BRACHT, Tieleman JANS VAN, 1625-1664. Der Blutige Schau-
    Platz oder Martyrer Spiegel der Tauffs Gesinten oder
    Wehrlosen-Christen. Ephrata in Pensylvanien, Drucks
    und Verlags der Brüderschafft, Anno MDCCXLVIII.

Die Schule der Weissheit Iter Theil in Poesie, als das Hoch-
    Teutsche A.B.C. vor Schuler und Meister in Israel.
    [Ephrata?] Gedruckt in Jahr, 1748 [?].

RINGWALDT, BARTHOLOMAEUS, 1530?-1599. Neue Zeitung und
    wahre Prophezeyung Hans Frumans. In liebliche Reimen
    verfasset durch [Ephrata] Verlegt von Mich: M:
    [Michael Müller] 1749.

1750

Liebreicher Zuruf der Väter, Freunden u. Göher in
    Europa, gethan an die, von ihnen gesandte, Hirten in
    Pensylvania, an ihrem Lob und Danck-Fest, wegen derer
    glücklichen Ankunfft, so jährlich fället auf den
    15. Januarii. Ephrata: Typis Societatis. 1750.

1752

Erster Theil der Theosophischen Lectionen, Betreffende die
    Schulen des einsamen Lebens. Ephrata gedruckt in Jahr
    1752.

1752

Neuer Nachklang des Gesängs der einsamen Turtel-Taube.
[Ephrata, 1752?]

[BEISSEL, JOHANN CONRAD] 1690-1766. Paradisisches Wunder-
Spiel. Welches sich in diesen letzten zeiten und
Tagen in denen Abend-Ländischen Welt-Theilen als ein
Vorspiel der neuen Welt hervor gethan. Bestehend in
einer gantz neuen und ungemeinen Sing-Art auf Weise
der Englischen und himmlischen Chören eingerichtet.
Da dann das Lied Mosis und des Lamms, wie auch das
hohe Lied Salomonis samt noch mehrern Zeugnüssen aus
der Bibel und andern Heiligen in liebliche Melodyen
gebracht. Wobey nicht weniger der Zuruf der Braut des
Lamms, sammt der Zubereitung auf den herrlichen
Hochzeit-Tag trefflich Praefigurirt wird. Alles nach
Englischen Chören Gesangs-Weise mit viel Mühe und
grossem Fleiss ausgefertiget von einem Friedsamen, Der
sonst in dieser Welt weder Namen noch Titul suchet.
Ephrata Sumptibus Societatis: 1754.

BUNYAN, JOHN, 1628-1688. Eines Christen Reise Nach der
seligen. Ephrata in Pennsylvania. Drucks und Verlags
der Brüderachafft, Anno 1754.

Erster Eingang und Gebät. Im Namen dess HERREN JESU Amen.
Andächtige und Geliebte in dem Herrn! Merkwürdig
ist die Beweg-Red darmit ehmal der Prophet Hoseas
seine Vermahnung an des Volck Israel, zur Verbesserung
ihres Lebens und Wesens unterstüzet hat ...
[Ephrata, 1754].

FREAME, JOHN, d. 1745. Scripture-instruction; Reprinted at
Ephrata in Pennsylvania 1754.

HILDEBRAND, JOHANNES. Ein Gespräch zwischen einem Jüng-
ling und einem Alten von dem Nutzen in Gottseeligen
Gemeinschafften. [Germantown, Christoph Saur, 1754].

1755

Nachklang Zum Gesäng der einsamen Turtel Taube, Enthaltend
eine neue Sammlung Geistlicher Lieder. Ephrata,
Drucks der Brüder-schaft Im Jahr 1755.

[KEMPER, HENRICH]. Treuhertizige Erinnerung und Warnung
bestehend in vielen Klag-Reden vom Verfall des
Christenthumes in ausserlichen Gottes-Dienst. Mit
samt einer Anweisung von dem wahren bleibenden und
ewigen Gottes-Dienst...Heraus gegeben auss Liebe zu
aller Menschen Seeligkeit. von einem auf der Wacht
stehenden Ermahner. Germanton: gedruckt bey
Christopher Saur im Jahr 1755.

1756

Ein Angenehmer Geruch der Rossen und Lilien Die im Thal der
Demuth unter Dornen hervor gewachsen. Alles aus der
Brüderlichen Gesellschafft in BETHANIA. [Ephrata]
Im Jahr des Heils 1756.

WAGNER, TOBIAS, M. Tobias Wagners Abschieds- Rede an unter-
schiedlichen Zeiten ... Ephrata Typis Societatis,
MDCCLIX.

1760

Durch Adams Fall ist ganz verderbt Menschlich Natur und
Wesen ... [Ephrata? 1760?]

KONIG, SIMON. [Eine Schrift über Ephrata] [Ephrata?
1760?]

Beissel, Johann Conrad. Die Kirche Gottes, geschrieben von
Johann Conrad Beissel, an Peter Becker, Ephrata deu
[sic] 20ten des 3ten Monats 1756. [Snow Hill?, ca.
1860?]

1761

[BOHLER, ELISEBA (HENNRIETHA WILHELMINE VON HONING)].
Abgeforderte Relation der Erscheinung eines entlebten
Geists Den Publico zur Nachricht getreulich aus dem
Mund derer, die von Anfang bis ans Ende mit
interessiert aufgeschrieben ... Ephrata Typis &
Consensu Societatis, Anno Domini MDCCLXI.

1762

ES Ist noch recht. Ephrata, 1762.

Jetzt ist mein vieler Schmertz. Ephrata, 1962.

Neu-vermehrtes Gesang der einsamen Turtel-Taube, zur
gemeinschaft-lichen Erbauung gesammelt und ans Licht
gegeben ... Ephrata Typis Societatis Anno 1762.

POTTS, JOHN. Confusion is fallen, and a Seal of the Gospel
is opened. [Ephrata?] 1762.

WUDRIAN, VALENTIN, 1584-1625. M. Valentin Wudrians seel.
Creutz-Schule. Ephrata, Drucks u. Verlag der
Bruderschaft, Anno 1762.

1763

[BENEZET, ANTHONY] 1713-1784. Eine kurtze vorstellung des
theils von Africa. Ephrata Drucks der Societat auf
kosten etlicher freunden Anno Domini MDCCLXIII.

1764

[BIBLE. N.T. APOCRYPHAL BOOKS.] Von der Historia Des
    Apostolischen-Kampffs, Zehn Bücher Wie sie der Abdias
    anfänglich in Hebräischer Sprache beschrieben,
    Eutropius aber ins Griechische, und Julius Africanus
    ins Lateinische übersetzet haben. Welchen dann
    Wolfgangus Lazius aus alten Scribenten auch beygefüget
    hat Das Leben des Apostels Matthasi, und des heiligen
    Marci Olementis Cipriani und Apollinaris; Nunmehre für
    einige unpassionirte Liebhaber der Wahrheit ins
    Deutsche übersetzet; Nebst etlichen Merckwürdigen
    Reden JESU die man swar nicht in den Evangelien, aber
    bei andern bewährten Scribenten findet: Auch der
    Marter-geschichte der heiligen und hochberühmten
    ersten Märtyrin und Apostolischen Jungfrau Theclä.
    Vormals in Amsterdam; nun aber in Ephrata gedruckt
    durch die Bruderschafft, auf Kosten dor Bruder in
    Cane-gotshiken, im Jahr 1764.

[FRANKLIN, BENJAMIN] 1706-1790. Historische Nachricht von
    dem neulich in Lancaster Caunty durch unbekante
    Personen ausgeführten Blutbade über eine Anzahl
    Indianer, welche Freunde dieser Provinz waren.   Mit
    einigen hinzu gefügten Anmerkungen. Aus dem
    Englischen übersetzt. [Ephrata?] Gedruckt im Jahr
    1764.

Lebens-Regul Wie sie zu Rom aus Päbstlichem Befehl an der
    Päbst-lichen Cantzley-Thür angeschrieben Stehet.
    [Ephrata, 1764?]

A Letter, from Battista Angeloni, who resided many years in
    London to his friend Manzoni. Wherein the Quakers are
    politically and religiously considered. To which is
    added, The clovenfoot discovered ... Ephrata [?]
    Re-printed and sold by several store-keepers in the
    county of Lancaster [1764?].

1765

[BEISSEL, JOHANN CONRAD] 1690-1768. A dissertation on mans
    fall, translated from the High-German original.
    Printed: Ephrata Anno MDCCLXV. Sold at Philadelphia
    by Messieurs Christoph Marshal and William Dunlap.

1766

Paradisisches Wunder-Spiel, Welches sich In diesen letzten
    Zeiten. Sammlung andächticher und zum Lob des
    grossen Gottes eingerichteter geistlicher und
    ehedessen zum Theil publicirter Lieder. Ephratae:
    Typis & Consensu Societatis A:D: MDCCLXVI.

1767

[BARTON, THOMAS]. The Family Prayer-Book ... Ephrata:
Printed for William [sic] Barton MVCCLXVII.

1768

Ein Lob-Lied dem in GOTT geehrten Vatter Friedsam zum
Andencken abgesungen. Als die ehrwürdige Jungfrau
und Schwester ATHANASIA seinen Hingang aus der Zeit
mit einem Liebesmahl beehrte. Geschähen den 29sten
August, 1768. [Ephrata, 1768]

1769

[BOOSEN, GERHARD] 1612-1711. Christliches Gemüths-Gespräch.
Ephratae Typiz Societatis Anno MDCCLXIX.

1770

Die Ernsthaffte Christen-Pflicht ... Ephrata, Drucks u.
Verlags der Brüderschafft Anno MDCCLXX.

[BOOSEN, GERHARD] Christliches Gemüths-Gespräch ...
Ephrata: Typis Societatis Anno MDCCLXX.

1771

Der Americanische Calender Auf das 1772ste Jahr Christi ...
Ephrata eit Bewilligung der Bruederschaft gedruckt von
Albert Conrad Reben [1771].

1773

[BEISSEL, JOHANN CONRAD] Deliciae Ephratenses, Pars I. Oder
des ehrwürdigen Vatters: Friedsam Gottrecht, Weyland
Stiffters und Führers des Christlichen Ordens der
Einsamen in Ephrata in Pennsylvania, Geistliche Reden
... Ephrata: Typis Societatis, Anno MDCCLXXIII.

[BEISSEL, JOHANN CONRAD] Deliciae Ephratenses, Pars II.
Oder des ehrwürdigen Vatters Friedsam Gottrecht,
Weyland Stiffters und Führers des Christlichen
Ordens der Einsamen in Pennsylvanien, Theosophische
Episteln ... Ephratae: Typis Societatis, Anno
MDCCXLV.

1775

Inwendige Glaubene- und Liebes-Uebung einer Seelen gegen
Gott und dessen Gegenwart. Kurtz und einfältig
entworffen und ange-wiesen Von und vor eine Seele so

1775 - con't.

nach Gottes Gegenwart und Vereinigung durch seine Gnade ist begierig worden. Parthenopolis [Ephrata] Gedruckt Anno 1775, vor Jacob Kimmel.

1776

SCHNEEBERGER, ANDREAS. Das Raben-Geschrey.   Durch Br. Andreas auf Antitum. [Ephrata, 1776].

SCHNEEBERGER, BARBARA, d. 1777.   Die Stimme der Turteltaube, durch Schw. Barbara Schneeberger. [Ephrata, 1776].

1782

Ausbund geistlicher Lieder, Gestellt in der Gemeinde an Antitum. [Ephrata?] Gedruckt Anno 1782.

1784

Ein Denckmahl aufgerichtet zum heiligen Andencken der H. Jungfrau und Schwester Melania in Saron, als sie den 11ten September, 1784 ein erbauliches Liebesmahl vor die Gemeinschaft gehalten. [Ephrata, 1784]

1785

Ausbund Geiztreicher Lieder. Ephrata, Gedruckt im Jahr 1785.

Christlicher-Haus-Segen, nebst der Zwölf Stunden Gedächtnise. Ephrata, 1785.

1786

[BENEZET, ANTHONY] Etliche Anmerkungen über den Zustand und Gemüths-Beschaffenheit Der Indianischen Einwohner Dieses Welttheils.   Aus dem Englischen übersetzt. Ephrata, Gedruckt Im Jahr M,LCC,LXXX,VI.

[HOCKER, LUDWIG] Kurz gefasste. [sic] Nützliches Schul-Büchlein Die kinder zu unterrichten, in Buchstabieren, Lesen, und auswendig lernen, Deme angehänget ein kurzer doch deutlicher, und gründlicher Unterricht Zur Rechenkunst. Aufgesetzt zum Nutz und Gebrauch vor Kinder. Von L. H. Zweyte Auflage. Ephrata, Gedruckt und zu bekommen bey dem Schulmeister, Drucker und Buchbinder 1786.

LAMECH, BROTHER. Chronicon Ephratense, Enthaltend den Lebens-Lauf des ehrwürdigen Vaters in Christo Friedsam Gottrecht, Weyland Stiffters und Vorstehers des geistl. Ordens der Einsamen in Ephrata in der Grafschaft Lancaster in Pennsylvania. Zusamen

1786 - con't.

getragen von Br. Lamech u. Agrippa ... Ephrata:
Gedruckt Anno MDCOLXXXVI.

Die merkwürdige Indianer-Predigt oder Verantwortung auf
    sine Predigt, welche von einem Schwedischen
    Missionario gehalten worden, an der Canestoga, Im Jahr
    1710. Ephrata, Gedruekt Im Jahr M,LCC,LXXX,VI.

1787

Das Ganz Neue Testament Unsers Herren Jesu Christi, Recht
    gründlich verdeutschet. Ephrata in Pennsylvanien,
    Anno 1787.

1788

Geistlicher Irrgarten. Ephrata, Im Jahr 1788.

[MACK, ALEXANDER] Anhang zum Widerleyten Wiedertaeufer,
    Enthaelt Zwei Unterredungnen und den gaentzlichen
    Abschied Theophili ... Ephrata 1788.

[MACK, ALEXANDER] Apologie, Oder schriftmäsige Verant-
    wortung Etlicher Wahrheiten. Herausgefordert durch
    eine neulich aufgesezte Schrift, unter dem Namen Der
    Widerlegte Wiedertäufer, In einem Gespräch
    Geschrieben für den Gemeinen Mann. Es wird das ganze
    Gecpräch von Wort zu Wort in diesen Blättern
    mitgetheilet, und die Apologie Zur Verantwortung Der
    beleidigten Wahrheit, Darzu gesezt, durch Theophilum.
    Ephrata, Gedruckt auf kosten der Bruder, im Jahr 1788.

Das Vergnügte Leben eines Einsamen, namens Joergel.
    Glueckselig ist der Mann, Der so wie Joergel leben
    kan! Ephrata 1788.

Eine Widerlegung des Freyen Willens, und behauptung der
    Gaenzlichen Restitution, oder Wiederherstellung was
    durch den Fall verlohren ward. Aus der H. Schrift,
    wie auch aus der Erfahrung und verschiedenen Exempeln
    hergeleitet und erwiesen. In zwey Theile verfasst.
    Addressieret an ainen Freund und Correspondenten.
    Ephrata: Der Klosterpresso [sic], 1788.

1789 – con't.

[BEISSEL, JOHANN CONRAD] Göttliche Wunderschrift, Darinen
entdecket wird, wie aus dem ewigen Guten hat können
ein Böses urständen. Desgleichen, Wie das Böse wieder
in das Gute vergestaltet, und der ewigen Mutter ... in
den Schoos geliefert wird ... Denen Irrthümern des
Naturalismi und Atheismi entgegen gesezt, und zum
Heiligen Nachsinnen den Kindern der Obern Weisheit.
Ephrata, Gedruckt im Jahr 1789.

1790

Kurtzgefasstes Arzney-Büchlein für Menschen und Vieh,
darinnen CXXX auserlesene recepten. [Ephrata, 1790].

Das Leben Eines jungen Herzogs, Welcher 300 Jahr im Paradies
gewesen, Glänzend wieder zurück in sein Reich kam,
Folgende Geschichte erzehlt beym ersten Bissen Brots,
sich in Gestalt eines sehr alten Mannes verwandelt,
und stirbt, Ephrata, Gedruckt im Jahr 1790.

SCHROEDER, JOHANN GEORG. Merkwürdige Geschichte ...
Ephrata, gedruckt im Jahr 1790.

Kurzgefasstes Arzney-Büchlein, für Menschen und Vieh,
Darinnen 128 auserlesene Recepte, nebst einer
prognostischen Tafel. Wien gedruckt: Ephrata
nachgedruckt, Im Jahr 1791.

1791

[ROEMELINGS, CHRISTIAN ANTON] Der bussfertige Beicht-Vater
und Seel-Sorger, Aaron ... Ephrata, gedruckt auf
Kosten der Liebhaber, 1791.

1792

[MARTIN, GEORG ADAM] 1715-1794. Christliche Bibliothek ...
Ephrata, Gedruckt im Jahr M,DCC,XCII.

SCHNEIDER, PETER. Merkwürdige Prophezeyung eines
Einsiedlers... [Ephrata?] Gedruckt fur den Verfasser.
1792.

TERSTEEGEN, GERHARD. Vom Christlichen Gebrauch der Lieder,
und des Singens ... Ephrata, gedruckt im Jahr 1792.

[MACK, VALENTINE]. Ein Gespräch zwischen einem Pilger und
Bürger auf ihrer Reise nachund in der Ewigkeit.

1792 - con't.

Welchen noch hinzugefügt ist, ein Gespräch, das der Tod
    mit beyden gehalten ... Chestnut-hill: gedruckt bey
    Samuel Saur, 1792.

1793

Abgesungen auf Pfingsten an der Antittum [sic], bey der
    Ehrwürdigen Schwester Elizabeth Knepper ihrem
    Liebesmahl. [Ephrata, 1793?]

Anonimus' travels, throu Europe and America, and some vis-
    ions of many heavenly mansions in the house of God ...
    Ephrata, printed in the year MDCCXCIII.

BOLTON, JAMES. Of the universal restoration, [Ephrata,
    1793].

[BEISSEL, JOHANN CONRAD] Geistliche Briefe eines Friedsamen
    Pilgers, Welche er von 1721. bis an seine 1768.
    darauf erfolgte Entbindung geschrieben. Ephrata,
    gedruckt im Jah [!] 1794.

1794

ARNDT, JOHANN, 1555-1621. Geistreiche Morgen- und
    Abend-Gebethe, auf jeden Tag der Woche. Ephrata,
    Gedruckt: und zu haben bey Henrich Dorn in der
    Donegal-strass. [Brotherhood? n.d.]

Von der Richtigkeit [Nichtigkeit?] des Menschlichen Lebens.
    [Ephrata?] n.d.

STUDIES IN AMERICAN RELIGION

2932